The Academic Novel

The Academic Novel

New and Classic Essays

Edited by Merritt Moseley

Chester Academic Press

First published 2007
by Chester Academic Press
University of Chester
Parkgate Road
Chester CH1 4BJ

Printed and bound in the UK
by the Print Unit
University of Chester
Cover designed
by the Graphics Team
University of Chester

A catalogue record for this book is available from the
British Library

ISBN 978-1-905929-38-2

CONTENTS

Contents

PREFACE

The following collection of criticism on the academic novel gathers together the most illuminating commentary of the past forty years and adds to it new essays especially written for this volume. I have selected from the criticism of the academic novel - which is quite copious, as befits a genre which is itself copious - pieces which seem to me to contribute to the reader's understanding and appreciation of the genre itself, of one or more of its major practitioners, or of both. The classic essays range from academic articles published in learned journals to commentary contributed to the books section of a newspaper.

The new essays were commissioned to fill in areas where the published critical corpus needed augmentation.

The term "academic novel" is, like the other words applied to this type of writing, only partly satisfactory. Alternatives are "university novel," "college novel," and "campus novel," and these are all used by critics. "Campus novel" seems inadequate for the modern version which is often set at an institution which hardly has a "campus" in the old, pastoral sense (we recall the origins of the word in the Latin for "field"); and "campus novel" also seems more appropriate for the novel focused on the student body. *This Side of Paradise* is a campus novel; *Coming From Behind* is not. Since, at least in the United States, a distinction is made between the "college" and the "university," I have chosen "academic novel" as more inclusive. It has a useful secondary reference, as well, to the "academic" qualities of many modern academic novels - their self-referentiality, their flaunting of theoretical knowledge, their allusiveness and postmodern playfulness.[1]

In a very few places I have shortened these pieces, omitting material not immediately relevant in this book; I have also tried to bring the systems of documentation into greater conformity, but have not otherwise changed such things as variant British and American spellings; neither have I considered it necessary to add bibliographical information to those essays which, being first published as reviews or essays in literary quarterlies, appeared without footnotes.

Though very little annotation should be needed, there are three historical notes which may deserve mention:

1). *F. R. Leavis.* American readers, especially, are sometimes baffled by the invocation of Leavis, who is known in the United States primarily as a literary critic. In England he occupies or occupied a much larger role, as a sort of cultural critic, an educational reformer, and a prophet. Glyn Turton, for instance, refers to "the Cambridge of F. R. Leavis where belief in the saving, morally therapeutic value of literature had become an orthodoxy." Though Leavis, as he never tired of complaining, was undervalued by the Cambridge establishment, it is not too strong to say that he prescribed the study of English Literature, preferably at Cambridge and ideally under himself, his wife, and a few other people who agreed with them about everything, as almost the only medicine for a civilization in decline. For instance, in one of his last works, he argues as follows:

---

[1] Leslie Fiedler's coinage, the "anti-college novel," is a thought-provoking alternative. See his essay later in this volume.

The Academic Novel

> I have intimated something, then, about my reasons for insisting
> that the critical discipline – the distinctive discipline of university
> "English" – is a discipline of intelligence, and for being explicit
> and repetitive in associating the word "intelligence" with the
> word "thought." . . Having said this, I will go on to say further that
> the discipline is a training in fidelity to – which must be delicate
> apprehension of – the living principle.[2]

And he goes on to argue (p. 36) that "an account of how a
poem exists is a pregnant hint of the way in which the
Human World is created and, in constant renewal,
maintained." It is easy to see how such noble aspirations
must seem to be traduced in the typical modern English
department, or at least in the typical modern academic
novel, almost always written by an English professor.

2. *Vietnam*. Writing in 1964, Leslie Fiedler asks about the
generation of the Sixties: "What public events, for instance,
move them as the generation of the Forties-Fifties was
moved by the Depression and the war in Spain, and that of
the Twenties by the first great prosperity and World War
I?" He was writing just too early to know that the
explosive answer to his question was: the war in Southeast
Asia. The rise of student protest – first in the United States
and then in other countries – is the consequence of this
crucial generational development. The importance of the

---

[2] *The Living Principle: "English" as a Discipline of Thought* (London: Chatto
& Windus; New York: Oxford University Press, 1975), pp. 13-14. The
quoted passage is a fair illustration of Leavis's clotted prose style and
self-congratulation, as well as his noble expectations of "English."
Leavis deplored the decision of Cambridge to appoint Kingsley Amis,
author of one of the best academic novels, calling him a
"pornographer."

war in changing the ethos of students and the atmosphere of colleges and universities, especially (but not only) in the United States, cannot be overestimated. The consequences were felt in Britain as well, as George Watson's reflections on the 1960s, with their denunciation of the "collective hysteria that was once called the New Left," and "Violence-worship among intellectuals," testify.

3. Americans may need a reminder that British universities may be classified as the ancient universities (mostly but not exclusively Oxford and Cambridge); the "red brick" universities, mostly nineteenth-century metropolitan foundations in cities like Liverpool, Birmingham, Leicester, Leeds, Manchester; the "new universities" of the sixties and seventies - sometimes called "white tile" universities - including Sussex, York, East Anglia, Essex, and so on; and a new intake of universities converted from the polytechnics - themselves created in the postwar period to provide more technical education than was then available in the universities. Big cities often have a red-brick and a former poly: hence Liverpool University and Liverpool John Moores University, or Manchester University and Manchester Metropolitan University, and even Oxford has the ancient university and Oxford Brookes University, formerly Oxford Polytechnic. Former "colleges of higher education," the descendants of non-degree-granting teachers' colleges, are now joining the ranks of the universities.

I thank all those who have agreed to contribute to this volume; my colleagues in the Department of Literature and Language at the University of North Carolina at Asheville and - my academic second home - the Department of English at the University of Chester for fruitful conversation and good fellowship; the library staff at the

University of North Carolina at Asheville for help in acquiring materials; my family, for all they are for me; and the authors of all the academic novels, who make this subject endlessly diverting.

CONTRIBUTORS

Adam Begley is the books editor of *The New York Observer*. He lives in England.

Ian Carter is Professor in the Department of Sociology at the University of Auckland, New Zealand. He became interested in university fiction more than thirty years ago, outraged by reading Malcolm Bradbury's *The History Man*.

Benjamin DeMott received his PhD from Harvard University and, after some years as a journalist, joined the faculty of Amherst College in 1951, where he was Mellon Professor of Humanities until his retirement. He was the author of two novels and several books of essays and a frequent contributor to periodicals, including *Harper's*, *The Nation*, *The New Republic* and the *Atlantic Monthly*, of which he was a long-time contributing editor. He commented widely on American literature and American culture; his two most recent books are *The Trouble With Friendship: Why Americans Can't Think Straight About Race* (1995) and *Killer Woman Blues: Why Americans Can't Think Straight About Gender and Power* (2000). He died in October 2005.

Aida Edemariam is a feature writer for *The Guardian* in London. She has a BA in English Language and Literature from Oxford University, and an MA in the same subject from the University of Toronto. She was an assistant editor at *Harper's Magazine*, and a deputy literary editor at the *National Post*, and her work has been published in *The Times Literary Supplement, Lingua Franca, The New Statesman* and *Routledge's World Encyclopedia of Contemporary Theatre*, among other publications.

Leslie Fiedler, who died in 2003, was Samuel Clemens Professor of English and State University of New York Distinguished Professor at the University of Buffalo. He was famous for his provocative views and for his passionate devotion to a non-elitist look at popular culture. The author of more than twenty-five books, including most famously *Love and Death in the American Novel* and most recently *The Tyranny of the Normal*, Fiedler earned numerous awards and prizes for his criticism and fiction. He lectured all over the world and many of his writings were translated into other languages.

Philip Hobsbaum was a Professorial Research Fellow in English Literature at Glasgow University. He was educated at Cambridge and Sheffield Universities and was a Lecturer in English at Queen's University, Belfast, before moving to Glasgow in 1966. Among his numerous books are *A Theory of Communication, A Reader's Guide to Charles Dickens, Tradition and Experiment in English Poetry, Essentials of Literary Criticism,* and (as editor) *A Group Anthology, Ten Elizabethan Poets,* and *Wordsworth: Selected Poetry and Prose.* He died in June 2005.

J. P. Kenyon was a fellow at Christ's College, Cambridge, Professor of History at Hull University, and, from 1987 until his retirement in 1994, Distinguished Professor of Early Modern British History at the University of Kansas. He was the author of *The Stuarts, The Popish Plot, The History Men: The Historical Profession in England Since the Renaissance,* and *The Civil Wars of England.* He died in January 1996.

Contributors

David Lodge is a novelist, critic, and Honorary Professor of Modern English Literature at Birmingham University. His academic novels include *Changing Places*, *Small World* and *Nice Work*. His most recent novel is *Author, Author* and his most recent non-fiction book is *The Year of Henry James: The Story of a Novel*.

Merritt Moseley is Professor of Literature at the University of North Carolina at Asheville. He is the author of critical books on David Lodge, Kingsley Amis, Julian Barnes and Michael Frayn and has edited four volumes of the *Dictionary of Literary Biography: British Novelists Since 1960*, and, most recently, the *DLB* volume on *Booker Prize Winners*.

Dale Salwak is Professor of English at Southern California's Citrus College. He was educated at Purdue University and then the University of Southern California. His publications include *The Literary Biography: Problems and Solutions* (1996), *A Passion for Books* (1999) and *Living with a Writer* (2004), as well as studies of Kingsley Amis, John Braine, A. J. Cronin, Philip Larkin, Barbara Pym, Carl Sandburg, Anne Tyler, and John Wain. He is now completing a memoir on thirty years of teaching.

Samuel Schuman has recently retired as the Chancellor of the University of Minnesota at Morris; he had earlier been a professor and administrator at Guilford College and the University of North Carolina at Asheville. He is the author of *Vladimir Nabokov: A Reference Guide* and numerous articles on Nabokov, focusing particularly on the author's use of Shakespearean source materials. Dr Schuman is Past President of the Vladimir Nabokov Society.

J. A. Sutherland is emeritus Lord Northcliffe Professor of Modern English Literature at University College London; he also has an appointment at the California Institute of Technology, where he taught full time, 1983-1992. Among John Sutherland's many books, the most recent are *Stephen Spender: The Authorized Biography* (Viking, 2000) and *The Literary Detectives* (Oxford, 2000), literary quizbooks on Austen and Hardy, and *How To Read a Novel: A User's Guide*. He chaired the judging panel for the Man Booker Prize in 2005.

Glyn Turton retired in 2005 as Senior Assistant Principal at the University of Chester. He holds a Bachelor's degree in Russian Language and Literature from the University of Oxford and took his Master's and PhD at the University of Warwick. His interests include nineteenth-century European writing and contemporary British fiction and poetry. He is the author of *Turgenev and the Context of English Literature, 1850-1900*. He lectured in Literature for eighteen years at a polytechnic in the English West Midlands.

Chris Walsh is Dean of Humanities and Professor of English Literature at the University of Chester. He has published widely on nineteenth- and twentieth-century fiction and poetry. His publications include: *Studying Literature: A Practical Introduction, A Reader's Guide to the Poetry of Robert Browning*, and *The Practice of Reading: Interpreting the Novel*. He is editor of the *Longman Literature in English* series.

Susan Watkins is Senior Lecturer in English Literature at Leeds Metropolitan University, England. She is the co-editor of *Studying Literature: A Practical Introduction* (Harvester, 1995) and the author of *Twentieth-Century*

Women Novelists: Feminist Theory Into Practice (Palgrave, 2001). Her first degree is from the University of Liverpool; her doctorate is from the University of Sheffield. Her specialisms are nineteenth- and twentieth-century literature, women's writing, and feminist theory.

George Watson, who is a Fellow of St John's College, Cambridge, has been a Visiting Professor of English at the University of Georgia and at New York University, and Sandars Reader in Bibliography at the University of Cambridge. He is the editor of the *New Cambridge Bibliography of English Literature,* and the author of *The Literary Critics, Politics & Literature in Modern Britain, The English Ideology, The Story of the Novel, The Certainty of Literature, British Literature Since 1945,* and *Never Ones for Theory?: England and the War of Ideas,* and has edited Lord Acton, Coleridge, Dryden and Maria Edgeworth.

ACKNOWLEDGEMENTS

The editor acknowledges, with thanks, the owners of copyright for permission to reprint the following works:

Adam Begley, "The Decline of the Campus Novel," from *Lingua Franca* (September 1997), pp. 39-46, reprinted by permission. Ian Carter, "Barbarous Women," from *Ancient Cultures of Conceit: British University Fiction in the Post-War Years* (London: Routledge, 1990), pp. 159-66, reprinted by permission. Benjamin DeMott, "How to Write a College Novel," from *Hudson Review 15*, (1962), pp. 243-52, reprinted by permission. Aida Edemariam, "Who's Afraid of the Campus Novel?" from *The Guardian* (October 2, 2004), p. 34, reprinted by permission. Leslie Fiedler, "The War Against the Academy," from *Waiting For the End* (New York: Stein and Day, 1964), pp. 138-53, reprinted by permission. Philip Hobsbaum, "University Life in English Fiction," from *Twentieth Century 173*, (1964), pp. 139-46, reprinted by permission. J. P. Kenyon, "*Lucky Jim* and After: The Business of University Novels," from *Encounter 54* (June, 1980), pp. 81-4, reprinted by permission. David Lodge, "Robertson Davies and the Campus Novel," from *Write On: Occasional Essays '65-'85* (London: Secker & Warburg, 1986), pp. 169-73, reprinted by permission. J. A. Sutherland, "Campus Writers," from *Fiction and the Fiction Industry* (London: The Athlone Press, 1978), pp. 148-62, reprinted by permission. Susan Watkins, "'Women and Wives Mustn't Go Near It': Academia, Language, and Gender in the Novels of Alison Lurie," from *Revista Canaria de Estudios Ingleses 48* (April 2004), pp. 29-46; online at http://webpages.ull.es/users/rceing/, reprinted by permission. George Watson, "Fictions of Academe: Dons and Realities," *Encounter 51* (November, 1978), pp. 42-5, reprinted by permission.

I

The Fiction of Academia

INTRODUCTORY: DEFINITIONS AND JUSTIFICATIONS

Merritt Moseley

The essays assembled in the following pages examine the academic subgenre of the modern British and American novel. Their authors bring criticism to bear both on the species, *the academic novel*, and on specific examples. The academic novel raises a number of important literary, philosophical, and even sociological questions. What is an academic novel? Why do people like to read them? Is the popularity, or at least generous supply, of academic novels a sign of cultural illness? Are they good or bad for the academy?

We begin with an awareness that some readers, particularly those who are themselves professional academics, deplore the whole genre, and some would like to see the entire subject go away. Cambridge don George Watson writes "I have several reasons, all partly selfish, for hoping that Anglo-American campus fiction will fade away and die."[1] Bruce Robbins refers to "the generally unflattering treatment academics have received from the so-called academic novel" and says that "over the past half-century or so, novelists who turned their attention to the university have arguably contributed more than a little to the acute lack of respect and understanding of which academics . . . tend to complain."[2] John O. Lyons ends his book, *The College Novel in America*, with an apologetic

---

[1] George Watson, "Fictions of Academe: Dons and Realities," (*Encounter*, 51, November 1978), p. 43; reprinted below.

[2] Bruce Robbins, "What the Porter Saw: On the Academic Novel"; from James F. English, Ed., *A Concise Companion to Contemporary British Fiction* (Malden, MA; Oxford: Blackwell, 2006), p. 249.

acknowledgment of his urge to "carp at the lack of distinction in the novels about academic life."[3] Janice Rossen refers to "the mass of University novels, which are admittedly minor."[4] David Holbrook is concerned about something far more serious than mediocrity:

> But surely there is something terribly wrong, when in a Humanities department of a university, students are introduced to works which confuse them morally, and which tend actually to endorse the false solutions of hate and barbarity? This is one of the chief embarrassments today, for anyone concerned with literature and the Arts. Perhaps the process came to a head with the emergence of the "campus" novel, not least with *Lucky Jim* ....[5]

If Holbrook considers the academic novel culturally and morally dangerous, he is joined by the much younger D. J. Taylor, who decries "the academic romp, which began to be fashionable at about this time[6], the campus frolic of sexual and scholastic indignity," as an example of a new relativism, of "the disregard for absolute standards."[7] Gore Vidal is more worried about its circularity, or narrowness:

> As most of our novelists now teach school, they tend to tell us what it is like to be a schoolteacher, and since schoolteachers have been

---

[3] John O. Lyons, *The College Novel in America* (Carbondale, IL: Southern Illinois University Press, 1962), p. 186.

[4] Janice Rossen, *The University in Modern Fiction: When Power is Academic* (New York: St. Martin's Press; Basingstoke: Macmillan, 1993), p. 185.

[5] David Holbrook, *The Novel and Authenticity* (London: Vision; Totowa, NJ: Barnes & Noble, 1987), p. 184.

[6] i.e. the late 1960s [Ed.]

[7] D. J. Taylor, *After the War: The Novel and English Society Since 1945* (London: Chatto & Windus, 1993), p. 183.

Introductory

Undoubtedly the proliferation of academic novels *is* related to the fact that many novelists teach in higher education and most others have at least been students at a college or university. But Vidal implies, here and elsewhere, that the kinds of novels he dislikes are written by teachers and only read by other teachers and those to whom teachers have assigned them. This is clearly not true. Publishers do not usually publish books for which there is little or no voluntary market. And some "campus novels" have been very popular.

An instructive case is that of A. S. Byatt's 1990 novel *Possession*. Byatt was an academic herself (having taught at University College, London, until 1983) and a literary scholar. Some of her earlier novels, notably *The Game* and *Still Life*, featured university students and situations. But *Possession* is in a completely different category from her previous novels, and after it she was in an entirely different category of writer. *Possession* is a 550-page book which makes considerable demands on the reader; much of it is accomplished pastiche of Victorian poetry and prose.

---

[8] Gore Vidal, *At Home: Essays 1982-1988* (New York: Random House, 1988), p. 180. George Watson says that "there is something wrong with a literature in which universities are felt to be consumingly interesting; I hear myself murmuring, with Coriolanus, that there is a world elsewhere."

Moreover, the main twentieth-century characters are all academics, seen in their roles as scholars. The novel is *about* scholarship – the discovery of documents, the forming of judgments, the revision of critical understanding. There are some mildly sensational elements, notably two American scholars, one roguish and one radical, who complicate the search for truth by the English academics Roland Mitchell and Maud Bailey, but the novel lacks most of the requirements of the blockbuster – crime, fashion, exciting sex, exotic locations, and particularly ingratiation of the reader.

Possession won the 1990 Booker Prize, given for the best novel written by a citizen of the United Kingdom, the British Commonwealth or the Republics of Ireland and South Africa, and published in Britain. But what is more surprising is its enormous popularity. There is no reliable source for information on book sales in the United Kingdom; the fact is, though, that within seven months of its publication, the novel had sold about 100,000 hardback copies in the United States (where many English novels do poorly or are never published because of cultural differences); in 1991 it sold about 250,000 copies in paperback; it was translated into sixteen languages by 1995 and bootstrapped Byatt's reputation, bringing her earlier books back into print and leading to high expectations and good sales for her future ones.[9]

Possession is clearly an unusual book; but *Bertram Cope's Year*, a novel written by Henry Blake Fuller and self-published in 1919, recounting the adventures of a Midwestern university's new instructor, was republished as recently as 1998, certainly not with a view to university syllabi. And the interest of readers seems to be lasting. *The*

---

[9] Richard Todd, *Consuming Fictions: The Booker Prize and Fiction in Britain Today* (London: Bloomsbury, 1996), pp. 25-54.

Introductory

Groves of Academe, Lucky Jim, Pnin, and *Pictures from an Institution,* all academic novels of 1952-1959 focusing on professors, remain in print; so do all of David Lodge's major academic novels, *The British Museum is Falling Down* (1965), *Changing Places* (1975), *Small World* (1984), and *Nice Work* (1988); and Malcolm Bradbury's *Eating People is Wrong* (1962), *The History Man* (1975), and *Rates of Exchange* (1983). Novels of undergraduate life still evidently earning their places on publishers' lists include Philip Larkin's *Jill* (1946) and even Max Beerbohm's *Zuleika Dobson* (1911). And, for that matter, *Tom Brown at Oxford* (1859).

Why do writers and readers favor academic novels? Unsurprisingly, there have been many attempts to answer this question. It is interesting that such efforts assume that interest in reading about the professorial life is an anomaly to be explained; no one suspects that Cormac McCarthy's novels about cowboys are read only by cowboys, or by anomalous non-cowboys for whom some excuse needs to be found, and the same seems to be true of Irvine Welsh's fictions about Scottish junkies; on the other hand, George Watson declares academia an odd subject for fiction, since the "university, after all, is a place for students who have barely started to live, and professors who have done all (or nearly all) the living they are ever likely to do."[10]

One line of interpretation assumes that satire is the key determinant of the academic novel. If satire is the act of ridiculing a person, belief, or situation in order to expose its evils, then, by this reasoning, the academic novelist writes out of an urge to reveal, and perhaps punish, the follies and shortcomings of the academic institution in which he or she has been a dweller and participant. The novelist's relation to academia, then, is like the relation of earlier novelists to Hollywood; they may have gone there

---

[10] Watson, p. 42.

as a condition of earning a living, but their resentment fueled a savagely satirical novel later on - Nathanael West's *Day of the Locust* being a classic example. Adam Begley has recently deplored the tone of today's campus novels, contrasting them with classics of the genre like Mary McCarthy's *The Groves of Academe* and Randall Jarrell's *Pictures from an Institution*. Begley believes that "the decline of the Campus Novel," as he calls it, results from novelists being too dependent on the campus and as a result not satirical enough about it. That is, "the campus novel" by rights is a satire on campus life, but academia's dependents dare not offend it.[11] "Campus," Begley writes, commenting on *Lucky Jim*, "is the province of the pretentious, the dangerously dull and self-absorbed, the militantly complacent, and the resolutely hypocritical. Amis's Jim Dixon is lucky mainly in that he is leaving it all behind."[12] Janice Rossen, who believes that academics are a natural subject for satire, concurs that "many of the best University novels are about someone leaving academe at the end of the book." Rossen even declares that novelists have often "raided the University for fictional material and

---

[11] Adam Begley, "The Decline of the Campus Novel," (*Lingua Franca*, September 1997), pp. 39-46; reprinted below. A recent study, Kenneth Womack's *Postwar Academic Fiction: Satire, Ethics, Community* (New York: St. Martin's Press; Basingstoke: Palgrave, 2001) is dedicated to showing, not always very clearly, how "the practitioners of Anglo-American university fiction utilize academic characters and institutional themes as a means for exploring, through the deliberately broad strokes of their satirical prose, the ethical and philosophical questions endemic to their genre that impinge upon such issues as culture, morality, romance, and commitment" (p. 2). Robbins writes that, from *Lucky Jim* on, "there has been no need to ask whether satire would be the chosen mode. The only relevant questions have been how satiric the collective portrait would be and what institutions, schools of thought, or character types would be singled out for ridicule" (p. 249).
[12] Begley, p. 44.

gutted it with crude malice"[13]: a concept of the relationship between the novelist and his or her subject matter which is indeed unsettling. Throughout her assessment of academic fiction, in fact, Rossen assumes an adversarial relationship between novelists and their readers, and (often) between novelists and their subject – raiding and gutting – which reminds one of the Juvenalian satires of Shakespeare's day, with their rhetoric of stripping and whipping, and makes the academic novel a tense arena of struggle and conflict. Elaine Showalter takes a different tack, complaining that overall, "contemporary academic fiction is too tame, substituting satire for tragedy, detective plots for the complex effects on a community of its internal scandals, revelations, disruptions, disappointments and catastrophes."[14]

While reading satires of higher education might give professors a shock of recognition or perhaps even, in Janice Rossen's words, "satisfaction in seeing one's enemies held up to ridicule,"[15] what appeal could such satires hold for their non-academic readers? Some may derive pleasure from "finding out" how weak, pointless, and ineffectual the professor – a member of an ancient profession, a highly educated man (usually), even (particularly in the past) a well-paid and comfortably environed man – can be. John Lyons points out that "Even professors have a tendency to present the professor as a befuddled, chalk-covered, impotent half-man."[16] One of the conventions of the academic novel is that the professor is sexually unimpressive. Presenting the professor this way invites the

---

[13] Rossen, p. 88, p. 2.
[14] Elaine Showalter, *Faculty Towers: The Academic Novel and Its Discontents* (Philadelphia: University of Pennsylvania Press; Oxford: Oxford University Press, 2005), p. 119.
[15] Rossen, p. 2.
[16] Lyons, p. xiv.

non-academic reader – by implication a libidinous powerhouse – to enjoy an agreeable pity or contempt for the pedagogue. More seriously, readers may respond to the academic satire with outrage. Particularly in the past few decades, when the public has been targeted by a steady fusillade of alleged exposés of what is wrong with higher education – of which Dinesh D'Souza's *Illiberal Education: The Politics of Race and Sex on Campus* (1991), Roger Kimball's *Tenured Radicals: How Politics Has Corrupted Our Higher Education* (1990), and Allan Bloom's *The Closing of the American Mind: How Higher Education Has Failed Democracy and Impoverished the Souls of Today's Students* (1987) are the most damaging, and *This Beats Working for a Living : The Dark Secrets of a College Professor* (1973), by "Professor X", perhaps the most outrageous – members of the public may feel that *The History Man* or *Moo* is another dispatch from another "Professor X," an academic mole driven to write a novel to let the taxpayer know that the truth is out there. The flip side of this view is the insider's anxiety, as represented by David Holbrook (a Leavisite and thus a powerful believer in the moral power of university education): the campus novel

> seeks to portray the English academic at the university as a lustful fool, whose values are impotent and hypocritical, and who is "really" driven by lust, ambition, and egotism. The effect, as Boris Ford has pointed out to me, is that the public's view of the Humanities in the universities has been seriously damaged, and, more important, the view held by politicians of the status of the Humanities on the campus. There is no doubt that many now see us as incompetents who do not subscribe to the values we are supposed to uphold, not the least despicable because we seem to regard the

intellectual life with an air of superior disdain and ironic self-interest.[17]

But of course not all academic novels *are* satires.[18] Many of them, indeed, are loving celebrations of the academic life. More than anywhere else, Oxford inspires this sort of treatment, which includes awed celebration of the quality of human relations (if undergraduate) or quirky but life-giving humanistic intellectuals (if donnish), amid a place of beauty, serenity, and history. Some of these novels fall into the category I call Dappled Quads. Their appeal can be difficult to explain. The vast majority of readers have not been members of Oxford colleges (or Cambridge, or Harvard, which share some of the wish-fulfillment elements with Oxford in fiction). Any nostalgia they may feel is a nostalgia for that which was never experienced. Malcolm Bradbury comments on how reading academic novels prepared him for a beautifully unrealistic picture of university life:

---

[17] Holbrook, p. 184. Bradbury has acknowledged that *The History Man,* its effect magnified by being made into a television show, had some such ill effects on English higher education; see Peter Widdowson, "The Anti-History Men: Malcolm Bradbury and David Lodge," (*Critical Quarterly, 26,* 1984), p. 20.

[18] Brian Connery suggests that "a work is not a satire – or at least not a successful satire – if the people being satirised do not feel themselves as the target of satiric attack" ("Inside Jokes: Familiarity and Contempt in Academic Satire"; from David Bevan, Ed., *University Fiction,* [Amsterdam; Atlanta, GA: Rodopi, 1990], p. 124). But this idea, that the existence of satire requires the cooperative recognition of its targets, is an old and debatable one; such a definition would exclude a great many works with good claims to be satirical, including *The Shortest Way With Dissenters* and *A Modest Proposal.*

... rooms shared with a son of the aristocracy, hours spent writing poems that had better be modern, or else, late night philosophical conversations, mostly about G. E. Moore's *Principia Ethica*, conducted over a mixture of claret and cocoa, and so on.[19]

Though Oxford and Cambridge enroll a tiny minority of the British students going on to higher education, a group which is itself a minority of the age cohort, the interest of the public in them continues to be enormous. The popularity of *Brideshead Revisited* as a television series owed much to the picture of life among the privileged, the languid and effete, in 1920s Oxford. The Oxford-Cambridge boat race is still televised on the BBC and, presumably, watched by millions (somewhat as the Harvard-Yale football game used to be a significant athletic event in the US despite the negligible quality of the football). C. P. Snow's series of novels about Cambridge contrives to make the mundane details of life there – particularly such events as the election of a college master – seem somehow romantic and urgent.

John Kenneth Galbraith's *A Tenured Professor*[20] has almost no literary merit, but may serve the subsidiary function of making readers denied a Harvard education – almost all of us, that is – feel more knowing, after reading that "Sessions with one's tutor at Harvard favor an argumentative technique" and, "for all Harvard men and women" Harvard Yard "is thought a place of great symbolic, nostalgic and liturgical importance" and that, at

---

[19] Malcolm Bradbury, *No, Not Bloomsbury* (London: Andre Deutsch, 1987; New York, Columbia University Press, 1988), p. 329.
[20] There is no end to the surprises, when one first begins to discover all the writers who have published an academic novel. Galbraith was an economist and whilom chair of the President's Council of Economic Advisors and Ambassador to India.

the Harvard Faculty Club, "the room and the furniture are unattractive and give the impression of having been shabby even when new."[21]

The novel as satiric exposé or denunciation of university life and the novel as lush, usually nostalgic, celebration of that life share an assumption that the novel is based on, or related to, the reality of academia. We have all been taught to acknowledge the problematic nature of this relationship, to disbelieve in a one-to-one correspondence, or "homology", between the particulars of fiction and those of the world. Both David Lodge and Malcolm Bradbury have playfully alluded to the problematic relationship between the novel and life; Bradbury insists in the author's note to *The History Man* that

> It is a total invention with delusory approximations to historical reality, just as is history itself. Not only does the University of Watermouth, which appears here, bear no relation to the real University of Watermouth (which does not exist) or to any other university; the year 1972, which also appears, bears no relation to the real 1972, which was a fiction anyway; and so on.[22]

Lodge's *Changing Places* comes with the following warning, which is a bit more informative on the way fiction is connected to life:

> Although some of the locations and public events portrayed in this novel bear a certain resemblance to actual locations and events, the

---

[21] John Kenneth Galbraith, *A Tenured Professor* (Boston, Houghton Mifflin; London: Sinclair-Stevenson, 1990), p. 24, pp. 1-2.
[22] Malcolm Bradbury, *The History Man* (London: Secker & Warburg, 1975).

characters, considered either as individuals or as members of institutions, are entirely imaginary. Rummidge and Euphoria are places on the map of a comic world which resembles the one we are standing on without corresponding exactly to it, and which is peopled by figments of the imagination.[23]

Fiction is not a simulacrum of life. Nor, however, is it independent of life outside the text; the academic novel would not, could not, exist were there no academic system, no colleges and universities, no professors and students. Academic novels assume the real world. For example, British academic novels since the rise of Margaret Thatcher reflect, or react to, the changes in status and funding for higher education under the Conservative administration. Frank Parkin's *The Mind and Body Shop* (1986) posits a situation in which unfunded students sleep in unheated hovels while ignorant businessmen elevated into university administrators sell academic services to the highest bidder. This is a satiric response to Thatcherism and, consistent with satire's procedures, an exaggeration.

Though it is true that every academic novel has *some* relationship to academia, most academic novels neither revile nor romanticize the life they present. They are neither savage satires nor mellow incitements to nostalgia or envy. Perhaps the *conflict between* these two stances is the key. Terry Eagleton, writing from a position hostile to David Lodge's works[24], begins by contextualizing Lodge's subject matter:

---

[23] David Lodge, *Changing Places* (1975; Harmondsworth: Penguin, 1978), p. 6.
[24] Eagleton's ideological position is antithetical to Lodge's; perhaps the distance between his position at Wadham College, Oxford, and Lodge's at the University of Birmingham was relevant in some way, too.

Introductory

The success of the "campus" novel in England is not hard to account for. Ever since Burke and Coleridge's testy polemics against the Jacobins, the English attitude to the intelligentsia has been one of profound ambivalence. Intellectuals are seen as faintly sinister figures, bohemian and nonconformist, treasonable clerks whose heartless celebrations pose a threat to the unreflective pieties of ordinary life. But they are also pathetically ineffectual characters - crumpled figures of fun pursuing their ludicrous abstractions at a remote distance from the bustle of daily life. The anxiety and resentment they inspire can thus be conveniently defused by a sense of their farcical irrelevance .... The intellectual combines the fascination of the offbeat with the comic relief of the harmless eccentric, and is thus fit meat for a kind of fiction which equivocates between a satiric criticism of everyday middle-class life and an unshaken commitment to its fundamental values.[25]

Eagleton sees both Lodge and Malcolm Bradbury as defenders of liberal humanism – a characterization both would probably accept, though with qualifications, particularly by Bradbury – whose novels are ideological constructs designed to disarm a more radical critique of things as they are.

One does not have to accept Eagleton's view of the campus novel as a conservative genre dedicated to recuperating middle-class values to agree that its energy is often the result of a tension between contrasting forces, which may be the urge to celebrate and the urge to condemn or deride; or a self-consciousness about the compromises required by participation in academic life

---

[25] Terry Eagleton, "The Silences of David Lodge," (*New Left Review*, 172, 1988), p. 93.

complicated by an unwillingness to foul one's own nest. And the university, dedicated as it apparently, and really, is to noble purposes, is a particularly vivid site for another disparity, that between the ideal and the real.

Both critics as well as novelists, Bradbury and Lodge have also commented on the attractions of the academic novel. Lodge argues that "the university is a kind of microcosm of society at large, in which the principles, drives and conflicts that govern collective human life are displayed and may be studied in a clear light and on a manageable scale."[26] We should note that the view of the university as a microcosm of society at large contradicts both the view that the university is a place where people are more, or differently, venal, lazy, sexually profligate and hypocritical than in other parts of society and the contrasting view of the university as an arcadian remove, the land of lost content. Lodge's academic life, spent at the Universities of London and Birmingham, may make him less convinced of the divide between college and the world than the celebrants of Oxford and Cambridge. Bradbury is another non-Oxbridge observer. J. P. Kenyon, another don, comments in a similar vein, accepting the attraction of the university-as-community:

> The theme of a closed community, outside the mainstream of modern life, has always had obvious attractions. It explains the appeal of much science fiction, which is concerned with closed communities, whether on a space ship or on an alien planet.[27]

---

[26] David Lodge, *Write On: Occasional Essays '65-'85* (London: Secker & Warburg, 1986), p. 169; reprinted below.
[27] J. P. Kenyon, "*Lucky Jim* & After: The Business of University Novels," (*Encounter*, 54, June 1980), p. 83; reprinted below.

Introductory

And Malcolm Bradbury refers to the large number of novels "which have taken the university or campus as. a significant setting, and read the world of student, academic or general intellectual experience as an emblematic place in culture."[28]

Whether or not the campus is a representative or emblematic place, we should not overlook the *aesthetic* advantages deriving from it as a place. Henry James wrote in the preface to *Roderick Hudson*: "Really, universally, relations stop nowhere, and the exquisite problem of the artist is eternally but to draw, by a geometry of his own, the circle within which they shall happily appear to do so."[29] The university, or college, or campus novel helps the artist by drawing that circle. The traditional campus is even an enclosure, or a cloistered space, and, though many modern universities are decentralized and urban, they are in a sense psychically cloistered and intellectually enclosed. This is an advantage for both author and reader.

Another benefit the academic novel affords is a handy temporal scheme. The academic year provides the time period for any number of academic novels; for others, it is a semester or a term. Each has its boundaries, its rhythms, its predictable points of crisis. Other novelists choose a narrower focus - the first week of college, perhaps; in Oxford novels the period called Schools (when students are supposed to be finishing their studies and taking their exams at the end of their final year) exercises a potent appeal for the novelist. Eights Week, also in the spring but defined by rowing rather than exams, is another such emblematic time. Lionel Trilling's fine short story "Of This Time, Of That Place" puts it nicely:

---

[28] Bradbury, *No, Not Bloomsbury*, p. 330.
[29] Henry James, *Roderick Hudson. The Novels of Henry James, Vol. 1* (1875; New York: Scribner, 1907), p. vii.

17

The Academic Novel

Academic time moves quickly. A college year is not really a year, lacking as it does three months. And it is endlessly divided into units which, at their beginning, appear larger than they are - terms, half-terms, months, weeks. And the ultimate unit, the hour, is not really an hour, lacking as it does ten minutes.[30]

Fiction needs indices of change, and what setting is so rich in them as the college or university, where degrees, graduation, classes and ranks form so central a structure. And the academic year combines a cyclical principle (the faculty and the institution, which return each year to the same points) with a linear one (the students, who are always new, always in motion, always leaving).

There is one more useful point to make about the academic novel: about its tone.

Discussions of the academic novel are, by and large, too humorless. *Most academic novels are comic.* This does not, or need not, make them satiric; and the non-satiric comic novel is not necessarily less worthy than the satiric novel or the so-called "serious" novel (in the lingeringly Puritan sense whereby comic works cannot also be serious).[31] The academic novel may pursue some of the ideological projects attributed to it by Terry Eagleton or Peter Widdowson; it may be, as Janice Rossen argues, an analysis of power relations; but it is also very often *funny*.

---

[30] Lionel Trilling, *Of This Place, Of That Time, and Other Stories* (New York; London: Harcourt Brace Jovanovich, 1979), p. 101.

[31] See A. N. Wilson's distinction between Bradbury and Lodge: Lodge's "comedy is self-referential, and his books are not really any more satires on the university system than P. G. Wodehouse's comedies are satires on the English landed class; whereas *The History Man*, I believe, is pure satire." (*Penfriends from Porlock* (London: Hamish Hamilton, 1988; New York: Norton, 1989), p. 247. This does not make Bradbury superior to Lodge.

18

Introductory

John O. Lyons, introducing his 1962 study, decides that "Another category which can be eliminated on grounds of frivolity is the comic novel of academic life. They merely exaggerate and revel in the pat conventions which plague the serious novels."[32] This is most unfortunate. The idea of "eliminating" *Lucky Jim*, or *Coming From Behind*, or *Pictures from an Institution*, or *Changing Places*, or *Straight Man* on grounds of frivolity is not only painful: it is wrong. While obviously there are some topics which do not lend themselves to comedy, there is no reason why higher education should be among them. Analysis of humor is of course nearly impossible and trying to persuade one person to laugh at what another finds funny is vain; but I take it as evident that humor adds to the pleasure of readers. I am convinced that the high incidence of comedy, ranging from the most delicate verbal touches to broad farce, in academic fiction is one of its most valuable and welcome traits.

---

[32] Lyons, p. xviii.

UNIVERSITY LIFE IN ENGLISH FICTION[1]

Philip Hobsbaum

The place where young people gather at an impressionable time of their lives is bound to be, among other things, a forcing-house of experience. And it is in fiction that such experience tends to be most vividly rendered. It is this concern for the individual that tends to be left out of our discussions about universities. What one misses among the statistics is the human sense of place. A White Paper can give us the general pattern, but it may not tell us how it feels to be an undergraduate in the 1960s. And yet this testimony, too, is admissible evidence.

But the tendency to abstraction is by no means new in the writings of educationalists. It can be found in Cardinal Newman's strictures on the Oxford of his time. His memorandum of 1830, quoted by Meriel Trevor in her recent biography of Newman, discusses the low intellectual standards then prevalent. But it is left to Miss Trevor herself to show the drama of Newman pitting himself against the university authorities. The courses followed were, indeed, mediocre, and the colleges favoured the sons of the rich – gentlemen-commoners, as they were called. Individual tuition[2], and especially the tuition of scholars, was frowned upon. Such shortcomings may help to explain the wistful tone of Newman's *Idea of a University*, which followed a quarter of a century after. Newman was in advance of his time, and grounded these proposals for a new university in Ireland on the desirability of reform, rather than on anything very clearly

---

[1] Previously published in *Twentieth Century, 173* (1964), pp. 139-46.

[2] In other words, teaching, instruction, not fees [Ed.].

to be discerned in the world around him. None of his expository writings give us the feel of the university milieu in the way that *Loss and Gain* does; and this is a piece of fiction. Here, for example, is something that is constant among academics: resentment of a colleague's intellectual stature. This is rather a stupid tutor attempting to advise one of his pupils.

> As to Doctor Brownside, there certainly have been various opinions entertained about his divinity, still, he is an able man, and I think you will gain *good*, gain *good* from his teaching. But mind, I don't *recommend* him; yet I respect him, and I consider that he says many things very well worth your attention. I would advise you, then, to accept the *good* which his sermons offer, without committing yourself to the *bad*. That, depend upon it, Mr Reding, is the golden though the obvious rule in these matters.

Things don't seem to have changed very much: these were the terms in which undergraduates used to be warned against the undue influence of Dr Leavis. And, like Newman, Leavis committed himself to wholesale reform: outlined in his *Education and the University*. The difference is in the airs which the university gives itself. In Leavis's time, it is a matter of getting it to live up to its pretensions; but Newman had first to settle what those pretensions were. And then, as now, there were plenty of people who thought that proposals for reform were out of touch with reality; meaning, usually, that they did not square with the material values held by the gross average of humanity. For instance, the clownish novels of Cuthbert Bede hold the Victorian don in very low esteem. He is dubbed with a name like Slowcoach and is given physical characteristics that are ludicrous. One can't take this sort of thing too seriously, of course, but the Victorian university seems to have been unable to do much in the way of counteracting the natural loutishness of its undergraduates. Practical jokes provide the plot of Cuthbert Bede's *The Adventures of Mr Verdant Green, an Oxford Freshman* and seem to have met with Bede's approval. It appears that the study of the classics did not, any more than the present one of technology, conduce to the creation of serious standards. And, equally, one is unlikely to come across any criterion in these novels by which we can judge their prevailing buffoonery.

But such criteria, it was felt, were needed; and if they could not be supplied by the dons, they were imported from the public schools. Tom Brown got to Oxford in 1861, some twenty years after Mr Verdant Green; and found his lectures a bore and his tutor with little to offer him in lieu.

> He asked me and two other freshmen to breakfast the other morning, and I was going to open out to him; but when I got there I was quite shut up. He never looked one of us in the face, and talked in set sentences, and was cold, and formal, and condescending. The only bit of advice he gave us was to have nothing to do with boating – just the one thing which I feel a real interest in.

So Tom takes this up with great solemnity, if only as a way of avoiding the horse-dealers, cricket-cads and dog-fanciers favoured by the gentlemen-commoners. One chapter proudly sports as its title, "Muscular Christianity"; and the appeal is to temperance and a clean body. But of any form of intellectuality, we find not a sign.

And if the junketings approved by Thomas Hughes are less debauched than those of earlier novels, they still amount to no more than horse-play – town-and-gown battles, and the like. This sort of thing was being celebrated as late as 1913, when Compton Mackenzie produced his notorious *Sinister Street.* At the end of their first week in college, Michael Fane and his associates assert their independence by lighting a bonfire. But there is a difference: such exploits are no longer the overflow of animal spirits, for "the complexion of the gravel was tanned by the numberless bonfires of past generations.... From their windows second-year men, their faces lighted by the ascending blaze, looked down with pleasant patronage upon the traditional pastime of their juniors." Nostalgia has crept in, and the buffoonery of the past has hardened into custom. Their elders, too, are indulgent: the "tall hunched don" whom they insult gives them, next morning, only the mildest of reprimands, and indeed, throughout the book, the Fellows are shadowy, insubstantial beside the hearty figures of the undergraduates. Fane himself has no need of tuition to take his First; and this, for Mackenzie, is the seal of intelligence - not surprisingly, since the dons have no better way of encouraging it than the barren treadmill of study represented in his pages.

Education, as provided by the university, looked rather more attractive to those outside the college gates. One remembers the disputes about Hellenic metres that intersperse the struggles of the hack writers in Gissing's *New Grub Street.* Such people long to live in a world where the only hunger felt is for a pleasing cadence. But, if Gissing had got there, he would have found it populated with Pattisons and Liddells - hard, dull, slogging men, not much preferable to the critics and editors of his own terrain. In the end, one can't feel that a gifted novelist would have done better to be a classical scholar. Consider Hardy, for instance, who identifies himself with the young stonemason in *Jude the Obscure.* He wanders about Oxford, but is somehow excluded from it. His longing, however, is almost an aesthetic one - for cloisters and quadrangles, for processions decked out in academic regalia. What Hardy has in common with Mackenzie and Gissing is a nostalgia that is typically late-Victorian and Edwardian; but what they yearn after was never a live force. Old-world courtesy and regard for scholarship, if indeed they existed in the Victorian university, are no substitute for intellectual force. And here we remember that Arnold, Mill, Morris and Ruskin did their work outside the academic framework.

The Edwardian ideal, then, is hardly an exalted one. Rather it is a desire to be cloistered away from the difficulties of the world. Dramatic expression of a very high order is given to this longing by H. O. Sturgis, in his forgotten novel *Belchamber*. The central figure of this book is master of a great estate, but he would far rather have been a scholar. And the university, to a limited extent, provides a standard throughout. Its attraction is, initially, one of sheer personality: his lordship finds a Gamaliel at whose feet he can sit. At first sight this would seem to be the sort of tutor that, according to Newman, was so wanted in the Victorian university; and certainly the relaxation of the religious requirements and increase in the stipends had attracted a better class of don to college fellowships. About this time we hear of university teachers who were an inspiration to their pupils: Raleigh, for instance, Quiller-Couch, Lowes Dickinson. But Sturgis's hero comes to find that his mentor is adept at arguing either side of a case, using reason to rebut reason. In the end, academic practice seems suspect, and we are left with what we had in the beginning: a longing for the cloister without any conception of the intellectual discipline that such a seclusion might involve. The notion is that of a grammarian: the task, the elucidation of difficult passages. It seems that, for this particular Edwardian, the ideal university would be a retreat from life.

One finds an answer to this in *The Longest Journey*, published only three years after *Belchamber* and owing an immense debt to it. Forster's novel, also, has a crippled hero and a mentor who loves discussion for its own sake. This leads them into a liberal-humanist wilderness, where any decision is likely to be bad, and so is indecision. The feeling is that the university's day is over and that it no longer offers anything to thinking people. The thinker therefore has to leave – to live "out of doors" – and find some way of expressing himself beyond the college gates. The feminine side of this is seen in Rosamond Lehmann. Farewell, Cambridge; and now what? *Dusty Answer*, of course: the total recall of hectic friendships and indulgence in aching nostalgia – for the Backs in springtime, for King's College chapel at Evensong. The book is an argument in a circle familiar in the lives of those who were at university at this time and never quite escaped from it: one goes to Cambridge in order to write about going to Cambridge. Like the Edwardians, her predecessors, Rosamond Lehmann feels critical about the university without knowing how to make use of her criticism. What is certain is that no panacea is to be found in academic life: her heroine is resentful of the entrenchment of books that prevents her from joining in the riot of spring.

But it was possible for novelists to be more constructive than this. At the beginning of the century, new colleges had been started in the provinces, and these gave higher education to people who would never have had such an opportunity before. With the influx into the universities of the working classes, more searching questions were asked. When the dons withdraw from the world and the students deaden themselves at the academic grind, what, in the way of education, is going on? New voices began to be heard – angry ones. They belonged to writers who had expected the university to be a place of enlightenment and culture, and who expressed themselves in tones of bitter disappointment.

The Academic Novel

The professors were not priests initiated into the deep mysteries of life and knowledge. After all, they were only middle-men handling wares they had become so accustomed to that they were oblivious of them. What was Latin? - So much dry goods of knowledge. What was the Latin class altogether but a sort of second-hand curio shop, where one bought curios and learned the market-value of curios; dull curios too, on the whole.

Lawrence, of course; and one of the many things he started off was the red-brick novel. This is Ursula at Nottingham, and she is not at all Edwardian, but wants the university to be more than a retreat for poor bruised souls. It is true that Lawrence's conception of the university has something of the mediaeval in it; but it is the mysticism of the early Church that gives him a standard from which to criticize. Lawrence therefore attacks the linguistic side of the humanities, which the Edwardians took as being the seal of scholarship. What good, he asks, is Anglo-Saxon when one learns it only to answer examination questions in order to get a good job later on?

But in recent times there has been a tendency to let the standards of the world decide those of the university. One thinks most immediately of C. P. Snow: *The Two Cultures and the Scientific Revolution* is practical in the wrong sense. Snow's idea of the university is a preparation for life in a sense very different from that of Lawrence. It is the training of healthy people so that they may take their place in a sick society. But the university as it appears in his novels is rather different from this. For one thing, it is exclusively don-centred. It comes as rather a surprise that there are any undergraduates at all: but they appear very seldom, and then only as a pause in more important proceedings. Snow's fictional college seems to exist mainly in order to elect its officers. His dons intrigue and compete with each other like

26

so many politicians or civil servants. Yet ultimately we need to take a larger view. These men, after all, are in a key position: guardians of culture, explorers of new intellectual territory, instructors of the young. If they are really so content to be mediocre, and to admit mediocre men among them, there isn't very much hope for the university.

There is a case to be made out against such a system, but only its superficialities were sniped at in *Lucky Jim*. The villain of the piece, evasive Professor Welch, exposes himself all too readily. It is no good putting up a stuffed dummy and triumphing in its downfall. In real life, there are professors far more formidable than any Kingsley Amis deals with: empire-builders who boast of the number of work-hours per student in their departments, desiccated pedants whose power to bore is lethal. And Amis's lecturer-hero is in no position to be healthily sceptical: he is himself the author of a paper entitled "The Economic Influence of the Development of Shipbuilding Techniques, 1450-1485." No lively interest in history there! With such a hero, Amis has very little ground from which to launch his attack.

Malcolm Bradbury was shrewder, perhaps, in pinning his novel to a professor in a profound state of doubt. The first chapter of his *Eating People Is Wrong* gives one more of the essential malaise of a provincial university than all the lectures and chapbooks of advanced educationalists. Consider, for example, this description of student life:

> They appeared each year, to eat for three more years in the university refectory, to join sports clubs, and attend the students' union dances held each Saturday night, sliding gracelessly through weekly waltzes and tangos, drinking down beer at the impromptu bar, tempting girls out into the grounds in order to kiss them on damp benches; to throw tomatoes at policemen on three successive rag days, to go out in three years with perhaps as many girl friends,

and finally to leave with a lower second or third class degree, passing on into teaching or business seemingly untouched by what, Treece thought, the university stood for – whatever that was.

This is certainly authentic, but what one might object to is the superior tone. Supposing these students have no values, may not this be a failure on the part of their teachers? Such a failure need not be a defect in tuition so much as an unwillingness to join in the life of the community of which they – equally with the students – are part. There is in many provincial universities a gulf between staff and students which seems impassable; and yet one would have thought it was part of a university teacher's job to make himself available.

Co-exploration, that is to say; not dogmatic pronouncement on the one hand and passive acceptance on the other. Unfortunately it doesn't seem that the university novel is likely to get much further than diagnosis; but even this can be more sympathetic than anything Mr Bradbury provides. The stupidity which he chronicles from on high can be agonizing for the student.

What sane person would lie in bed, as he had lain all morning, trying to screw up enough will-power to get up, alternately deluding himself that another few minutes didn't matter, then silently screaming at the knowledge that he had missed yet another of Macrae's lectures, and then deluding himself that that didn't matter either? He stared at the sloping ceiling above his head. At the moment he felt that he could go on floating amidst the delicious warmth of the bed for ever, secure as an ostrich in its little patch of sand. The outside world was a dream. The final-year student, who wrote essays and drank coffee and all the rest of it, and who was in danger of being thrown out on his neck because he never got up in time to go to lectures, and handed in his half-length coffee-stained essays a week late, was some unreal Doppelgänger.

This is from a neglected novel by Keith Walker called *Running on the Spot*. Its great merit is that it looks at the university from a student's angle, and describes the idiocies that he is driven into through the situations that he is expected to undergo. Too little grant, for instance, or the academic treadmill: Lucky Jim's paper is required reading for the history student. Teacher and pupil share in common only their frustration, and wrangle joylessly like Orwell's O'Brien and Smith in *1984*.

"I know all your theories and arguments. I know all the answers to them. You're inside me."

"That's only because you're cleverer than I am .... It would only need someone more intelligent than you to know all the answers to your argument and you'd be inside them."

As Sturgis maintained in *Belchamber*, there is no appeal to reason which cannot be rebutted by an appeal to reason. But, in this case, the sterile controversy seems inseparable from academic life; and what might be a way of demonstrating one's intuitions has become a substitute for intuition itself.

The conclusions that can be drawn from this relate to far more than university life alone. In their several ways, Amis, Bradbury and Walker are criticizing the universities as portrayed by C. P. Snow: a microcosm of the great world outside. But none of them succeeds in reversing Snow's view completely: one would have to insist that the neurotic student is sane and that it is the criteria by which he is judged that are unbalanced. This is a stand which Peter Ferguson takes in *Autumn for Heroes*, where four different people react against the society they live in, and are, consequently, punished. One of these people is an Oxford girl: we are made to question very searchingly the sort of education she is getting.

> "The whole principle of reading English here is that you don't read something to appreciate it. You've got to look for something solid and reliable to test people on, dates, sources, manuscripts, all the irrelevant muck that keeps an establishment of inspirationless deadbeats in the money. If anyone wrote in schools that he liked so-and-so's poetry, he'd be suspected of naive padding."

The character who says this, however, is no more than a critic. His satire is negative, damaging beyond repair, and all the more authentic for that. But it is by no means baseless. Put a young girl through such a course, and she may indeed be taught to formulate intellectual concepts; but they will be pitiably out of phase with her stunted emotional development. The gap between intellect and emotion is, ultimately, what brings about the breakdown of Mr Ferguson's heroine.

This kind of failure – and stress – is very characteristic of modern universities. Philip Larkin wrote a fine novel on this theme, just after the war (*Jill*, reissued this year[3]). Here the young provincial student, crammed for the ancient university, finds himself completely at odds with the life there. But it would be equally easy to point to the lost people wandering through the red-brick novels of Bradbury and Walker: first-generation students ill-prepared by

---

[3] i.e., 1964 [Ed.].

municipal grammar-schools. No wonder the flow of university novels shows no sign of drying up.

And the stresses seem to be getting worse. The Victorian university appears in fiction as a place of tedious studies which can readily be forgotten in mindless leisure pursuits: it is a university for the moneyed, where a degree need not be taken seriously. With the Edwardians, the university relies far more on spurious traditionalism – mainly because so many sensitive plants seek shelter within its protecting walls. But through the twentieth century come more and more novels about the provincial university, or – what comes to the same thing – the grammar-school student at an ancient foundation. And the criticisms become more trenchant year by year.

These criticisms are disturbing; doubly so, when one considers the statistics of undergraduate suicides and the glib talk that goes on about the further expansion of universities and the broadening of the syllabus to include more and more subjects. More material to be learned by rote for examinations; less time to pause, reflect, enjoy. The facts about university life are chronicled in their abundance: it is common knowledge that the country cannot afford to provide a life of leisure for the deserving few. It isn't yet so obvious that it cannot afford not to: the facts are there, too, but the novels provide the fine focus by which they may be assessed.

Perhaps we are expecting too much from the universities. There is very little evidence that they were ever the palaces of enlightenment visualized by Lawrence's heroine, or Ferguson's. And yet the continuing tide of rancour suggests that they are expected to be, and that undergraduates are not content to be disappointed in their expectations. Certainly the anger of creative writers cannot be left out of our calculations. Universities are melting-pots for human endeavour, where people are trying to find themselves, and have, even now, just about enough time to make the attempt – before the shades of the office and the mortgage close in and leave neither curiosity nor energy for exploration. The question that novelists keep asking is how far the universities have helped them to map out new territory.

FICTIONS OF ACADEME: DONS AND REALITIES[1]

George Watson

Academe is an odd subject for fiction. A university, after all, is a place for students who have barely started to live, and professors who have done all (or nearly all) the living they are ever likely to do. And yet the spate of academic plays and novels goes on: the nearest thing English fiction has had to a new subject since 1945. The theatres are full of it. On the last three occasions when, eager to shake off a taint of the academic, I have travelled from Cambridge to London to see a new play, or at least one new to me, they have all turned out to be about universities - an experience that makes you wonder if it was worth leaving the gates of your college. There is Michael Frayn's *Donkey's Years*, a brisk farce about the wife of a college master not quite having it off with an old flame during an Old Boys' reunion; Simon Gray's *Otherwise Engaged*, which is set in London, indeed, but where the references to Oxford and Cambridge are embarrassingly numerous; and Tom Stoppard's *Jumpers*, a parody of an academic lecture accurate enough to be worth resenting.

The university novel, meanwhile, stumbles on. It has its 19th century forbears: but it started what by now looks like its continuous life with C. P. Snow's *The Masters* in 1951 and Kingsley Amis's *Lucky Jim* two years later. Since the 1950s, academe has provided fiction with a major theme for the first time in our literary history: William Cooper's *Struggles of Albert Woods*, Angus Wilson's *Anglo-Saxon Attitudes*, and a fistful of novels by David Lodge and Malcolm Bradbury – both of whom are professors of

---

[1] Previously published in *Encounter, 51* (November 1978), pp. 42-5.

English in real life, if reality it be. The species is by now old enough to have engendered its own little breed of nostalgia; Philip Larkin, now a university librarian at Hull, has recently reissued *Jill*, his first novel, with an introduction about what undergraduate life in War-time Oxford was like and how he first came to meet Kingsley Amis there, and Malcolm Bradbury, in a new introduction to his first novel, *Eating People Is Wrong*, has told what it felt like to be a first-generation student in a civic university like Leicester in the 1950s, puzzled and fascinated as a newcomer with the liberal values of an unknown style of life. And nostalgia has fuelled two recent collections of essays, *My Oxford* and *My Cambridge*, assembling undergraduate reminiscences for a public apparently insatiable in its thirst for revelations about university life, whether literary or sexual.

The phenomenon is Anglo-American, and hardly shared by our continental allies. Americans have had it for about as long, as Mary McCarthy's *Groves of Academe* and Randall Jarrell's *Pictures from an Institution* demonstrate – a fact powerfully confirmed by the play and film of Edward Albee's *Who's Afraid of Virginia Woolf?* In the 1950s and 1960s, and for the first time, universities suddenly became at once hot news and the main stuff of fiction. It is a mood that may have faded, though revivals of *Jumpers* suggest it has not simply faded away. A. Alvarez, better known as a poet and critic, produced his first novel in 1974 when he was in his late forties; it was called *Hers*, and its hero is a sort of young Jewish D. H. Lawrence, who satisfies the neglected wife of his professor before deciding to quit academe forever. (It is an established fictional convention that the professor is better at footnotes than in bed.) Most people who read, it is now probable, have either been to a university themselves, or have a close relative who has: the first age in history of which this could be said, even though

Britain remains the only considerable nation in the industrial West *not* to have yielded to the temptation of mass higher education.[2] It may be true that universities have recently suffered in funds and in prestige. But they still have a terribly permanent air about them, even the newest, and it would be unrealistic to suppose they could simply fold up or go away.

Let me make my own general view clear at the start. I hope, as well as believe, that universities will survive and prosper; I draw my own academic salary, diminished as it lately is in real value, with a good conscience, and encourage pupils to draw their grants in a similar spirit. When it comes to Academe, I am for it, groves and all. On the other hand, I have several reasons, all partly selfish, for hoping that Anglo-American campus fiction will fade away and die.

For one thing, it cannot be good for universities, or any other institutions one can easily think of outside politics, to operate under a blaze of glamourising publicity. For another, the very nature of that publicity, which is critical but still titillating, may (as Sex Education is credibly reported to have done) weaken a taste for the real thing. It may also cause disappointment in the young; I am haunted by the fear that many a freshman expects a university to be more than it is and more than it can reasonably hope to be.

And then again, my deepest convictions urge that there is something wrong with a literature in which universities are felt to be consumingly interesting; I hear myself murmur, with Coriolanus, that there is a world elsewhere. When I challenge friends and colleagues, in the interval of *Jumpers* or any similar play, with my own troubled sense that public interest in academe is vastly overdone, they

---

[2] The total number of those in Higher Education [in Britain] in 1976-77 was 519,000, of which the estimated proportion of working-class students applying was 25%.

assure me that this is simply a fact of the age we live in. Universities, the wife of a colleague remarked the other day, "... are the only communities left in the modern world." A remark like that is enough to spoil anybody's evening. If it is really true, as I desperately hope it is not, then it is a judgment on the age that Jeremiah might have hesitated to loose. Is our sense of community really so impoverished that universities are all there is?

A backward glance may help to create a sense of perspective. Of course university fiction did not literally begin with Snow and Amis a quarter of a century ago. The Victorians had their occasional farces on the subject, like *Mr Verdant Green* and *Charley's Aunt,* as well as thoughtful novels about young clergymen losing their faith. And it is common enough for the hero of a Victorian novel, like Thackeray's Pendennis or Trollope's John Caldigate, to spend a chapter or two in an ancient seat of learning, sometimes idling, or falling in debt or in love, before he leaves for the world that really counts. Like Thackeray himself, and many others down to the Second World War, he can depart without taking a degree. That phrase, common as it is in the *Dictionary of National Biography,* is already impressively archaic in its implications. Nowadays we call those who do that "drop-outs." The career of Evelyn Waugh, who tippled his way through three years of Oxford undergraduate life before utterly failing to satisfy the examiners, is no longer encouraged in an age where the Exchequer foots the bill. Indeed it is barely possible. Even heirs to thrones now sit exams and pass them, which is more than Edward VII or George VI troubled to do; and the United Kingdom now looks ready to greet, at some future day, its first graduate monarch.

Nobody can say that universities are not behaving seriously. The fact is that the college life depicted by Evelyn Waugh in his first novel, *Decline and Fall,* no longer exists. I do not call that immortal little book a university novel, since it merely begins and ends in academe. Its central assumption is nearer to *Pendennis* than to *Lucky Jim*, and by now dated enough to be interesting: that nobody but a complete muff would bother with a university at all, except as a swift passage from school to real life, and that anyone who remains in one is an existential failure. The university was a place for well-born idlers, on the one hand, and solemnly assiduous scholarship-boys on the other, and that system lasted right down to the 1940s. I am just old enough to remember the end of it. But by the 1960s it was so remote that it was hard to persuade students it had ever existed. How could we explain, to that passionate generation, that there had once been a time when statesmen like Disraeli or Churchill did not bother with a university at all, and with only passing regrets, and when other notabilities like Sir Thomas Beecham left of their own accord after a year or two because there was "no one there worth talking to"?

Nobody can understand the vogue for university fiction in the 1950s and '60s without understanding the vogue for academe itself. By now, I suspect, that vogue is withering, as we return to something a little nearer the Victorian condition. Whether because high prices make work necessitous, or because a collective hysteria is fading, there are once again intelligent young people who prefer on leaving school not to enter a university. But that view, in the first flourishing time of the university novel, was rare to the point of being almost inconceivable. The world of C. P. Snow's *Masters* and Kingsley Amis's *Lucky Jim* is based on one enormous and unspoken premise: that any intelligent person would go to a university if he had the choice.

To explain that mood, which already looks remote, one needs to examine the claims then made by the professoriate itself, and made in a calm expectation of acceptance. Student militancy in the 1960s was a solemn parody of donnish pretensions in the 1950s. It is only because the middle-aged looked and sounded powerful that the young conceived there was power to be had in academic committees; and it was only when they won the right to sit on those committees that they discovered their mistake. There is no power in universities, in any serious sense of that word: only a facsimile of power. In the wider world of affairs, they are charmingly impotent institutions, dependent on pleasing others to survive at all.

But dons looked powerful in the 1950s, and plainly saw universities as cockpits of intellectual influence. This was the decade that spawned the media-don. A New York philosopher once told me how, walking across the campus of Columbia University, Lionel Trilling had turned to him and remarked: "You know, I have power ... ". It was an accurate remark in those years, soon after 1945. I have visited American homes where volumes of Trilling stood on the shelves and were quoted with little less veneration than Holy Scripture a century or two earlier. An ambitious young man, entering a university during or soon after the Second World War, might easily feel he was entering an arena where power over countless minds was there for the taking, if he worked and planned for it. His mood as a freshman might resemble André Gide's silent address to the city of Paris in 1889, on the first page of his journal: *"Et maintenant, à nous deux."*

The Lucky Jim of those days was nothing like a Pendennis. The university novel might be a study in disillusionment, but it was always a study in illusions too. All these young heroes believed, until they ceased to believe, that academe might be their working place and their abode forever. And they believed it because their first, though fast fading, image of a don was of something more than a scholar, and certainly a world away from the comic derelicts of Victorian fiction. The don was suddenly a public figure: a voice on *The Brains Trust,* carried by radio or television around the globe; a prophet and pundit in Sunday newspapers; and a sage on the parental bookshelf.

He was also a creative artist. Perhaps this was the most surprising new possibility of all in that post-War age: that the academic need remain no mere pedant, but could dazzle the world as a Poet, Dramatist, or Novelist too. The university novel is after all largely a novel written by dons. C. P. Snow had been a scientific Fellow of Christ's College, Cambridge, and its Senior Tutor, though by 1951 he had ceased to be a resident member of a university; but *The Masters* was supposed to lift the lid on the intrigues of college men. By the time *Lucky Jim* appeared Kingsley Amis was a lecturer in English at Swansea, and though the novel is based on earlier and reported experience, it was widely imagined to have been built on observation; and *Eating People Is Wrong* was written by a graduate student who had observed his own mentors too closely for their own comfort and who was shortly to become a university teacher himself. The prolific fiction of Iris Murdoch, once a Fellow in Philosophy in an Oxford college, touches on academe only occasionally, but it demonstrates that the two roles were highly compatible, and that the one might take strength from the other.

In that same expansive era, many American universities appointed "Writers on Campus." A wall of suspicion had tumbled down. I do not know how many British or American academics published a novel before the Second World War under their own names - Snow himself, certainly, and my late colleague at Cambridge, F. L. Lucas, are among the few that spring to mind. But by the 1940s, arts faculties in our English universities had moved out of one assumption about the creative act into another and far more arresting one. It was no longer disgraceful, or even odd, for an academic to be known to have written a poem or a novel or a play. So much the more exciting, then, to be an academic.

One odd misunderstanding about that post-War world now seems rooted in literary history, so it may be worth a moment's thought to root it out. It now seems to be widely believed, even more in the USA than in Britain, that the Angry Young Men of the 1950s were of inferior social standing to the run of Victorian or Georgian novelists and poets; and that they owed their presence in Oxford (or, less commonly Cambridge) to the Butler Education Act of 1944.[3]

The last part of all that, at least, must be mistaken. Whatever contributions to education and culture are owing to the Master of Trinity College, Cambridge, he cannot be held responsible for Philip Larkin or Kingsley Amis. Both were undergraduates at St John's College, Oxford, well before his Act reached the statute book: Larkin in October 1940, and Amis months later, in April 1941, followed by John Wain in 1943. Iris Murdoch went up as early as 1938. Nor can their social origins have seemed in any way odd there. In his new introduction to *Jill*, Larkin has explained that War-time Oxford was austere with rationing and free of social distinction, the impulse being to minimise such differences. That is certainly the atmosphere I recall shortly after the War. At all events, there is nothing exceptional about our ancient universities admitting scholarship boys: they have been doing that since their medieval foundations. Myths die hard; none harder, surely, than that of Oxford and Cambridge as aristocratic preserves.

The humility of my own social origins I would prefer

---

[3] Legislation which provided state funding for students to attend universities, in the form of grants [Ed.]

not to unveil, for fear they may not prove shocking enough. But a tutor of Trinity College, Cambridge of the 1930s once told me that in those pre-War years more than half his undergraduate pupils were from maintained schools or the public sector. The Butler Act formalised certain existing practices, and pushed a partly open door a little wider open still. But it was not a revolution; and it was in no way responsible for the New Novel of the '50s. Most of those novelists were already at a university; and not one of them, I may add, was of a social origin as humble as that of Charles Dickens, whose father was imprisoned for debt and who managed to be a better novelist than any of them without going to a university at all.

The new academic hero, like his creator, had one toe in the ocean of academy and kept the rest of himself out of it. Lucky Jim leaves that life for good at the end of the novel, convinced that its corruptions are subtler than those of moneymaking, and joyfully enters the world of City finance. The hero of *Hers*, 20 years later, makes a similar choice, selling off his hardbacks in a final gesture of intellectual resignation. The rash fierce blaze of academic enthusiasm did not last; and these novels, after all, are in a clearly recognisable sense autobiographical. After a dozen years at Swansea (1949-61) interrupted by a year at Princeton (1958-59), Amis tried Cambridge for two years before resigning academe altogether in 1963 for literary London. The author of *Hers*, now his near-neighbour in Hampstead, has made the same choice in abbreviated form, lecturing at times but preferring his liberty from the timetable. In all these authors, academe is something to exorcise: it needs to be lived for a time, but lived in order to demonstrate that it is ultimately unlivable. There *is* a world elsewhere.

The borderline instances are equally instructive. Philip

Larkin is a university librarian, but does not teach. John Wain has spent five years as professor of poetry at Oxford - as temporary as all such professors are. And Iris Murdoch has long since resigned her teaching fellowship. The seeming exceptions are instructive too: David Lodge's *Changing Places* and Malcolm Bradbury's *History Man*, which both appeared in 1975, are by active university teachers. But the first novel is a resounding farce about an Anglo-American academic exchange where wives are swopped (and reswopped) as casually as curricula; and the second, a savage satire on a trendy-lefty sociologist in a new university, stands well beyond disillusionment, biting acidly into the heart of modern academic pretension. The fiercest sceptics of academe are no longer those who leave it. But why, one cannot help wondering, did the author of *Lucky Jim* wait more than ten years before following his own hero to the metropolis?

As universities are brought within a sense of scale, with cuts and perhaps more cuts, we may expect their fictions to fade with them, though the old and the middle-aged may still choose to write of their remembered youth. Meanwhile, these fictions offer a sizeable charge-sheet against the institutions we know, or have recently known. I believe them to be seriously plausible charges; and will distinguish three, in mounting order of gravity.

1) *The sin of Pygmalion.* Those who teach sometimes suffer from a professional deformation of wanting their pupils to resemble themselves. The illusion has its farcical aspects, if you pause to consider what a whole nation of dons would look like. "There was one allowance they never under any circumstances made," remarked Randall Jarrell of his colleagues in *Pictures from an Institution*: "that the students might be right about something, and they wrong." Lucky Jim's exploitation by his ruthless professor is Amis's

version of the same point.

2) *Hypocrisy*. Does the enlightened don really mean what he says? His style of life does little to suggest it. The Lefter your views, the higher and fatter you live: that is the burden of *The History Man*, the most withering exposure of academic hypocrisy since *The Groves of Academe*.

3) *Righteousness*. A sage cannot afford to be wrong. And our universities – or at least their most vocal and highly publicised elements – were publicly wrong in the 1960s about public events. There can be little appeal in history against that collective hysteria that was once called the New Left. Violence-worship among intellectuals is not a fact to be forgotten or excused. Few among the young, it is true, knew they were being manipulated by middle-aged professionals hell-bent on promotion. They were easy fodder. But the spectacle is one that ordinary men will not quickly forget or forgive.

Our intelligentsia, to speak bluntly, has a lot of egg on its face. It can choose now to distance its indignation through farce, as in *Jumpers* or *Changing Places*; or blur it with cynicism; or pretend that nothing really happened. But a memory of the 1960s lingers guiltily on. Those who shouted then, all shouted for dictatorship and the glamour of the gun: the rest failed to shout at all. The moral purity of violence - that was the greatest of all the fictions and falsehoods that academe once took to its heart, and from which it must now find its painful way back to a world of rational debate and tolerant hearts.

THE WAR AGAINST THE ACADEMY[1]

Leslie Fiedler

Indeed, it is the revolt against school, and in particular against the university, which most clearly distinguishes the generation of the Sixties from those which immediately preceded it. Given the opportunity, that generation prefers (theoretically at least) to go on the road rather than into school; and even, if forced so far, would choose the madhouse over college, prison over the campus. Yet, at the very center of the generations immediately before them, there stands a group of novelists bound together, whatever their social origins, by a common social fate: that is, by a commitment, primary with some of them, secondary with others, to the university. Among distinguished recent American writers of fiction who have taught, or are teaching, in universities are Saul Bellow, Isaac Rosenfeld, Bernard Malamud, Philip Roth, Mary McCarthy, Randall Jarrell, John Hawkes, John Barth, Wright Morris, Walter Van Tilburg Clark, Robert Penn Warren, Peter Taylor, Robie Macauley, Herbert Gold, Lionel Trilling, Vladimir Nabokov, and a host of others.

As a matter of fact, its role as teacher in the university may seem in the long run the truly distinguishing characteristic of the generation of the Forties-Fifties, more critical even than its urban origins, or the particular flavor lent it by the Jewish writers who constitute so large a part of it. Naturally, the writers of that generation have distilled out of their experience a kind of fiction new at least in theme, a sub-genre of the novel which treats the academic community as a microcosm reflecting the great world, an

---

[1] Previously published in *Waiting for the End* (New York: Stein and Day, 1964; London: Jonathan Cape, 1965), pp. 138-53.

adequate symbol of our total society. The college novel is a form as clearly defined for us as the historical romance or the tale of terror; and, indeed, it usually is a tale of terror, with appropriate comic overtones. In this respect, it resembles the war novel of the Twenties, and especially the Hollywood novel of the Thirties: that other product of the American writer's dream of finding a job not wholly at odds with what he is driven to do, whether it pays or not. The encounter between such a dream and reality is bound to eventuate in a catastrophe at once comic and horrible, a pratfall from which the comedian does not rise again; and models for such pratfalls are provided in Fitzgerald's unfinished *The Last Tycoon*, as well as Nathanael West's *The Day of the Locust*.

Fitzgerald's book provides, in addition, suggestions for introducing into such new versions of Gothic Burlesque, elements of the class struggle. And, indeed, the college or more properly, anti-college novel of the Forties-Fifties is distinguished from earlier American books with academic settings by its quasi-Marxian or Popular Front view of the relationship between professors and administrators. As early as Hawthorne's *Fanshawe*, there had been novels in which college-educated authors returned in imagination to the scenes of their youth; but unlike *Fanshawe*, and the scores of middlebrow entertainments with campus settings which followed, from *Fair Harvard* to *Stover at Yale*, or even such works of serious novelists as Fitzgerald's *The Beautiful and the Damned* and Faulkner's *Sanctuary*, recent academic novels deal primarily with professors rather than students. When students enter at all, they enter briefly to seduce, or be seduced by, their teachers, thus providing erotic relief from the struggle of faculty and administrative officers at the barricades. In this light, George Stewart's *Doctor's Oral* seems a transitional book, representing, as it were, the American author in the process of getting his PhD, and thus graduating from the distillation of undergraduate reminiscence to the dispensing of post-graduate gossip.

Yet despite the large number of talented writers who have taught in college and have been willing to tell the tale (Robert Penn Warren, Randall Jarrell, Mary McCarthy, Bernard Malamud, Howard Nemerov and Robie Macauley come to mind), we do not yet have a college novel to compare with West's account of the artist in Hollywood or with Hemingway's of the writer at war; perhaps because, in the university, tragedy tends to be reduced to the pathetic, and the comic to stir a titter rather than a belly-laugh. Or perhaps it is the incestuous nature of the academic novel, the apparently irresistible temptation implicit in it that makes its practitioners abandon their administrator villains in favor of writing about those most like them in the university. Randall Jarrell's *Pictures from an Institution* typifies the genre, being a book about a writer writing a book about a college; and beyond it we imagine a counter-counter-novel about a writer writing about a writer writing about a writer in the academy.[2]

Or perhaps the failure of the anti-college novel has to be explained on the grounds that failure is its very subject, and that its authors typically cannot maintain enough distance between their protagonists and themselves to keep the inadequacies of the former from seeming their own. As accounts of the writer's continuing doomed battle

---

2 Most recently Jack Ludwig has written, in *Confusions* [(Toronto: McClelland and Stewart; London: Secker & Warburg, 1963)], a college novel intended to end all college novels. At least his protagonist, contemplating one of his own (surely the one in which he appears), attempts to make a pact with the Devil to help him achieve so improbable an end. "Devil, tell me," he says, "if I merge with you will you guarantee ... that this book will kill off, once and for all, the Jewish novel *and* the campus novel?" To which the Devil answers, "What, what? Should I bargain away my primary vehicles?"

with the establishment in its manifold forms, latter-day academic novels tend to fall into self-pity or self-exculpation, since they are inevitably histories of defeat, a defeat which the institution the writer berates may consider his, but which he asserts (without final conviction) is the institution's. In any case, the feelings which motivate such books are primarily frustration and impotent rage - secondarily the desire to strike back and be revenged by making a last-minute success out of failure: i.e. a best-selling or critically acclaimed novel. And precisely such successes wrested from such failures have been achieved in books which present the writer's case against the army, or even Hollywood.

Why not then in the anti-college novel? Is it because such novels are often too circumstantial, too much *romans-à-clef*, or personal justifications, ripped unaltered from the diary, or directly transcribed from the complaint to the American Association of University Professors? But once more, precisely such undisguised apologies have survived the occasions they bewailed, and outlived the friends and enemies they travestied or praised, Hemingway's *The Sun Also Rises*, for instance, or Henry Miller's *Tropic of Cancer* - so why not academic novels, too? Is it simply that no one has ever succeeded in making typical university events seem at once as banal and surreal as they actually are? Most college novels are, in fact, not nearly grotesque enough for their subjects, and end up seeming not the descents into hell their authors had surely intended, on one level or another, but merely descriptions of obstacle courses devised by minds more apt at tedium than terror. They are, that is to say, hopelessly middlebrow, muted where they pretend to be moderate, melodramatic where they pretend to be tragic, commonplace where they pretend to be wise. And this is, surely, their essential flaw, the clue to why they inevitably end by falling into the very

47

attitudes they begin by satirizing. Certainly most of them seem not so much transcendent explorations of the failures of institutions of higher learning as depressing symptoms of the way in which such institutions subserve the flight from excellence and the parody of high art represented by the triumph of midculture in our lives.

Some literary forms appear to be born middlebrow, while others have to be radically debased to suit middlebrow ends; and the college novel, like, say, the earnest exposé of advertising in such sub-novels as *The Big Ball of Wax*, or attacks in satirical science fiction on organized religion, is an innately vulgar form. Certainly two of its major themes which we have already noticed – the teacher as liberal and innocent victim of social repressions and the teacher as lecher and guilty seducer of the young – belong respectively to the stock subjects of sentimental, popular-front politics and to garden-variety pornography. Both of these demand cliché rather than truth, since their end is titillation rather than insight; and both are hard to avoid, since they are as old, or older than, the form itself.

Long before the kind of college had been invented to which the writer can come to be disillusioned, the archetypal story of Abelard and Heloise had been adapted to novel form by Jean-Jacques Rousseau in his *Julie, or the New Eloise*; and the notion of the teacher burning with lust behind his pretense to detached wisdom has continued to excite the popular imagination on levels progressively more and more debased. The truth is, of course, that the relationship of teacher and taught is a passionate one in essence, though no official theory of education has taken this into account since the collapse of the Greek synthesis of pedagogy, gymnastics and pederasty expounded in Plato's *Symposium*. But middlebrow writers have never forgotten it, taking advantage of relaxing taboos to make more and more explicit the aura of sex which the mass mind connects not only with teachers but with coeds as well, even when quite unencouraged.

Lowbrow fantasy has always conceived of college as a place where atheism and communism are taught, while middlebrow liberalism has thought of it rather as one where those two challenges to orthodoxy are persecuted; but both have agreed that within its walls good girls are likely to be deflowered by their mentors as well as their fellow students. And the writers of college novels have done much to sustain this view. Herbert Kubly's recent *The Whistling Zone* is a case in point, not only describing a pair of professorial love affairs and an academic cuckolding, but culminating in a campus orgy dripping with more sperm than has flowed in any American book since *Moby Dick*; but Kubly intersperses his sex with pious exhortations to political tolerance, and righteous sermons about freedom in the classroom. More sophisticated, and consequently more frankly pornographic, though not without some satirical intent, is the account of the adventures of a particularly luscious college girl (saved from her lubricious teacher only by the intervention of a boy lover of that teacher) in "Maxwell Kenton's" *Lollipop*, one of the latest books to have passed from a first publication by the Olympia Press, which launched *The Ginger Man* and *Lolita*, to the list of a respectable American publishing firm.

If, however, the relationship of teacher to student in the university is unconfessedly passionate, his relationship to the administration is avowedly political; and since the time of Senator McCarthy, at least, has been seen in the light of the middlebrow liberals' defense against all attacks on the intellectuals' flirtation with communism. For serious writers, however, the mass of obtuse clichés associated with that defense have seemed as formidable an obstacle to

49

art and truth as those which have grown up around campus love life; and they have sought to redeem the former, as they have the latter, by ambiguity and parody and inversion. Their models in this regard have been Nathanael West's *A Cool Million*, which attempted to rescue Horatio Alger for literature by standing him on his head, and Saul Bellow's *The Victim*, which succeeded in refurbishing the liberal-sentimental novel about anti-Semitism by dissolving into ambiguity the relationship which joins anti-Semite and Jew.

So more ambitious and subtle novelists have tried to free the academic novel from the limitations of erotic reverie and ritualistic liberalism, by making, on the one hand, a sexual victim rather than an aggressor of the professor, and, on the other, by turning him from the guileless butt of reaction into a disingenuous exploiter of the clichés of the politically enlightened. Quite early on, Faulkner had portrayed Temple Drake, the University of Mississippi student in *Sanctuary*, as more seduced than seducing, but no teachers were numbered among her prey; and not until Robie Macauley's *The Disguises of Love* was there a detailed, self-conscious study of the seduction of a professor by a coed, in that ironic mode which we are likely to associate these days with Nabokov's *Lolita*. So extraordinary, however, did this pursuit appear at first to one critic, conditioned by conventional notions of who pursues whom in the classroom, that he accused Macauley of having fallen back on what that critic called the "Albertine strategy," of having, like Proust, presented a really homosexual relationship in the guise of a heterosexual one.

In an analogous way, Mary McCarthy's *The Groves of Academe* parodies the political platitudes of the academic world by portraying a grossly inefficient professor, a monster of self-pity and self-adulation, who hangs on to his job by pretending to have been a communist – thus becoming the beneficiary of the stereotype propagated by a hundred middlebrow novels and ten thousand middlebrow tracts proving that a commitment to the radical movement (at the proper moment, of course) was the noblest of human errors. *The Groves of Academe* is a witty and satisfying book; but it is essentially a parasitic one, its satisfactions, like those of parody always, depending on a knowledge of, and contempt for, the kind of literature which it inverts and mocks. Finally, that is to say, it does not transcend its occasion, though in its failure it provides many more incidental pleasures than most books of the genre to which it belongs. In no case, at any rate, has a fictional work of independent power and enduring appeal been created against the drag toward middlebrow banality that besets even the most wary writer of academic fiction.

Nevertheless, we keep trying. The number of academic novels turned out in the Forties and Fifties exceeds many times over the number of Hollywood novels produced in the Thirties, in part because the professor, and even the administrator, is driven to turn writer in emulation of the writer turned professor (think of Carlos Baker, one-time chairman of the Princeton English Department and then anti-academic novelist, or of Stringfellow Barr, first president of St. John's at Annapolis and then author of *Purely Academic*), in part because so many writers have sought the numerous college posts opening wholesale in a time of academic expansion. Is it an accident that Hollywood shrinks as the academy grows, or is it an essential part of the comedy of our cultural life? Driven from one kind of cover, the writer seeks another, the ironic prayer of Melville always on his lips: "Oh time! Oh cash! Oh patience!"

In any case, we must be careful to understand the precise nature of the joke which the community plays on the professor-author at the moment he believes he is playing a joke on it; and to understand this, we must disabuse ourselves of all conventional notions of the "academic" writer and the kind of "academy" he inhabits, particularly those sponsored by Europeans. The American writer who teaches in a university and lives in a college town necessarily inhabits neither a cultural center nor an "ivory tower." Rather than being protected from the bourgeois world, he is plunged into it, immersed in its small politics and petty spites, its institutionalized hypocrisy, its self-righteous timidity, and its endless bureaucratic ineptitude. If it is a refuge from the pressures of real life he is after, he can find that more easily in the artificial paradises of North Beach or Greenwich Village; the world he inhabits may be artificial, too, but it is likely to be a small artificial hell, in which not only the demons who torment him (i.e. deans and administrators) but even his fellow damned are likely to be members of the local Rotary Club.

It must be remembered that the presence of the intellectual in an American university community is bound to be an anomalous one, even when he is a full-fledged PhD, but more especially when he is a writer-in-residence without the customary academic degrees. His appointment is likely to represent (quite like the Hollywood producer's quest for big-name writers) the tribute middlebrow vice pays to highbrow virtue, a tribute inevitably withdrawn when cultural shame feelings yield to hostility and suspicion. And, after all, this is fair enough, for the writer is likely to regard his non-writing colleagues with a certain amount of genial contempt, based on his sneaking conviction that all their differences are to his advantage. The difficulty of his position is compounded in cases where he is not merely an intellectual among anti-intellectuals, but also, say, a Jew among Gentiles, an Easterner among Westerners, a radical among conservatives, a European refugee among the native born, or simply an urban type among defensive provincials.

Two recent attempts to deal with the tragicomedy involved in such situations (though in each a tribute has also been paid to the standard middlebrow problems of sex and politics) are Bernard Malamud's *A New Life* and Vladimir Nabokov's *Pale Fire*: the former, Malamud's valedictory to one college he was about to leave for another; the latter, Nabokov's farewell to teaching. But there is no way out for the teacher-writer in the end. Even when he has exchanged a less sympathetic set of colleagues for a more amiable one, or has fled all academic colleagues forever, he hears still his own hectoring voice demanding: *Why were you there to begin with? What on earth did you think you were after?* And this voice is not really appeased by the answer: *I went to make a book, to turn the very experience in question into art like Mary McCarthy in* The Groves of Academe *or Randall Jarrell in* Pictures from an Institution, *or John Barth in* The End of the Road; *to show how funny it all is, to make clear the joke on everyone, including myself.* To which the first voice answers: *Not funny enough!*

Indeed, there have been some who have found the whole adventure, the entry of the free intellectual into the university, and his future there, not funny at all; but most of these have feared self-pity and have camouflaged their pathos with quips and funny sayings (like Malamud and Barth and Nabokov), though a few have tried to reveal the naked horror behind the superficial humor. The suicide of F. O. Matthiessen, late professor at Harvard and author of that astonishingly non-academic critical work, *The American Renaissance,* has twice over tempted novelists to try their hands (more successfully in May Sarton's *Faithful*

Are the Wounds) at academic tragedies in which his self-destruction and the betrayals that presumably prompted it are made parables of the intellectual's defeat in the university. Unfortunately, in America no fictionist with the gifts and sensitivity of the Italian Cesare Pavese has been moved as Pavese was moved by the death of Matthiessen; and for Pavese no possible novel seemed an adequate response to his feelings about that death. What followed for him was his own suicide - cued, doubtlessly, by many other things beside the example of the American critic he loved, though his suicide note was, like Matthiessen's, the quotation from Shakespeare that had been underlined for them both by Herman Melville: "We must endure our going hence even as our coming hither. The ripeness is all."

For a younger generation of Americans and their spokesmen, however, those who represent the final horror of academic life are not the defeated intellectuals who fled the campus or died on it, but those who have adapted to the demands of the university and stayed in the classroom – most usually to teach literature, and, presumably, to write novels on the side. The viewpoint of the latest generation is not, in any case, that of the professor, licked or victorious, but that of a bright and skeptical student looking *at* the professor, particularly at the kind of professor who, for over two decades now, has helped create the new academic novel. Sometimes, as in William Goldman's *The Temple of Gold*, the eye that looks and the voice that speaks belong to an actual child of the university, a professor's son, whose values, unlike his father's, are derived from popular culture rather than the classics, from the screen version of *Gunga Din* rather than the plays of Euripides.

More usually they are the voice and eye of a sensitive freshman, unattached to the academy except by wavering choice; and what he sees or hears is rendered by some recent college graduate or by one moved in sympathy and love to emulate the undergraduate role, as Salinger is moved to play Franny in the story called by her name. But here is Franny's version of the "section man," the kind of young teacher, proud, as she does not even trouble to note, of his difference from the old-fashioned scholars who taught him, and of his intimate knowledge of recent or currently prized books, and likely, as she has no way of knowing, to end by writing a conventional anti-academic novel.

> ... where I come from, a section man's a person that takes over a class when the professor isn't there or is busy having a nervous breakdown or is at the dentist or something. He's usually a graduate student or something. Anyway, if it's a course in Russian Literature, say, he comes in, in his little button-down-collar shirt and striped tie, and starts knocking Turgenev for about a half hour. Then, when he's finished, when he's completely *ruined* Turgenev for you, he starts talking about Stendhal or somebody he wrote his MA on. Where I go, the English Department has about ten little section men running around ruining things for people, and they're all so brilliant they can hardly open their mouths ....

Only Lionel Trilling has attempted to treat a similar situation from the teacher's, which is to say the adult, point of view, though there is an anticipation of such an approach – much confused by overtones of anti-Semitism – in the section of Thomas Wolfe's *Of Time and the River* which deals with his relationship at NYU with an undergraduate whom he calls Abe Jones. Trilling, more sure of what he is after, has made of his attempt his only wholly successful piece of fiction, the short story "Of This Time, of That Place," which has won an extraordinary kind of fame for so brief a work. Indeed, a recently inaugurated television series based on campus life has as its hero a young instructor, called Joseph Howe after the protagonist of Trilling's story, though the actual shows since the pilot program, which was an adaptation of that story, have had nothing to do with Trilling's vision or the actual plight of the universities. Worthy of much better treatment, Trilling's story invites, by virtue of its subject matter, middlebrow degradation and dilution, despite the fact that it first appeared in the almost archetypically highbrow pages of *Partisan Review*.

And how much more easily is the fiction of Salinger assimilated to the same level; for his earlier stories appeared in *Good Housekeeping, Collier's,* and *The Saturday Evening Post* while, at the height of his career, he has been content to write for the kind of reader to whom the *New Yorker* represents ultimate sophistication. Yet even if the young for whom Salinger means most come out of the social circles to which the readers of the *New Yorker* aspire when they do not belong, this does not make them unrepresentative, nor the stories which appeal to them untypical. This audience consists, it is true, of the cleanest, politest, best dressed, best fed, and best read among the disaffected youth and his protagonists reflect (or explain) that fact. Not junkies or faggots, nor even upper bohemians, his chief characters travel a road which leads from home to school and from school either back home again or to the nuthouse or both. They have families and teachers and psychiatrists rather than lovers or friends; and their crises are likely to be defined in terms of whether or not to go back for the second semester to Vassar or Princeton, Dana Hall or St Mark's. Their *angst* is improbably motivated by such questions as: "Does my date for the Harvard weekend *really* understand what poetry is?" or "Is it possible that my English instructor hates literature after all?"

I do not mean by reduction to mock the concerns of Salinger's characters; they cannot in any case be reduced, and I should only mock myself making fun of them. For better or worse, a significant number of young Americans live in a world where politics is meaningless, words in the newspaper repeated by the solemn old; and sex unreal – a threat or a promise, a compulsion or a curse, but never a pleasure; and in that world, the classroom and the football game provide adequate arenas for anguish and joy, both to the dull majority who go to them, and to the more sensitive minority who stay away from them. To that world, at any rate, Salinger has been more faithful than it perhaps deserves; more faithful than one would have expected of a writer who, far from remaining in it, with whatever ambivalence, like Trilling, for example, was busted out of it for good early in his college career. For this reason, Salinger, unaffiliated as he is, must be understood as an academic novelist, though one fixed forever in the student's stance at the point he had reached when he flunked out; and in this regard, he resembles such other notable flunkees, returning forever in the imagination to the sophomore year they never quite attained, as Faulkner and Fitzgerald.

If Faulkner's Temple Drake stands as the classic coed of the Twenties, the Franny of Salinger's Glass stories bids to become her equivalent for the Fifties, her only rival Denise, the young lady in search of an orgasm who shuttles back and forth among T. S. Eliot, her psychoanalyst, and two lovers in Norman Mailer's short story, "The Time of Her Time." Mailer's story preserves much of the brutal impact of Faulkner's novel; and if there is a decline in terror and intensity in Salinger's, this is not only because of the markets for which he writes, but also because he is more faithful to the general experience of the middle class young in our cushy times. Not the orgasm, as Mailer would theoretically insist, but madness, as Salinger instinctively knows, what politer circles call a "nervous breakdown," is the fatal Cleopatra of the young; for they are fighting now new enemies in new wars, not the Anthony Comstocks with whose ghost Mailer still jousts, but precisely the most enlightened of their elders. And this, of course, those elders find harder to understand in direct proportion to their enlightenment. Indeed, the females among them, earnest readers of the *New Yorker* one and all, revealed the depth of their incomprehension, when "Franny" first appeared in that magazine, by interpreting her collapse in the face of impending insanity as a symptom of pregnancy.

The revolt they remember, and are braced to understand and forgive in the young (as their parents did not understand and forgive it in them), is the sexual revolt, the attack on vestigial Puritanism and obsolescent chivalry which had set Temple in motion and had led her to take up the weapons of booze and promiscuity and getting away from home to college. But Franny's is a revolt against literature and the New Criticism, and her weapons are the "Jesus prayer" and the quick retreat from school to home. Certainly this is fair enough, for in the thirty years that separate the two coeds, the culture religion of western Europe has replaced Christianity as the orthodox faith of those most eager to send their children to college, at least if they are urban, middle class Americans; and the pastors to whom our hungry sheep look up in vain are not ministers of the old-time religion, but PhDs in literature and those section men who serve as their acolytes. In a society presided over by this new clergy, to play with Vedanta or Buddhism, or even Christian orthodoxy, except as reflected in certain poetic texts like Eliot's *Four Quartets*, i.e. to seek a salvation beyond the reach of art, is considered heresy or insanity, or some particularly blasphemous compound of both, for which the recommended cure is psychiatry.

Franny, at any rate, who will not write the proper critical papers or go out for the next college play, seems, not only to her elders and her more submissive peers, but even to herself, a heretic guilty as charged and therefore self-condemned to a "nervous breakdown." Certainly, she enters the scene in which Salinger asks us to be interested as an academic "drop-out": one of that group of quiet protesters who adapted passive resistance to American conditions long before it was taken up by CORE, and who have managed to shake our society or at least to impress it to a point where the President himself had begun to set up committees to study the problem. Certainly, the suggestion that college has failed our young men and women stirs in us feelings of guilt and confusion. The specter that haunts a world, secure economically, but culturally uncertain to the point of panic, is precisely this threat; and Franny, in her own way, embodies it.

Despite her final submission to that unspeakably false guru, her brother Buddy, with his pop-culture dogma that "Christ is the Fat Lady," she remains a sister in rebellion, a fellow traveler, at least, to Ferdinand R. Tertan of Trilling's "Of This Time, of That Place," the student always right in his literary judgments, of whom his poet-instructor is nonetheless forced to decide: "Oh, the boy was mad. And suddenly the word, used in hyperbole, intended almost for the expression of exasperated admiration, became literal." Yet that instructor must finally prefer, at the same time he must inevitably betray, Tertan's madness to the sanity of his "well-adjusted" and "well-rounded" classmate, bound for success in the same world in which the instructor seeks to be recognized, though the latter will publish poetry, while the former sells insurance or real estate.

Interestingly enough, Tertan was modeled in part, at least, on a leading member of the generation of the "beats," who had turned up in Trilling's own classes and has survived to tell much of his own story, though he has never treated his college years in any detail. Such self-conscious devotees of un-reason, to whom the phrase "to flip," i.e. to go out of one's head, represents a supreme achievement, do not ordinarily write about classroom experience, for they are likely to be well out of it, and immune to nostalgia, before they have begun to define themselves. It is their teachers, therefore, loved for having, with whatever doubts, protected the right of others to "flip," but despised for not having dared cross that frontier themselves, for having preferred academic security to insanity, who must write the record as best they can. Such teachers can, moreover, in baffled affection and unconscious desire for revenge, invite their madder students back to the campus to lecture or read from their works; but it does not really help, for such occasions are likely to end in frustration and scandal. In any case, even after we have seen him in an academic auditorium, we cannot imagine Jack Kerouac, for instance, in any relationship to the college community except one of mockery and evasion; and the brief valedictory of Allen Ginsberg's *Howl* remains in the mind ("who passed through universities with radiant cool eyes hallucinating Arkansas and Blake-light tragedy among the scholars of war, who were expelled from the academies for crazy & publishing obscene odes on the windows of the skull ... "), no matter how often he has returned since to read it to undergraduates in scheduled class meetings.

We have come full circle to the Twenties and the attitudes of Ernest Hemingway: the centrifugal young, once more running away from school to strange lands, if not to strange wars, in search of salvation, instead of the centripetal young going to school to sit at the feet of the writer-in-residence. And the former is, alas, the more typical American way. Though enormous numbers of novelists and poets are still sustained by the colleges and still make themselves visible there to the less enlightened young who seek them still, we begin to feel that we have reached the end of an era; begin to see that it was perhaps only a single generation which tried, against the grain of our tradition, to bring about a marriage of literature, at its freest and most advanced, with the university.

Yet it was not an utterly ignoble dream, this hope of compromising yet another of the polarities that have disrupted American life, and the generation of the Forties and Fifties could not have foreseen how soon it would be disavowed. Certainly that generation continues to consider naive and ignorant the contempt for the professor so rampant in the Twenties (and so attractive once more in the Sixties); just as that generation tends still to despise the cult of raw experience, which usually accompanies such contempt, and which has for so long helped keep American literature callow and immature. It was not just in search of security (which in any event they did not find) that the children of the Depression turned to the colleges, but also in pursuit of the long-delayed adulthood of American culture, and of a kind of independence never possible in bohemias.

Isolated in small academic communities hundreds of miles apart, seeing each other rarely at brief, ritual, and often drunken gatherings, it was possible for writers in colleges to remain lonely eccentrics, protected from each other by precisely the lonely crowd which surrounded and despised them.

Finally, the most terrible threat to the freedom of the writer is the chumminess engendered by the ghetto life of bohemian refuges, the rubbing up against each other of flocks or schools with common dogmas, easily represented or travestied in the popular press. Early or late in their careers, it has been in universities that such anti-flock writers as Walter Van Tilburg Clark, Wright Morris, John Hawkes and John Barth have found sustenance and protection; and if Barth seems at the moment the most promising novelist of those now in the neighborhood of thirty, it is because he has, like the generation before his, found in the provincial college that vacuum which nature abhors and art loves.

With the publication of *The Sot-Weed Factor*, his third novel, which begins in English academia and ends in the American wilderness, Barth has passed from seeming merely the most promising of a new generation to seeming the best, the most achieved. But the very disciplined intelligence, which, along with his wild invention and outrageous wit, constitutes his strength, isolates him from his contemporaries. To be a trained philosopher in a time of required misology is, like being neither Negro nor Jew in a time of required ethnic roots, to be isolated, indeed. But where, really, is the new center against which such a new eccentric as Barth defines himself? What are the essential experiences that influence the generation of the Sixties, besides the lust for madness and the aversion to schools? What public events, for instance, move them as the generation of the Forties-Fifties was moved by the Depression and the war in Spain, and that of the Twenties by the first great prosperity and World War I?

HOW TO WRITE A COLLEGE NOVEL[1]

Benjamin DeMott

(Memo from an Academic Grove to a Sensible Senior Editor. Written after a weekend with the college fiction of Mary McCarthy, Stringfellow Barr, Carlos Baker, John Aldridge, May Sarton, Randall Jarrell and others.)

Choice of author:

Stay away from insiders: they are too killingly predictable. A man in course of an honorable and successful career as a teacher produces books in which the campus is swathed in Quiet Cultivation and Sunny Selflessness and populated only by stereotypes – the Good Dean, the Evil Trustee, the Wise Chairman – most of whom were invented by college catalogues. (A defensive ploy, obviously.) When the writer is an academic gypsy – a character who lacks the credentials or ingenuity or stamina required for a lifetime university career, or who feels that (on those occasions when he was "in residence") colleagues and students treated him with less than the appropriate adulation – it offers either a metaphor of the College as a snakepit, or a mean, nose-picking little drama that rests on incredibly simple assumptions, as for example that the only dirty diapers and undefrosted refrigerators in America are the property of assistant professors of Slavic languages with lazy but fertile wives. You can best avoid these clichés by retaining an outsider. Find some brainy chap whose attitude toward his own formal education is that the latter is merely something that happened to him as a boy; buy him a room in a campus inn for three months (rates are low except on Football and

---

[1] Previously published in *The Hudson Review*, 15 (1962), pp. 243-52.

Commencement weekends), and leave him alone to smoke in and smoke out The Truth. Not a word of it has ever been put in a book, to judge from recent samples.

Notes on tone:

Behold the professor, the fresh hope of the age: should you encourage the writer you hire to treat him as a New Man? At first glance, yes. After decades of abuse – first for not meeting payrolls, then for meeting Reds – the professor is coming into his own. Nobody but speaks well of him in public. Nobody but wants more of him by the tens of thousand. Nobody in the corporations (show us how to test our young men), or in politics (give us some unconventional wisdom), or even in the churches (define for us the faith of the free-thinker) but pleads for the top of his mind. What is more, no one in the university itself is unaware that the slickest current pitch of the Fund Drive is: Alumni! fatten the profs. For these reasons, you'd assume that the new professor would be all exhilaration and glow. The assumption, though, isn't worth a damn. Academic purses are heavier and the professor has learned more about the basic comforts, but exhilaration is still outside his gates. Partly this is because the academic thinks that the people who have lately taken it into their heads to admire him have no better grasp of his nature than those who in former days detested him. (A well-founded suspicion.) Partly it's because he's suffered too long from the habit of self-contempt. (If the writer you hire plans to attend public College lectures, tell him to keep a book on *introductions*. To this day, one professor introducing another on a public occasion normally finishes a recital of the guest's accomplishments with the nervously jocular words, "And now, eschewing the word professor in favor of a more honorable title, I introduce to you *Mr. X----Y----*"!)

There's nothing mysterious about this habit, of course. For almost a century the professor figured as the most available target of every onslaught of American anti-intellectualism – and it would be foolish to claim that the abusers were all real estate operators and used car salesmen. The typical American writer or artist of this century felt obliged to assure the audience that he was a dumb fellow, a bad speller, a famous truant, a teacher-hater from early youth to his election to the American Academy. And the fervor and justice of his claim to stupidity, coupled with his reputation or achievement, have told impressively against the learned. The latter, whether they leave the groves or hang on, are riddled with scars. Those who clear out often spit over their shoulders at the Chapel tower as they depart. (The economist headed for Washington mutters about impractical, mathematics-maddened collegians; the literary journalist maunders about professor poets or novelists.) Teachers who remain often betray, through their on-campus behavior, inadequate trust in the standards of their calling. They are easily victimised, for example, by students who, blessed with a trace of a talent, claim regard as persons too gifted to muck about with common assignments. Faced with such a claim, teachers sometimes go so far as to agree that learning is the enemy of art: they encourage the talented boy in his fantasies, carry him piggy-back through the hateful turbulence of exam week and then, when the graduation ceremony is over, wait patiently and gratefully outside the Quad for the new AB to bestow them a scornful parting crack in the shins.[2]

---

[2] An amusing episode of this sort occurred recently at a small New England college. A gifted, angry, coddled young man was brought effortfully through final examinations by his department -- it was considered "bad public relations" to harass an Artist with intelligent questions -- and then awarded (by a group of teachers he had frequently characterized as pedants) a rich fellowship enabling him to travel abroad.

It follows that if the novelist you hire is seeking to render contemporary fact, he must represent (somewhere) the ambiguities of the teacher's confidence in the standards and values he upholds. The public is, at the moment, swinging hastily from extreme to extreme in estimating the professor, but a new and thoroughly positive definition of the ideals of the profession will be required before the academic can share other people's confidence in himself. In short: avoid both beamishness and cynicism, and let the mixed nature of the present situation appear even in the final draft.

Suggestions for character-analysis I: Some bearings of vanity

An acceptable characterization of a teacher *cannot* be worked up casually: sweat the opposite idea out of the man you hire *before* you offer an advance. No novel of academe has ever produced a believable prof. The teacher's strengths – intelligence, relative freedom from greed – are (perhaps) obvious, but they do not exempt him from analysis any more than they qualify him for abuse. Where could such analysis begin? Possibly at the beginning – with some rendering of the unique circumstances of academic careers that affect the development of character. What are these circumstances?

Consider: The professor-to-be is usually encouraged into his profession while an undergraduate. He is singled out from his fellows for heady praise at an extraordinarily early

---

When he returned, the same group of teachers arranged for a further financial contribution to his welfare, and successfully undertook to "place" him in a superior graduate school for which the character was in theory ineligible, though he signified his willingness to attend. Even at this point the people mentioned had not exhausted means for expressing their generosity. Offering them a chance to applaud their own destruction, the young recipient of their aid announced before leaving town that his next literary work would be a "murderous satire" upon them – and was roundly cheered.

age (17 or 18 or 19), awarded in adolescence the right to believe in the quality of his mind and in the validity of his opinions. (Note, incidentally, that academic praise in America tends toward powerful adjectives like *brilliant, incisive* and *masterful*, rather than toward condescending epithets like *clever* that remain in vogue in England.) While it is probably true that not every young man in his late teens wishes to take himself with great seriousness, the young man who is instructed to do so rarely finds it difficult to obey. And this obedience is, for definable reasons, a Bad Thing. A boy of eighteen, however bright, cannot possibly have in mind – at the moment when his abilities are being celebrated – everything that it is useful for a person to have in mind at such a moment. He lacks the proportioning senses of life – the sense of contradiction for one. He does not know that charm can be mistaken for brilliance, grace of movement for distinction of mind; he doesn't know that men of acknowledged gifts on occasion do fail to make their way; he doesn't know that some men regarded as clods in youth discover in mid-life a vein of truth or energy in themselves that yields them a splendid accomplishment; he doesn't know that even people like himself will die and may suffer pain; he doesn't know that marriages go sour, or that for some splendid accomplishment there is no audience, or that many late-found pursuits are enjoyable enough to make a man long to give himself over to them in scorn of his Career – or any of a thousand other truths which, when experienced, function in paradoxical ways as checks on vanity. Praise of a youth can set flowing a current of confidence that will bear the man forward to great achievement. In which event vanity ripens into wisdom and humor, and everyone has gained – including the novelist, who can build a golden character out of such a movement.

But only one such movement in *this* novel, please. The rule of life, after all, is that most men (even professors) can boast merely of middling achievement, can accomplish enough to establish that their first enthusiasts were correct in seeing lights of intelligence, but not enough to justify the voices that claimed to see genius.

When such men possess self-knowledge, their "failure" as geniuses can cause them to lapse into bitter negativism. (It is easy to flourish as a "brilliant boy" among ordinary boys, less easy to flourish as an aging "brilliant boy" in a society of former brilliant boys, a small minority of whom are becoming brilliant men.) When such men do not possess self-knowledge, they often seem not merely vain but oblivious, remote, completely off the pad. Perfectly all right to represent such a figure: but indecent not to seek understanding of him. In American fiction no one has ever tried; in English fiction there are some helpful hints – see George Eliot's Casaubon or even Virginia Woolf's Professor Ramsay. Neither figure is admirable, but both *are* fully seen. Tell your man to try to see fully: his goal is *not* to write a College Confidential.

Suggestions for character-analysis II: Some bearings of social position

A feature of the professorial nature closely related to vanity is the disposition toward *climbing*. Here again there are nice complications. The old English saw that maintains that whenever a professor enters an elegant company the social tone is instantly lowered is inapplicable in America, where little elegant company exists. And the charge that the average American professor in a good institution is a bright lower middle class person who is using the university as a ladder to carry him to some better social destiny has not been richly documented. But it is true that two significant academic social classes in this country have tics of manner that recall versions of the nineteenth-century climber. The first class is composed of intelligent men of private means who, rendered ineligible for the usual American career, must seek honor instead of money. The second is composed of men who, whatever their original status, regard themselves as "rising in the world." The man of means is marked by a curious air of embarrassment, a tendency toward careful self-effacement and reticence; he seems bent on assuring men of lesser advantage that he is ashamed of the superiority of his manners and tastes. The hustler is marked, on the other hand, by a tendency toward extreme volubility at faculty meetings, and by an eagerness to shock – symptoms of an uncontrolled need for recognition.

So much is simple. Complication enters because the types mentioned have something more in common than mere self-consciousness. Each is a character with an ideal vision, an unformulated but nevertheless deep belief in the existence (somewhere) of a thoroughly admirable social world that would admit him if it but knew that he existed. The imagined world is rather less like Proust's Paris, perhaps, than like the Boston that T. S. Eliot once described as refined past the point of civilization; or, saying the same thing in another way, it is often more like a superstition than a vision, and owes much to the preservation, even in tanktown colleges, of certain relics of aristocratic tradition. But it does have influence. Out of respect for it many academics display an intense anxiety about coarseness and vulgarity, become Anglophiles or Francophiles, restrain themselves from reading any item that has ever interested the common world, and sometimes even go so far as to invent private languages in order to suggest acquaintance with a standard unavailable to ordinary men.[3]

---

[3] If the author of the desiderated novel investigates this subject – the private languages and pronunciations of academe – he will discover that there is no uniformity in the field. Cambridge chic differs from Charlottesville chic and neither has much in common with Berkeley chic or Williamstown chic. Neither at Harvard nor at Chicago does an academic

What all this means is that snobbery and climbing have a moral dimension in academe that they often don't have elsewhere. Behind them both stands a passion for the ideal that needn't be an object of scorn. A subtle novelist would manage to hint that this passion, no matter how mean the particulars of its daily expression, is nevertheless a fructifying social force.

Suggestions for character-analysis III: The instinct for self-dramatization

Another significant element in the teacher's nature that existing academic fiction points at *sparsim* (never actually comprehends) is the tendency toward self-dramatization. According to the cliché, the teacher is the only American who still lives in a rigorously structured society, who still believes in Superiors and Inferiors, Juniors and Seniors – and there is some truth in the statement. The uninformed, though, think of the academic hierarchy as a mere business of professorial rank, which is a mistake. Divisions of rank vary in significance from institution to institution and within the departments of any single institution. The only distinction of absolute importance is of course that between teachers and students – and no other distinction works as powerfully in the cause of self-dramatization. This isn't to say that the relation between teacher and student lacks dignity; when unvulgarized by opportunistic Pals-ism, or by cheap psychological "counseling," it is an admirable human relation: the affection that a man can feel for a person to whom he knows he has taught something – even if only to tie a fly or to tack downwind – can be strong and ennobling.

"give a speech"; but in the East he "holds forth," while in the Midwest it is his "turn to utter"; neither in New Haven nor California is Thoreau Tho-REAU: but in the East he is THO-reau, while in the West he is Throw.

Unfortunately, however, the relation of teacher to student is less commonly a relation of individuals than of a leader to a mass. And in consequence moments occur when the academic community has about it an unpleasant flavor of Rome in the days of multiple tribunes. (You can look in vain for any hint of this in the academic novels of the last twenty years.) The student body is a kind of constant; it cannot revolt, or at any rate its revolutions injure – only the gods, to assign the deans a label that will satisfy them. Hence the student body takes on the character of a Populace, and the teacher comes to feel – unless he is forced into engagements with individual student minds – a swelling of the imperial theme within himself. If the swelling proceeds far, the professor is likely to give himself to the joys of personal mythmaking, hinting (by means of skilful self-dramatization) that the Populace might well find him more amusing or interesting than his Policies (or subject matter). He thus loses his position as a knower and sharer of knowledge, and moves toward the status of a performer.

Like each of the other tendencies of personality mentioned here, the tendency toward self-dramatization can be regarded as a positive quality of character. It does not follow that, if a member of one profession is vain of his mind, the members of all other professions are free of vanity, and in any case the man of reasonable intelligence who admires his own mind has hit upon an object of affection more respectable than a Countess Mara tie or a Porsche. Again, the conviction that snobbery is the hallmark of the academy can be used as a ground of contempt only by a fool: it is plain (to repeat) that in some instances snobbery is kin to pride, and, however un-Christian to acknowledge it, there is no deceit in the claim that civilization itself is a product of pride. And as for the impulse toward self-dramatization – it can be read as evidence of the presence of a latent personal vibrancy, a desire to make one's weight felt, a will to contend against the world rather than to remain passive in face of it, that fearful men can only envy.

In sum: there *are* interesting complications of character in the college grove, items that can be made to yield a good deal in the way of human truth. The academic novel of the past, with its ready-welded conflict of Selfishness against Selflessness, snobs against liberals, elegant aesthetes against hard-driving Jews, is at best a boyish fantasy: do not let it get past your desk. Hire a man who believes in the possibility that complication can exist even on a campus, and let him pursue that possibility far enough to win out over the stereotypes.

A possible theme:

A plausible theme for an academic novel now might lie in the new difficulties of professorial contention against the World. As everyone knows, this contention is a valuable key to professorial character: the professor is a man who, offered an opportunity to act out his life in terms of the generally accepted American values, has opted out. He conceives of his "career" less as a means, a way of providing for a family, a way of gaining position or security or power, than as an end in itself. He is a notoriously inefficient bargainer for money or promotion not merely because he is timid but because at one point in his life he rejected the goal of efficiency in these enterprises, and thereafter was led – by an impersonal force called scholarship, the tradition of learning, or civilization – into a round of study that assumed in its forms, if not in every practice, that his purpose was simply to seek truth. The professor's rebellion, to call it that, was always imperfect, subject to personal adaptations and needs. But when the professor took his first turning he faced in a direction that his country as a whole has not faced since the seventeenth century – away, that is, from the pursuit of physical comfort: and the memory of that first turning never fades.

But the memory in itself is not enough to underwrite the daily renewal of commitment and critical passion. Poverty once nourished the professor in his otherness, in his conviction of his own faithlessness to American convention (and faithfulness to original American ideals). But as his situation alters he finds himself faced with the problem of choosing a style of life, modes of consumption that will be in keeping with his own sense of his difference, his own expressed hostility to the conventions of affluence. Asceticism is no longer open to him – except as a strategy of evasion. He must buy, he must choose – what? (A president of an Eastern college of substantial reputation, addressing a mixed group of professors and administrators, spoke enthusiastically a year ago[4] of the likelihood that the average "teacher-scholar" at the rank of full professor will soon be earning at least $25,000 a year – provided, as the man warned, he is shrewd enough to husband his time, turn out lucrative textbooks, and avail himself of the various consultantships that will ever more frequently be offered him. Implicit here is the mistaken assumption that the professor has for years been biting the stable walls in anticipation of an opportunity to become a wheeler and dealer.)

On the one hand (pursuing this point), the professor tells himself that it is right for money-men to recognize his work. But the recognition he is offered is in fact an invitation to become less recognizable, to accept styles and norms invented by one or another slick magazine. Here lie the roots of a psychological conflict that, in time, will figure centrally in professorial character. It is true to be sure that there is always a crisis for the idealist in his moment of material plenty: the theme is common in American fiction. But the

---

[4] i.e. 1961 [Ed.]

case of the professor is uncommon: his gods and traditions are not obscure, and his effort to honor them and increase their dignity (without compromising it in the eyes of the godless and traditionless) creates situations of great strain and even of some poignancy. A novel that looked into this matter would at least be looking into the future.

A final word:

Above all, above all: let the professor think on the page: real thoughts in a real library or study or classroom. Let the contents of his mind be shown: nothing about the academic is more interesting than his rumination, yet no one ever exhibits it. In existing academic novels – this is what triggered the memorandum you are now reading – in existing novels teachers who are (in theory) fully conscious of Freud, Darwin, Durkheim and other heroes of the last century speak and act like medieval men, define moral problems in the vocabulary of Aquinas, accept a psychology that Dr Johnson would have thought outmoded, discuss political or cultural issues in the categories of Disraeli or Gladstone or Matthew Arnold, embrace ideas and modes of analysis that in fact have not been alive in most academic minds for a half century. Plainly the novelist will have to know something if he is going to give adequate representation to modern intellectual accents and idioms. He will have to believe in the mind, and he will also have to have some faint consciousness of the major revolutions in thought of this age. If he has this intelligence, if he can see the academy as a place *of* this world, if he can allow for the possibility that professorial character can be as complicated as, say, lawyerly or journalistic character, if –

But why run on? If your man lacks all these qualifications you will simply publish him anyway: and *The Saturday Review* will hint that he's written a *roman à clef*. and there will be that much more stupidity in the world for academics to cudgel their brains against. There will also, though, be yet another occasion for what is called the last laugh. For the professor knows, even if novelists, editors and Old Boys don't, that if he were as uninteresting in fact as he is made out to be in fiction, the attempt to take his likeness would have been given up ages ago. Up academe!, in short, and a gesture of hand and elbow to all the blind peepers of its past.

CAMPUS WRITERS[1]

J. A. Sutherland

1956: Nabokov, who in 1940 tried and was unable to obtain an academic position in England, is proposed for an important chair at a Great University. After a heated debate the proposal is defeated: "Gentlemen, even if one allows that he is an important writer, are we next to invite an elephant to be Professor of Zoology?"[2]

A running theme in Peter Firchow's book on English literary conditions, *The Writer's Place*[3], is the relative merits of the American "free enterprise" system of patronage via the university, and the semi-socialist British Arts Council. When it is put to him the English writer, as canvassed by Firchow, seems in two or three minds about the advantages of more university employment. Pamela Hanford Johnson approves:

> America has been awfully lucky to have patronage through the academies, awfully lucky. I've done some of this work myself in America. Americans are very generous in looking after their writers. We haven't done so at all, or only on a very small scale and that's why we're really down to BBC television and journalism. It would be very valuable to a lot of writers here if they had more

---

[1] Previously published in *Fiction and the Fiction Industry* (London: Athlone Press, 1978), pp. 148-62.

[2] Andrew Field, *Nabokov: His Life in Art* (London: Hodder and Stoughton; Boston, MA: Little, Brown, 1967), p. 11.

[3] Peter Firchow, *The Writer's Place* (Minneapolis: University of Minnesota Press; London: Oxford University Press, 1974).

76

university patronage.[4]

V. S. Pritchett, a writer who has always enjoyed a connection with London journalism, demurs. For him the campus entails a limiting kind of intellectual provincialism, a benign prison camp which keeps the writer away from the reviving metropolitan air: "For prose writers, playwrights, novelists, I think the university is dangerous, because the university is a specialised community. It is quite unlike the outside world.... Artificial worlds have a sterilising effect on writers."[5]

Kingsley Amis shares the antagonistic view, declaring himself "a little suspicious of any closer ties between the academic setup and the literary setup."[6] His objection is in line with his well publicised distaste for academic expansionism, and his phobic fear of takeover by intellectual trendies. A more indignant argument is often heard elsewhere from artists less financially successful than either Amis or Pritchett. Academics, they point out, make their living from creative writers – shouldn't they be prepared to pay something back?

To begin with, one would make a distinction between the various capacities in which universities can "employ" writers. In America, for example, most operate fulltime as writers teaching writing in universities (e.g. the late Theodore Roethke, whose career was entirely subsidised by the various academies in which he taught); others have a sabbatical or honorary arrangement with universities, entailing little or no teaching load (e.g. Vonnegut, who had two useful years at Iowa, which enabled him to get

---

[4] Firchow, pp. 217-18.

[5] Firchow, p. 280.

[6] Firchow, p. 21.

Slaughterhouse-Five into order); still other writers are employed by universities in incidental connections (e.g. Nabokov, who was a Fellow of the Museum of Comparative Zoology at Harvard when Edmund Wilson induced an American publisher to take an interest in *Bend Sinister*); finally there is the side benefit of the single public reading, or tour. American universities are generous in the number of paid visits which they sponsor. They are also generous in the scale of payment. The going rate in 1976-7 was $150-$400, plus expenses. A writer with an air timetable can put together an itinerary which will bring him $2,000 or so for a month's work.

***

[Several pages which explain the situation of American writers in universities, discuss the teaching of creative writing, and speculate on whether that subject will be added to British university curricula, have been omitted. Ed.]

***

There is already a small corps of campus novelists in Britain - probably as many as there are novelists in publishing or in the BBC and many fewer than there are novelists in journalism. A list of fulltime university-employed novelists would probably not include many more than David Lodge, Simon Gray, Gabriel Josipovici, Malcolm Bradbury, A. S. Byatt, Angus Wilson, Iris Murdoch, Dan Jacobson, J. I. M. Stewart, Rachel Trickett. With the exception of the recently retired Stewart, who continues, in one of his guises, the Dorothy L. Sayers tradition of elegant frivolity, all these novelists are serious. They are also academics who hold their jobs primarily by virtue of scholarly and critical achievement well above the average. In this last section, the present condition of the British university novelist is considered, in the presumption that it will not materially change in the near future.

Since the death of E. M. Forster the best known of the university novelists in this country is Angus Wilson, who has been a don for fifteen years. Wilson started late as a novelist (at thirty-five) and late as a university lecturer (at forty-five). Although he was invited to East Anglia, Wilson can be said to have earned his university place by academic rights; he is a distinguished critic, particularly of Dickens. But his conditions of employment are honoured ones, and might be thought near sinecure. He is a professor and has leave two terms in three (the average sabbatical entitlement is about one term in ten); and lives forty miles off-campus.[7] His teaching duties are very light, and take the form of a single seminar. Wilson, as he well might be, is "grateful" for "the kindness of the university" for whom he is as he over modestly puts it, "a very minor celebrity." He concludes:

> ... if one is going to be forced to do these things, I think perhaps it is better to teach at the university than it is to do very frequent reviewing or to be in the television world or to be in the editorial world of publishers.[8]

Wilson's opinions have to be taken in the context that he is, in a sense, *emeritus*. East Anglia treat him as they do because he is a very major celebrity. More typical are Malcolm Bradbury and David Lodge, who write directly

---

[7] "The Book Programme", BBC 2, March 2, 1976.

[8] Firchow, p. 343.

in the tradition inaugurated by Kingsley Amis in his university days (Swansea, 1949-61). Bradbury and Lodge are campus novelists through and through, having spent practically the whole of their post-adolescent lives in universities. Not surprisingly, academic life has provided the setting for much of Lodge's fiction and all of Bradbury's in such acclaimed novels as: *The British Museum is Falling Down, Changing Places, Eating People is Wrong, Stepping Westward, The History Man*. Bradbury and Lodge's fiction is so closely linked with their academic experience that it often partakes of the *roman à clef*. Certainly Bradbury's first novel was a reverberating subject of gossip at Leicester (his first university and, none too mysteriously, the setting of *Eating People is Wrong*), for years after he left. So too with *The British Museum is Falling Down*, and University College London. One imagines that Lodge's *Changing Places* was pored over with some eagerness at Berkeley and Birmingham, and *The History Man* at East Anglia.

All these novels display an in-group jokiness, a sense of shared jests among a coterie. The British campus novel easily converts to a kind of privileged literature, fully appreciated only by a few in the know. One still, for example, meets academics who remember the work in progress *Lucky Jim* being read aloud to them by the author. *Lucky Jim*, which is dedicated to Philip Larkin (then a librarian at Leicester) has a number of jokes which, again, are only obvious to someone who knew Leicester in its University College days. (Doubtless a thesis will be written one day about that unfashionable institution's role in post-war fiction: it figures centrally in the fiction of Bradbury, Snow and Amis and in the poetry of Larkin.) Clique interanimation remains an essential part of the campus novel, whose authors regard themselves as part of a fraternity writing for each other. The dedication of

Lodge's *British Museum*, for example, is to Malcolm Bradbury, "whose fault it mostly is that I have tried to write a comic novel." (Bradbury returned the compliment by dedicating *Possibilities* to "my friend" Lodge.) The same novel has an extravagant number of donnish parodies of fiction – most clearly picked up by fellow teachers trained in dating exercises. Intertextual games are common in the academic novel, both here and in America.

All this has to do with a large objection: is the university, *per se,* a stultifier of fictional talent? Bradbury's three novels are, on the face of them, only as various as the turns of his career. *Eating People* is set in a University College (Leicester, where Bradbury was a student, 1950-53), *Stepping Westward* on an American campus (Indiana where Bradbury was a visiting professor, 1955-6), and *The History Man* at a new university (East Anglia, where Bradbury has been since 1965 and where he is now a professor). Three more various academic settings it would be difficult for a British academic to find. Yet, one asks, is there enough variety within universities as a whole, even if one were to go from Patrice Lumumba to Bob Jones via the Sorbonne? The answer might, of course, be "yes" if one were actually talking about universities. But where the university novel is concerned "university" tends to mean the English department, traditionally the quietest and most self-engrossed corner of the university.

David Lodge bears out this last point. Writing a mock "Don's Diary" in *The Times Higher Educational Supplement,* Lodge expatiates on what is his most recent fictional theme: that the English English department (unlike the American) is a very undestructive element in which to immerse:

Monday. Intended to rise early to prepare today's teaching, but

The Academic Novel

stayed up late last night watching trashy film on TV and overslept in consequence. No time for breakfast, let alone preparation. Bluffed way through tutorial at 10; 11-12 coffee and gossip in Common Room. Bluffed way through seminar at 12. Drank too many beers at lunch and fell asleep in chair afterwards. Late for lecture at 3. Stumbled through old dog-eared notes, almost as bored as students. Drove home with splitting headache, kicked dog and quarrelled with wife. Somehow one cannot imagine it in the *THES* though I daresay that in a campus novel it would not seem wildly improbable.[9]

Certainly not improbable in Lodge's campus novels which deal with just such minor self-defeats, self-betrayals and lapses. But is it, one asks portentously, the stuff of fiction? Is there not a lack of necessary tension in the academic lifestyle? One may return here to the metropolitan V. S. Pritchett and quote his reservations in full:

Artificial worlds have a sterilising effect on writers. They begin to think of life in terms of specialised communities. There have, of course, been a number of rather good "academic" novels, though awfully small in their scope. The curse of academic life is the watchfulness of one academic on another. Writers can be as bitchy as they like about one another, but they've got the whole of London or the whole of England or the whole of Europe to be bitchy in, and it does not really matter. But in academic life, the infighting goes on day-by-day, inch by inch, hour by hour. Their jobs depend upon it,

---

[9] *Times Higher Education Supplement*, February 6, 1976.

the whole organization encloses them.[10]

There is, of course, one great compensation which goes a long way to answering such objections as Pritchett's. The English university teacher-novelist is forced to become an expert in the theory of his craft. Novelists testify to the value of enforced critical expertise. As Lodge puts it:

> As an academic critic and teacher of literature with a special interest in prose fiction, I am inevitably self-conscious about matters of narrative technique, and I believe this is a help rather than a hindrance. I certainly think that my criticism of fiction gains from my experience of writing it.[11]

Antonia Byatt argues that her academic tasks are actually necessary for her fulfilment as a novelist:

> I discovered, when I tried to give it up to write more, that I couldn't write if I wasn't teaching. I now teach at University College London ... the novelist Dan Jacobson who has just joined the
> department says he feels here part of a tradition, and that all this thought and talk is good for his writing.[12]

Bradbury echoes Byatt on the necessity of teaching: "I couldn't, myself, teach if I didn't write: I'm very doubtful

---

[10] Firchow, p. 280.

[11] *Contemporary Novelists*, Ed. J. Vinson and D. L. Kirkpatrick (2nd ed., London: St. James Press; New York: St. Martin's Press, 1976), p. 833.

[12] *Times Higher Education Supplement*, June 9, 1976.

if I could write if I didn't teach." His reasoning is much the same as the other novelists': "Teaching is a relief because ... it is human in intense ways, a line of primary relationship .... I also feel the need to link criticism with creation, teaching and reviewing with the run of public cultural debate."[13] One may have some doubts about the shimmering rainbow of staff-student relationships and it is easy to see how the Byatt-Bradbury belief in critical-creative reinforcement could in less sensitive hands lead to what Gore Vidal calls "plastic fiction." Nonetheless there is clearly a powerful defence here to allegations of dessication and sterility.

The argument then has two sides. The campus limits the actual fictional territory of writers at the same time that it widens a certain intellectual awareness. With this in mind one may consider one of the finest of university novels, Raymond Williams's *Border Country*. Williams's novel records the alienation and encapsulation of the self which the university produces in its more sensitive inmates. It is only when he returns home to his dying father that Matthew (Will) Price recovers a sense of personal reintegration by "measuring the distance he has travelled." And in writing the novel Raymond Williams is, one suspects, undertaking just such a measurement for himself. Williams, as one would expect from his critical writing, has a powerful grasp of the ways in which the academy obstructs the integration of province with metropolis, traditions with modernity, self with community. In essence the novel is a demonstration of how someone like Matthew Price (and by implication Williams himself) could never write a novel like *The Rainbow*; yet *Border Country* is, paradoxically, one of the nearest things to *The Rainbow* which modern times have

---

[13] *Times Higher Education Supplement,* March 5, 1976.

produced.

The notion of the border country, of being uneasily between two worlds, is central to Williams's thought. In this respect one can quote the testimony of a colleague, more frankly Marxist than Williams: "His particular social transition made him an extraordinarily 'typical' bearer of some of the classic contradictions of the social formation: proletariat/bourgeoisie, region/metropolis, rural/urban." To which one could add "university/outside world."[14]

The divided nature of the campus novelist is a study by itself, and it is subject matter to which the self-conscious university novel is constantly returning. Malcolm Bradbury candidly admits to being "schizophrenic." Hence it is that his novels, all of which he conceived of as satirical of the new universities (university colleges, the American campus, "new" post-Robbins universities), never seem to have conflicted with Bradbury's zeal and effectiveness as an educationalist in just those institutions. He joined a new university, at a time when the heat was strongest (this may be one reason why no fiction was produced between 1966 and 1975). He was instrumental in setting up one of the first American studies courses in Britain. His latest novel, *The History Man*, shows the influence of his interdisciplinary activities, particularly his love (and latterly love-hate) affair with sociology. Bradbury is the most distinguished of modern literary sociologists with *The Social Context of Modern English Literature* (1971) to his credit and another collaborative scheme with the sociologist Bryan Wilson projected. The interdisciplinary ideal, again, was a formative element in the make-up of the new universities.

Yet, when one reads the novels – particularly *The*

---

14 Terry Eagleton, *Criticism and Ideology* (London: NLB, 1976), p. 24.

History Man – they seem an elegy for the destruction of old humane "liberalism" by the "cannibalism" represented by the new order, particularly the new order of universities. Taxed on this, Bradbury affirms that there is a mutually reinforcing benefit from positive action and negative reflection. It would require a peculiarly modish approbation of his own term "schizophrenia" to accept this at face value. One is left with the constant sense that Bradbury is creating literature in the face of what he memorably calls the "sense of absent literariness" in modern university life[15], its lack of what should be central to it, and is no longer. This, it would seem, is Bradbury's border country: the liberal university behind, the barbarous campus in front.

David Lodge, Bradbury's partner in campus fiction, seems to have solved his problem differently, by a kind of guarded, retreated pose. For him the university has seemed a kind of refuge. His whole career has been served in the rather staid, municipal surroundings of Birmingham. He seems remarkably firm-minded about the way in which freedom has to be balanced against the administrative responsibilities which come with promotion. For a long time he was one of the most distinguished critics in England, yet one who was, surprisingly, not a professor. Only recently has he taken a personal chair (which carries less administrative duties). One cannot know, but it would seem likely that for the last ten years Lodge could have had any number of professorships in England or America, had he so wanted. But what he admires and covets most in the university set-up is the provision of free time; the fact that one can avoid pressure and write novels and critical books, turn and turn about:

---

[15] *The Times*, August 7, 1976.

Campus Writers

I am one of those who think that university teaching is a privileged profession though as the privileges are earned by a certain sacrifice of libido in youth and of income later I do not feel guilty about it. One of these privileges is being paid (however inadequately) to read and re-read great books. Another is certainly the sabbatical or study leave .... It is not only a question of having time to write, but of having a continuous span of time free, in which one's own work can develop a rhythm and thrust that can hardly emerge in something put together like a jigsaw puzzle in odd moments.[16]

The advantages, to sum up, are time and a high level of theoretical discourse on the nature of fiction constantly about one. The cost is paid in psychic division, controllable schizophrenia, financial and emotional impoverishments. The cost, if we are to credit the novelists themselves, is not exorbitant.

In contrast to some of the other areas examined in this book, it is unlikely that there will be a close assimilation of British and American practice with regard to writers and universities. It is just possible that over the next decade British universities may move more towards American patterns and hence open up a wider gap for Creative Writing. But the possibility is diminished by the fact that American higher education flourishes in a much more expanded condition than Britain's – teaching anybody anything. Similar expansion seems remote here. Britain will continue teaching a select few students a select few subjects.

The British university will continue, in all probability, to offer a niche for a modest number of creative writer-critics. And the fact that they are professional critics and teachers

---

[16] *Times Higher Education Supplement,* February 6, 1976.

87

will tend to establish them as importantly thoughtful practitioners. Their significance will not be in their number – which is unlikely to rise above a score – but in the links they make between theory and practice and the intellectual self-awareness they bring to their craft.

LUCKY JIM AND AFTER: THE BUSINESS OF UNIVERSITY NOVELS[1]

J. P. Kenyon

George Watson ... points to a notable post-War literary phenomenon, not always treated with the seriousness it deserves: the rise of the University Novel.

Watson is more concerned with the negative aspects of the genre, but there is still ample room in 1980, it seems, for the nostalgic, best-years-of-our-lives treatment, typified by J. I. M. Stewart in the "Pattullo Quintet," sired on *Gaudy Night* by *Sinister Street*. Stewart makes some concessions to modern trends, and he has clearly read and absorbed Philip Larkin's *Jill* (1946); but he is still mesmerised by the solid, timeless comfort, the faded chic, the phoney grandeur of Oxford academic life. He is much too willing to excuse the excesses of the odious Mumfords (grandfather, father, and son) and even his specimen "modern" undergraduate, Nicholas Junkin (significant name) has a distinctly Edwardian flavour.

C. P. Snow is nothing if not up-to-date, but in his Cambridge sequence, *The Light and the Dark* (1947), *The Masters* (1951) and *The Affair* (1960), he shows the same lotus-eating satisfaction as Stewart with the minutiae of the don's life: the hot muffins under silver covers, candlelight reflected in wood panelling, cosy bottles of claret behind sported oaks. Here Sir Lewis Eliot in old age returns to Christ's for dinner one summer night:

> Lights were shining, young men's voices resounded: the smell of wisteria was faint on the cool air: it brought back, not a sharp

---

[1] Previously published in *Encounter*, 54 (June, 1980), pp. 81-4.

memory, but a sense that there was something I knew but had (like a name on the tip of the tongue) temporarily forgotten.

Eliot himself, a detached, rather ineffectual observer, plagued by incomprehensible neuroses and uncharmingly self-obsessed, is second cousin to Stewart's Duncan Pattullo.

In fact, "young men" are conspicuous by their absence from C. P. Snow's novels, until in *The Sleep of Reason* he turns back to the civic university in his home town – and then its students are stylised to the point of caricature. His Cambridge combination rooms, in fact, are a back projection of the real corridors of power, in London.

Simon Raven's Cambridge has attracted less scholarly interest than Snow's, but it is certainly much jollier, even if his dons are afflicted by every perversion known to psychotherapy, and many not. *Doctors Wear Scarlet* (1966) is arguably a Gothic pastiche, but *Places Where They Sing* (1970), written in the aftermath of the student troubles of 1968, presents a Cambridge at least remotely recognisable to those who have lived and worked there; and to my mind Hugh Balliston is one of the few credible students or undergraduates in the whole genre, apart from Larkin's John Kemp. He is even seen doing some work, something surely unique. In one memorable scene he turfs his delectable girl friend out of bed in order to get on with his essay: "Hugh quivered with tenderness, gurgled slightly, and then turned back with a shrug to the papers on his desk. 'Go along, bottykins', he said softly, 'Come tomorrow at twelve.'"

Sad to say, when he presented the essay that evening, his tutor "screwed it into a ball, and tossed it through an open door into his bedroom." But the dons of Lancaster College are rather like that.

Lucky Jim and After

A recent Cambridge novel, Tom Sharpe's *Porterhouse Blue* (1974), is pure fantasy, of course, but the absence of students is still significant – apart from the unfortunate research student Zipser, of course, who is immolated together with his lascivious bedmaker in the explosion of a gross of gas-filled condoms. And when we turn to the Redbrick (or precast concrete) university novel, which has now taken a commanding lead, the suppression of the student is almost absolute. Malcolm Bradbury manages a few thumb-nail sketches in *Eating People Is Wrong* (1959), not surprisingly, since he was a student himself when he wrote it; but the book's "hero," Louis Bates, is a sad, self-destructive, hopelessly unattractive figure, with his blackheads, his reeking feet and gargoyle face. (Emma Fielding is only technically a student – yet another research student, though as usual her precise field of research is not explained – and as a full-grown woman she is associated in the reader's mind with her rival, Dr Viola Masefield.) In *The History Man* (1975), writing years later as a professor, Bradbury succumbs to a black disgust with students and with universities. Here we stand alongside Howard Kirk, high in the Social Sciences tower, as he watches his students filing on to the Watermouth campus at the beginning of a new session:

No longer do they look like an intellectual elite; indeed, what they resemble this autumn is rather the winter retreat of Napoleon's army from Moscow. For in the new parade of styles, which undergoes subtle shifts year by year, like the campus itself, bits of military uniform, bedraggled scraps of garments, fur hats and forage caps and kepis, tank tops and denims and coats which have lost their buttons have become the norm; the crowds troop along raggedly, avoiding the paths which have been laid out for them, hairy human bundles fresh from some sinister experience....

91

The whole paragraph is a remarkable attack on university life in the 1970s; there is no pity in it, no charity, no hint of tenderness.

Nor is this necessarily a post-1968 attitude. The anonymous university college in *Lucky Jim* (1954) – the novel that started it all – is scarcely distinguished for high living or sound learning; and the student body, it seems, is mainly composed of silly, giggling girls and suave, slightly bogus ex-servicemen like Mr Michie, with his barathea trousers and public-school manners, whom the unfortunate Jim Dixon finds it so difficult to cope with. In Kingsley Amis's recent novel, *Jake's Thing* (1978), only one student makes an appearance, and Jake Richardson silently apostrophises her thus:

> "One, see if you can't work out some way of getting yourself just a bit ashamed and scared of not wanting to know anything about anything or to be good at anything. Two, if that fails, at least try to spell a bit and write legibly and write a sentence now and then – you can forget, or go on never having heard, about punctuation. Three, when you see a word you recognise in a question, like Greece or Tyre or Malta, fight against trying to put down everything remotely connected with it that you may have – oh stuff it. And four, go away and leave your place at St Hugh's to someone who might conceivably – oh stuff it .... "

But, of course, it is the dons, the unfortunate lecturers and professors, who really come under the hammer in this kind of novel. Jim Dixon, the "hero" of *Lucky Jim* – and it is noticeable that all the heroes of these novels have to be qualified by inverted commas – is an abject failure in his job, and, up to the last reel, in his personal relations. His professional failure is only disguised by the fact that his colleagues are all incompetent has-beens, led by that classic professorial figure Ned Welch, too true to type to be funny – his personal failure is only redeemed by a *coup de théâtre* which throws him, not very credibly, into the arms of Christine Callaghan (and her millionaire uncle) in the last chapter. Across the years I now feel a belated sympathy for Somerset Maugham, who at the time solemnly denounced Dixon and his friends and was himself equally solemnly denounced by our literary cognoscenti, led by C. P. Snow.

> They do not go to the university to acquire culture [said Maugham] but to get a job, and when they have got one, scamp it. They have no manners, and are woefully unable to deal with any social predicament. Their idea of a celebration is to go to a public house and drink six beers. They are mean, malicious and envious .... Charity, kindliness, generosity, are qualities they hold in contempt.

As for Jake Richardson, sympathy is not even solicited for him, as it was, I think, for Jim Dixon, nor is his negligence offset by any obvious incompetence on his colleagues' part. His perfunctory performance of his academic duties is matched by a rather perverse sexual impotence, which is something rather different from George Watson's "established fictional convention that professors are better at footnotes than in bed." To Simon Raven, in *Doctors Wear Scarlet*, Richard Fountain's impotence is just one symptom of a complete psychic breakdown. It reappears more naturally, even conventionally, in the case of Tom Llewyllyn in *Places Where They Sing*, though it must be admitted that none of the fellows of Lancaster College seem to be "potent" in any recognised way.

The same trend is evident in Malcolm Bradbury's work. Professor Stuart Treece, in *Eating People Is Wrong*, is ill-adjusted and self-doubting, and quite unable to handle even the most elementary social situations. We are left to assume that he is not very competent as a teacher or writer, either, though this is not stressed. However, he is a figure with whom it is difficult not to sympathise. Very different indeed is "The History Man," Howard Kirk, a flashy intellectual scoundrel who is so dishonest that he cannot even recognise honesty when he sees it, whose wife commits suicide on the last page apparently for the sole reason – and not an implausible one – that she cannot put up with him any longer. *Stepping Westward* (1965), though milder in tone, and set in America, still portrays a profession riddled with hypocrisy, cant and sheer dishonesty. David Lodge's *Changing Places* (1975), a buffoonish version of Bradbury's classic, carries the same message.[2]

But it is time we stood back and asked ourselves the obvious question: Why do all these novelists, most of them with direct experience of University life from below and above, pillory the English universities in this way? And why does the reading public revel in it?

J. I. M. Stewart's Oxford and C. P. Snow's Cambridge are, I suppose, moderately attractive, though to me they smell too much of the antimacassar; but Kingsley Amis's and Malcolm Bradbury's universities, or for that matter Sharpe's and Raven's Cambridges, are so relentlessly unattractive, so intellectually null, that surely any sane person would reject them out of hand. Yet most of these

---

[2] Incidentally, I cannot follow those who assume that *The History Man* is an attack on sociology. Howard Kirk's academic discipline is surely chosen at random, probably to avoid offending Bradbury's nearer colleagues in the humanities. Nor can I understand those who are aggrieved because they don't find it funny. Bradbury can be ruthlessly witty, as in his classic exposé of a Social Sciences Faculty meeting, but he is emphatically in the business of tragedy, or at best black comedy.

novels have sold well, some of them spectacularly so. They are all in paperback; *Lucky Jim* has never been out of print; and *The History Man* was the cult novel of 1975. It is reasonable to suppose that their readership is mainly drawn from the hundreds and thousands of men and women who have graduated from our universities since 1945; in fact, much of the background detail would be incomprehensible to those who had not. Yet they are prepared to accept a profoundly unsympathetic picture of universities and their students, though they were so recently in this category themselves and devoted three precious years of their young lives to it. Most of them, too, are anxious that their children should enjoy the same "privilege."

For I do not accept George Watson's argument that the demand for university education has fallen off dramatically or significantly. It is falling relative to the number of places available; but the number of such places has steadily increased since 1965. A few intelligent and capable teenagers reject university education consciously and honestly (as a similar proportion always did); but the great majority of those who adopt this attitude do so because they know that, educated in our declining state schools, they are simply not equipped for it. In the meanwhile the McNair Report has recommended (and the Law Society has agreed) that all future lawyers should hold a degree; and it is the eventual aim to make school-teaching an all-graduate profession, albeit through the dubious mechanism of the BEd. Not surprisingly, the educated middle class continues to put enormous pressure on its offspring, usually with success, to proceed to university at eighteen almost as a matter of course. George Watson's "unspoken premise that any intelligent person would go to a university if he had the choice" is very far from out-of-date. (In my personal experience it is no longer unspoken.)

I doubt, in fact, if University Novels are regarded by those who read them as especially relevant to "real" universities. Firstly, the profound cynicism and disgust displayed by their authors is dismissed as a quirk of the cloistered academic. No layman regards a professor as being quite of this world.[3]

Secondly, the pharisaic attitude is very strong – "I thank thee, Lord, that mine own university is not as one of these," or, of course, "mine own college" in the case of Oxford or Cambridge. Given our capacity for self-deception, this is probably the strongest neutralising agent.

Next, I think Watson dismisses too cavalierly the lady who remarked that universities are "the only communities left in the modern world." The theme of a closed community, outside the mainstream of modern life, has always had obvious attractions. It explains the appeal of much science fiction, which is concerned with closed communities, whether on a space ship or on an alien planet.

But I also suspect that the University Novel fills a gap left by the absence of anything like a "Business Novel" in English. I suppose a majority of the middle class is engaged in business or administration of one kind or another; yet it is remarkable how few modern novels reflect their daily life in any convincing way. If we ignore,

---

[3] In fact Kingsley Amis and Malcolm Bradbury reflect a deeply worrying tendency on the part of those who teach in universities to reject them *in toto*. Nor is this reaction confined to universities, if Tom Sharpe's ineffable Fenland College of Arts and Technology is any guide But naturally this need not trouble those who have shared in higher education only as "consumers."

as I think we must, the American "Tycoon" novel, which is unreal even to Americans, then we can only fall back on Roy Fuller's *Image of a Society*, or perhaps Edgar Mittelholzer's *A Morning at the Office*, both of them set in a highly specialised environment. Yet if you substitute for "professor" the term "managing director," or for "College Council" or "Faculty Board" the term "Board of Directors," you realise that many University Novels are in fact "business-like," in a literal sense. What, after all, is *The Masters* about? Surely the intrigue to replace the dying head of an Organisation, which could just as well be a Company as a College. *The Affair* deals with the common case of a junior executive unfairly dismissed. One of the many intertwined plots in *The Sleep of Reason* describes how a Board chairman (Vice-Chancellor) loses the confidence of his key Directors (senior Professors).

It is easy to say that these novels deal in general terms with human nature, human greed, human failure. True, but they are unusual in that they portray human relationships which are also power relationships, and they are set in status-competitive situations which are equally important in business as in higher education – probably more so. The man's job is not just a background to the action, it is the action. The signal weakens slightly when we move away from C. P. Snow; but even then, *Lucky Jim* is really all about an unhappy junior executive striving to turn his post into a permanency, *Eating People Is Wrong* is an essay in directorial failure, and in *The History Man* a middle manager sets out to sabotage the whole firm. The meeting of the governing body of Lancaster College, which is recounted in some detail in *Places Where They Sing*, could be transposed into a Board meeting with very little change.

Why is this so? The fact is, a high proportion of senior academics are much more interested in what they call "politics" (when they mean "business") than they are in their teaching or research. After all, as long go as 1908 F. M. Cornford recognised the "Good Business Man" as a common Cambridge type. They spend much of their time bullying or cajoling their colleagues into doing things their way; and they delight in pushing their chosen measures through an increasingly intractable consultative and administrative machinery. They are also by nature voluble creatures, in speech and writing, who find it easy and agreeable to recount their experiences in an entertaining form. Thus the "University Novel."

I agree with George Watson that we have had too much of a good thing, but, as I have suggested, it fills a remarkable gap. What we need now are good "Business Novels."

TYPES OF ACADEMIC FICTION

Merritt Moseley

Dividing the mass of academic novels into manageable kinds is difficult because of their multiplicity. The temptation is to be too schematic: I think this is the seduction to which both Ian Carter and John Schellenberger have surrendered. Carter says (admittedly about British books only, but even there it is too stark a taxonomy):

> Despite their apparent diversity, almost all British university novels play modest variations on one of three linked stories: how an undergraduate at Oxford (usually) or Cambridge came to wisdom; how a don at Oxford (usually) or Cambridge was stabbed in the back physically or professionally, sometimes surviving to rule his college; and how rotten life was as student or teacher outside Oxford and Cambridge.[1]

John Schellenberger has distinguished four types of modern British university novel: "the university-comic, rooted in nineteenth-century Oxford undergraduate models; a more serious variant of this, 'an earnest and painstaking account of Oxford as an educational experience': the college detective novel; and the novel of redbrick disillusionment."[2]

---

[1] Ian Carter, *Ancient Cultures of Conceit: British University Fiction in the Post-War Years* (London and New York: Routledge, 1990), p. 15.
[2] As quoted by Carter, p. 19.

The Academic Novel

Carter's book is about the English university novel as a defense of privileged bastions – hence Oxford and Cambridge – against various barbarians at the gates, including women, scientists, and Americans. But even granted that, and granted that Oxbridge has a symbolic centrality in English thought that no American college can ever have, this reduction of academic novels to three (or four) categories is too reductive, as I hope to show with my own suggestions for taxonomy, which follow.

1. *Focus on Students*

1.1 *Dappled Quads.* I use this term to describe the novel redolent of nostalgia for the beauties and ineffable subtleties of undergraduate life, almost always at Oxford, Cambridge, or, if American, an Ivy League university. The characters here give little attention to lectures, writing essays, or sitting exams; instead, there are brilliant conversations with other gilded youths, exciting relationships with sympathetic dons, early morning walks along the river. Janice Rossen points out that learning and reading "do not dramatize well," and raises the question of whether, confronted with description of joys which are special largely because available only to a minority, "readers might not experience envy rather than delight in glimpsing this inner world of privilege."[3]

---

[3] Janice Rossen, *The University in Modern Fiction: When Power is Academic* (New York: St. Martin's Press; Basingstoke: Macmillan, 1993), p. 96. See Richard Sheppard on Oxford and the nineteenth-century assumption that "academic work is relatively unimportant" ("From Narragonia to Elysium: Some Preliminary Reflections on the Fictional Image of the Academic," from *University Fiction*, Ed. David Bevan [Amsterdam; Atlanta, GA: Rodopi, 1990], p. 40); and Philip Hobsbaum, "University Life in English Fiction" (*Twentieth Century, 173*, 1964, pp. 139-46;

Types of Academic Fiction

Several of the early twentieth-century classics of the academic novel are set in dappled quads: Max Beerbohm's *Zuleika Dobson* (1911), Compton Mackezie's *Sinister Street* (1913; in its university portion, Book Three, called "Dreaming Spires"). Like *Sinister Street*, a relatively small part of Evelyn Waugh's 1945 *Brideshead Revisited* takes place at Oxford, but these pages are its most memorable and evocative.

Hamish Miles and Raymond Mortimer by 1923 had detected the ripeness of the Dappled Quads and wrote an astringent parody of it in *The Oxford Circus: A Novel of Oxford and Youth by the Late Alfred Budd*, and in 1920 F. Scott Fitzgerald, an acknowledged follower of Mackenzie, provided an American variant in *This Side of Paradise*. *The Rule of Four* (2004) by Ian Caldwell and Dustin Thomson is a murder mystery set, like Fitzgerald's novel, at Princeton, still moderately idyllic.

The hallmark of the Dappled Quads novel is purple prose, "poetic" and often archaic, as in this from *Zuleika Dobson*:

Some clock clove with silver the stillness of the morning. Ere came the second stroke, another and nearer clock was striking. And now there were others chiming in. The air was confused with the sweet babel of its many spires . . . [4]

---

reprinted in this volume) on the "aching nostalgia" of early twentieth-century Oxbridge novels.

[4] Max Beerbohm, *Zuleika Dobson* (1911; Harmondsworth: Penguin, 1986), p. 33.

The Academic Novel

Or these reactions by Michael Fane, Compton Mackenzie's Oxford undergraduate, on his first night at Oxford:

> Michael wandered on in meditation. From lighted windows in the High came a noise of laughter and voices that seemed to make more grave and perdurable the spires and towers of Oxford, deepening somehow the solemnity of the black entries and the empty silver spaces before them. Michael pondered the freshmen's chatter and apprehended dimly how this magical sublunary city would convert all that effusion of naïve intolerance to her own renown.[5]

Waugh's Oxford is a "city of aquatint," a place where

> ... the bells rang out high and clear over her gables and cupolas, exhaled the soft vapours of a thousand years of learning. It was this cloistral hush which gave our laughter its resonance, and carried it still, joyously, over the intervening clamour.[6]

Fitzgerald's hero, Amory Blaine, also notices bells and spires, male voices and deep silences, and finds that "the Gothic halls and cloisters were infinitely more mysterious as they loomed suddenly out of the

---

[5] Compton Mackenzie, *Sinister Street* (1913; Harmondsworth: Penguin, 1960).
[6] Evelyn Waugh, *Brideshead Revisited: The Sacred and Profane Memories of Captain Charles Ryder* (London: Chapman & Hall; Boston, MA: Little, Brown, 1945), p. 21.

darkness, outlined each by myriad faint squares of yellow light."[7]

"Myriad" is good Dappled Quads vocabulary, and Miles and Mortimer catch the tone in passages celebrating "the long tenebrous quiet of the Turl ... the empurpled dusk of the narrow street ... the pinnacled soar of Exeter Chapel .... the darkling distance ... the decrescent moon and a myriad plangent stars."[8]

It is possible that some novelist has written, or will write, a description just as moving and redolent and aching and mellow as these about Heriot-Watt University in Edinburgh, or the University of Central Arkansas, or Stillman College, or Liverpool Hope University. But historically, and by powerful convention, dappled quads are found in novels about Oxford, Cambridge, and the Ivy League. Thus the topic itself, and the romantic attitudes it evokes, and the special language in which it is presented, contrive, like the quadrangle itself, a privileged enclosure. Reading about them presumably can give the actual Oxford/Cambridge/Ivy League undergraduate the pleasures of nostalgia. The vastly larger readership made up of outsiders becomes eligible for the same kind of satisfaction that the thousands of tourists visiting Oxford seek. Those tourists can enter the colleges during limited hours; they can see the halls but not climb the staircases, perhaps visit the dining halls when the meals are not being served, walk around the quadrangles but not

---

[7] F. Scott Fitzgerald, *This Side of Paradise* (1920; New York: Collier, 1986), p. 56.

[8] Hamish Miles and Raymond Mortimer, *The Oxford Circus: A Novel of Oxford and Youth by the late Alfred Budd* (London: John Lane, 1922; New York: Knopf, 1923), pp. 25-6.

across them. We can see the beauty, but as to the "magical" life which the initiates lead in the midst of that beauty, we are lookers in.

1.2 *Not so Dappled.* Other academic novels focusing on students are less dewy and bedazzled, less murmurous and empurpled. Frequently this difference is because they are about students who are not from the privileged classes (Philip Larkin, *Jill* [1946]), or the privileged gender, being much less favored female undergraduates (Rosamond Lehmann's *Dusty Answer* [1927] or Hilary Mantel's *An Experiment in Love* [1995]); or because they are in the wrong place – e.g. not at Oxford or Cambridge or an Ivy League campus (Keith Walker's *Running on the Spot* [1959]) or the wrong time (Wilfrid Sheed's *A Middle Class Education* [1960]).

These novels focus more firmly and perhaps clearly on the real conditions of student life; they are more likely to include eating disorders, suicide, unwanted pregnancy, study, and fear of failure than to celebrate leisurely laughter from pinnacled colleges resounding down thousand-year-old stone passageways. They are also much more interested in the grubby details of student life – love, for instance (Julian Gough's *Juno & Juliet* [2001]), or social-climbing (Auberon Waugh's *Path of Dalliance* [1963]), or drinking and partying (Kate Atkinson's *Emotionally Weird* [2000]) or work-avoidance, cleverly detailed in Walker's *Running on the Spot* or Jason Epstein's *Wild Oats* (1979), with its account of the protagonist, assigned a paper on *The Iliad*, desperately handing in something called "The Shoes of the Greeks," which his baffled teacher accepts as ironic.

Types of Academic Fiction

Postgraduate students are rarely at the heart of academic novels; instead, they figure more often as oddly intermediate characters, alike enough to undergraduates to be set off from their professors, different enough from undergraduates for affairs with faculty members without the opprobrium that attaches to entanglements with undergraduates. Two novels centrally about graduate students are David Lodge's *The British Museum is Falling Down* (1965) and an older and little-known book, George W. Stewart's *Doctor's Oral* (1939). Each covers one day in the life of a graduate student harried by characteristic woes. Lodge's Adam Appleby is struggling to write a dissertation (on "The Structure of Long Sentences in Three Modern English Novels"), while Stewart's Joe Grantland faces taking his preliminary oral examination (which occurs, at considerable length and with compelling detail, in the latter half of the novel). Meanwhile each is distracted: Joe by his girlfriend's suddenly announced pregnancy and Adam by the much-dreaded pregnancy of his wife Alison.

2. *Focus on Administration*

This is a small category of academic fiction. There are a few novels that focus on college presidents or other central administrators, usually from outside and scathingly.

The central administrator as destructive agent figures in Bradbury's *Eating People is Wrong*:

> The Vice-Chancellor, like all vice-chancellors, had clear ideas
>
> of what a university should look like, and taste like; vice-
>
> chancellors all share in common a Platonic ideal for a

university. For one thing, it should be *big*. People should be coming to look at it all the time. There should be a special place for parking Rolls-Royces. There should be big sports grounds, a science building designed by Basil Spence, and more and more students coming every year. There should be new faculties – of Business Administration, of Aeronautical Engineering, of Sanitation, of Social Dancing. Vice-chancellors want big universities and a great many faculties; professors want small universities and only the liberal arts and pure sciences. Vice-chancellors always seem to win.[9]

Dr Gerald Sidewinder in Howard Jacobson's *Coming From Behind* (1985) is similar but more monstrous; the disruptions of traditional university procedure chronicled in Frank Parkin's *The Mind and Body Shop* (1987) result from a radically changed educational landscape, but their implementation comes from a Vice-Chancellor who insists that Philosophy be thought of as a commodity, that students are customers, and that department heads should profit from his own experience as "East Midlands sales rep for Consolidated Tractor Fuels."[10] "Rationalization" – that is, laying off faculty – political correctness, and required assessment are all blamed on lavishly caricatured central administrators.

[9] Malcolm Bradbury, *Eating People is Wrong* (1959. Chicago: Academy Chicago, 1986), p. 172.
[10] Frank Parkin, *The Mind and Body Shop* (London: Collins, 1986; New York: Atheneum, 1987), p. 12.

Types of Academic Fiction

One of the bitterest treatments of university administration comes from the Australian Michael Wilding's *Academia Nuts*, where one professor complains:

> "What sort of academic would become a Dean, a Pro-Vice-Chancellor, or a Vice-Chancellor? Only one who was no longer concerned to teach, only one who was no longer concerned to research. The people who occupy these administrative roles are self-selected failures from the academy they presume to control. They are people whose teaching skills were so derisory that they avoided teaching by getting teaching relief for administrative duties, whose ability to write or research was so inadequate that they avoided research by hiring research assistants to do their research and write their publications for them, research and publications which have no credibility in the scholarly community ... They are the Judases of the profession, they betray what they have no skills in, they destroy the institutions in which they failed."[11]

Yet smaller is the subset of academic fiction that focuses on presidents as main characters, including R. V. Cassill's *The President* (1964), Ralph McInerny's *The Search Committee* (1991), and Phoebe and Todhunter Ballard's very odd *The Man Who Stole a University* (1967), in which "stealing a university" – that is, moving it to an abandoned military base to

11 Michael Wilding, *Academia Nuts* (Watsons Bay, NSW: Wild and Woolley, 2002), pp. 197-8.

The Academic Novel

break a faculty strike, for instance – figures as a very good thing to do.

3. *Focus on Faculty*

This is by far the largest category of academic novels. As Sanford Pinsker, a literature professor himself who claims that "novels about academe are to college professors what bodice-rippers are to the hoi polloi," acknowledges the presence of students in such fiction, but insists

> The truth of the matter is that when we think of college novels we tend to think of their more permanent residents – faculty members who grumble and plot insurrections, deans (and sometimes, presidents) who dream about signing their dismissal notices, and increasingly, flashy academic superstars who liven up a moribund campus with insider gossip and the latest trends in literary theory.[12]

Most academic novelists are, or have been, faculty members (of course, they've been students, too, but professors more recently).

3.1 *Minor subspecialties.*

3.1.1 *Mysteries.* Because a college or university is a closed community; because it is a place tolerant of eccentricity and social deviance; because it is, or at

---

[12] Sanford Pinsker, "Who Cares If Roger Ackroyd Gets Tenure?" (*Partisan Review, 66,* Summer 1999), p. 440, p. 442.

108

least is traditionally thought to be, a place devoted to reason, it makes a splendid setting for the mystery novel. Perhaps even more importantly, the academic murder mystery relies on the apparent antithesis between the values of higher education – tolerance, gentleness, the settling of differences by discussion rather than violence – and the homicide at the heart of the murder mystery. Likewise, at least according to fictional convention, professors make good sleuths. And Carolyn Heilbrun, writing as Amanda Cross, explains that she chose an academic sleuth because "the mind of a literary person who loves quoting, loves conversation, a comedy of manners, in short, is what appealed to me."[13] Sometimes the mystery is related to scholarly investigation, as in Michael Malone's *Foolscap* (1991), Lennard J. Davis's *The Sonnets* (2001) or James Lasdun's *The Horned Man* (2002).

3.1.2 *Science Fiction.* Not a large category – particularly considering that there is so much more science than murder at most universities – this one has been vivified in part because of the computer. The best examples, focusing on artificial intelligence and, in effect, the human qualities of computers, are Richard Powers's *Galatea 2.2* (1985) and Jonathan Lethem's *As She Climbed Across the Table* (1997); also exploiting the imagined properties of computing to more sensational ends is Stephen Fry's *Making History* (1996) about undoing the birth of Hitler.

---

[13] Interviewed in Diana Cooper-Clark, *Designs of Darkness: Interviews with Detective Novelists* (Bowling Green, OH: Bowling Green State University Popular Press, 1983), p. 187.

3.1.3 *Satiric Farce.* By far the largest number of academic novels falls into this category. The topics of their satire provide a rough approach to taxonomy.

3.1.3.1 *Satire on professors themselves.* Many of the classics of the genre satirize the professoriate because of its mental quirks, its pointless activities, its neuroses, its perversity. These include Kingsley Amis's *Lucky Jim* (1953), Mary McCarthy's *The Groves of Academe* (1952), David Lodge's trilogy of novels about Morris Zapp and Philip Swallow, Malcolm Bradbury's *Eating People is Wrong* (1959) and *The History Man* (1975), Vladimir Nabokov's *Pale Fire* (1962) and *Pnin* (1957). More recent examples are Anthony Burgess's novels about the poet Enderby under the aspect of professor and Alan Brownjohn's A *Funny Old Year* (2001).

3.1.3.2 *Satire on conditions that undermine college education or faculty liberty.* In Britain, these conditions seem to be the Thatcherite attacks on higher education – in novels like Bradbury's *Cuts* (1987), Lodge's *Nice Work* (1988), Parkin's *The Mind and Body Shop* (1987), and Alan Plater's *Oliver's Travels* (1994). The American Richard Russo's *Straight Man* (1997) is also about the discontent of academics facing financial stringency, and one of the fiercest depictions comes from Australia. Wilding's *Academia Nuts* includes the explanation that "Finance was the excuse" – for encouraging senior faculty members to take early retirement. "Budgetary considerations. But anyone who wanted to could see that that was only an excuse. Most didn't want to. They were already so fearful, demoralized or sycophantic they wanted to see nothing. The climate of insecurity was having its effect. Destabilising the academics, unnerving the already pretty well nerveless, it made central control easier to reimpose."[14] In the US the context is more likely to be the illiberal suspicion associated with McCarthyism, required loyalty oaths, and a nation's touchy suspicion of leftwing values: May Sarton's *Faithful Are the Wounds* (1955), Bradbury's novel of a British professor visiting in America *Stepping Westward* (1965), or Bernard Malamud's *A New Life* (1961).

3.1.3.3 *Satire on the publish-or-perish syndrome*: including James Hynes's *Publish and Perish: Three Tales of Tenure and Terror* (1997), James Pease's *The Associate Professor* (1967), John Williams's *Stoner* (1988), Michael Frayn's *The Trick of It* (1989) and Amis's *Lucky Jim* (1953).

3.1.3.4 *Satire on the political environment*, particularly racial and gender relations, in the late twentieth-century university. Most of these novels operate from what must be called the conservative side – that is, the position that sees "political correctness" as an excessive demand for self-suppression and punishment of offenders. There is a long list of novels on this subject including J. M. Coetzee's *Disgrace* (1999), Philip Roth's *The Human Stain* (2000), Edward Allen's *Mustang Sally* (1992), Anne Bernays's *Professor Romeo* (1989), Saul Bellow's *The Dean's December* (1982), Percival Everett's *Erasure* (2001), Philippa Gregory's *Perfectly Correct* (1996), Francine Prose's *Blue Angel* (2000), and Alison

---

[14] Wilding, pp. 114-15.

Lurie's *The War Between the Tates* (1974). Most of these concern impermissible sexual affairs between professors and students. Roth's novel is about racial insensitivity. The odd novels in this category are those which approach it from a position on the left, most notably Ishmael Reed's *Japanese By Spring* (1993) and Fedwa Malti-Douglas's *Hisland: Adventures in Ac-Ac-Ademe* (1998).

3.1.4 *Doubly Academic Novels.* By this I mean novels with an academic subject – professors, students, campuses – which also incorporate an "academic" theoretical interest. The early exemplars of this trend are Nabokov's *Pale Fire* (1962) and John Barth's *Giles Goat-Boy* (1966). More recent entries are more explicitly informed by post-modern concerns, flaunting their own fictionality and playfully exploring epistemological and ontological questions. Among the very impressive such novels are David Lodge's *Small World: An Academic Romance* (1984); Gilbert Adair's *The Death of the Author* (1992) and John Banville's *Shroud* (2002), both obvious explorations of the case of literary theorist Paul de Man; and four novels which deserve to be much better known: Andrew Crumey's *Mister Mee* (2000), in which an eighteenth-century encyclopedia vanishes under observation by a twentieth-century professor, Lee Siegel's rich and inventive *Love in a Dead Language: A Romance* (1999), David Caute's *The Occupation* (1971), which combines a plot involving campus rebellion in the 1960s with an involuted and self-referential technique, and Robert Grudin's *Book: A Novel* (1992). *Book* is simultaneously a mystery, a meditation on publish-or-perish conditions, and a

satire on literary theory: towards its end, the English
Department is divided to create a new Department of
Literary Theory, which attracts no students but
permits plenty of output:

> ... the irrepressible Emerson Baismacou was conducting a
> nonstop seminar on his recently published *Oracle, Orifice* and
> his soon-to-appear *The Text as Undergarment*. Supported by a
> massive government grant, E. F. Taupe was eloquently
> advancing the thesis that all known forms of heterosexual
> activity were processible rape; while Sandy Eule was rough-
> drafting a polemic which asserted that books were not
> written by people, or, if they were, they were not books.[15]

There are academic novels that fit none of these
categories – Tim Parks's novels about Englishmen
teaching English in Italy; Barbara Pym's books about
the academic fringes in Oxford; Tibor Fischer's *The
Thought Gang* (1994), about philosophers as bank
robbers, and Judith Dawson's *Judasland* (1989), about
a college secretary. But the multifariousness of the
genre – its vigorous resistance to being summed up
in any number of categories – is another tribute to its
fertility and brilliance.

---

[15] Robert Grudin, *Book: A Novel* (1992; New York: Penguin, 1993), p. 235.

BARBAROUS WOMEN[1]

Ian Carter

"Why," asked G. B. Shaw's Professor Higgins, "can't a woman be more like a man?" For much British university fiction this question is disastrously mistaken: the real task is to assert how irreducibly different men are from women, and to defend the difference. This colours accounts of women's experience in Oxbridge and not-Oxbridge universities as student, wife, or lover. In British university fiction women are subject to what a critic has called, felicitously, textual harassment.[2] Challenges to this harassment are interestingly modest.

Given their monastic origins, it is little surprise that novels about Oxford and Cambridge should treat women as threatening interlopers. "'I judged [Tandon] to be of the aggressively celibate type – such as still exists, you know, in the colleges,'" says Elinor Fontaney to Quail; "'A negative attitude to women in general, and a positive dislike for women of education.'"[3] The prospect of admitting women to Comyns College, Oxford, unmans Jake Richardson. This direct literary – and etymological – descendent of Jim Dixon finds his thing drooping in direct proportion to women's success in forcing open the doors of Oxford men's houses.[4] The prospect of admitting women to Porterhouse, Cambridge, is particularly abhorrent to the college's Senior Tutor: "Sickly unisex would replace the

---

[1] Previously published in *Ancient Cultures of Conceit: British University Fiction in the Post-War Years* (London: Routledge, 1990), pp. 159-66 [Ed.].

[2] M. Jacobus, *Reading Woman* (New York: Columbia U. P.; London: Methuen, 1986), p. 85.

[3] J. I. M. Stewart, *The Guardians* (London: Gollancz, 1955), p. 134.

[4] Kingsley Amis, *Jake's Thing* (London: Hutchinson, 1978).

healthy cheerful louts who had helped to preserve the inane innocence and the athleticism that were his only safeguard against the terrors of thought."[5]   Here, as elsewhere, opposition is based on more than simple homophilia. "'There has been no greater mistake made in Oxford,'"says the Bursar of St Thomas, "'than the abolition of compulsory chapel, except of course the admission of women and the abolition of compulsory Greek.'"[6] Secularization, decline of the classical curriculum, letting women in: these are three aspects of a single degradation, the erosion of difference between Oxbridge and not-Oxbridge.

We are shown that fears of this erosion have a long history. "'Nobody thought of women playing any part in University life when I was an undergraduate,'" says Winn of the 1890s; "'I really do not think that there were women in Oxford – certainly it never occurred to us to miss them.'"[7]   An Oxford don from this generation surfaces gently in the Bodleian Library:

A long low wheeze, as of air let gently out of a bicycle tyre, made Jane glance to her left. Dr Undertone had opened his eyes and was looking at her in great astonishment – rather as if, on returning to his immediate surroundings, he had discovered himself seated next to a studious walrus or erudite dromedary. This was disconcerting to Jane, but, on reflection, not at all surprising. During a large part of Dr Undertone's reading life, it had to be remembered, women – and

---

[5] Tom Sharpe, *Porterhouse Blue* (1974; London: Pan, 1978), p. 202.

[6] J. C. Masterman, *To Teach the Senators Wisdom: An Oxford Guide-Book* (London: Hodder & Stoughton, 1952), p. 140.

[7] Masterman, p. 105.

particularly young women – must have been an unusual sight in Bodley.[8]

Women are constructed by Winn as invisible, by Undertone as not-human. In either form they threaten culture's citadel. Once women have breached the walls of Oxford and Cambridge novelists start to give us distinctly unflattering representations of female education. The women's colleges are very different from the men's. Pursuing enquiries into yet another Oxford murder,

> The policemen walked through the huge, single quadrangle of Walpurgis, by lawns and gravelled walks, populous with litter-bins and tennis-courts. There was nothing here of the quaint, the cramped or the medieval: Walpurgis was large and airy and modern, and had been designed exclusively for big, normal, strenuous, red-legged young women with glasses.[9]

We are required to understand that Walpurgis is in Oxford but not of Oxford. It is a sham, a feeble emulation of a real college. Where a proper ancient men's college has rooms opening off staircases, these female places have "small, unsolidly modern"[10] bed-sitters ranged along corridors. It is not just that the corridors "swam in a strange effluvia composed in equal parts of floor-polish, cosmetics and cosy secrets"[11]; their very existence asserts

---

[8] Michael Innes, *Operation Pax* (London: Gollancz, 1951), p. 172.

[9] Robert Robinson, *Landscape with Dead Dons* (1956; Harmondsworth: Penguin, 1963), p. 54.

[10] Edmund Crispin, *The Case of the Gilded Fly* (1944; New York: Walker, 1979), p. 123.

[11] Robinson, p. 56.

women's colleges' kinship with not-Oxbridge universities, with their halls of bed-sitter residence. The architecture of another Oxford women's college evokes a much more specific redbrick comparison. St Mary's

> ... a rambling, uncoordinated sprawl of buildings in harsh red brick set off by occasional excrescences in white stone .... The front entrance ... was silent and spacious, its tiling and panelling suggesting a lavishly equipped mental hospital whose inmates pay enormous sums for the privilege of being shielded from the incomprehension of society.[12]

Since this is Oxford we are shown a privileged asylum, but the institution is recognizably of a kind with Bradbury's[13] minor redbrick university housed in a converted public lunatic asylum. Here, as there, the account of the building contaminates our view of its inmates.

Of necessity being, like lunatics, possessed of less than full citizenship, women cannot understand what it is to be an Oxbridge undergraduate. Where men display a varied aristocratic eccentricity, women demonstrate a depressingly uniform lower middle-class taste: "in every window the back of a postcard reproduction of Van Gogh's *Sunflowers* was clearly distinguishable."[14] The daily routine for men and women reflects this difference between aristocratic and *petit bourgeois* styles. Women get up too early.

---

[12] Louis McIntosh, *Oxford Folly* (London: Johnson, 1956), p. 25.

[13] Malcolm Bradbury, *Eating People Is Wrong* (1959; London: Arrow, 1978).

[14] Robinson, p. 55.

The women undergraduates were the first abroad – cycling along the streets in droves, absurdly gowned and clutching complicated files, or hovering about libraries until the doors should open and admit them once again to study the divine mysteries which hang around the Christian element in *Beowulf;* the date of the *Urtristan* (if any), the complexities of hydrodynamics, the kinetic theory of gases, the law of tort or the purposes of the parathyroid gland. The men rose more circumspectly, putting a pair of trousers, a coat, and a scarf over their pyjamas, shambling across the quadrangles to sign lists, and shambling back again.[15]

Women lack a proper sense of direction:

Outwards towards the Banbury or the Woodstock Road an unending stream of battered sports cars bore cohorts of male undergraduates, discreetly concealed amid golf clubs, shotguns, and riding kits. Inwards towards the lecture-rooms and libraries of the University rode an answering army of young women on bicycles bearing large baskets bulging with massive volumes, as if they were the delivery service of a community given literally to devouring books.[16]

These bicycling women lack academic discrimination: "Girl students in wringing-wet gowns were going to odd little afternoon lectures, of the sort that men would never be so foolish as to forsake their strong tea and anchovy

---

[15] Edmund Crispin, *The Moving Toyshop* (London: Gollancz, 1946), p. 27.

[16] Innes, *Operation Pax*, p. 158.

toast for."[17] Arrived at their destination, these females –
not-Oxbridge "students," note, rather than Oxbridge
"undergraduates" – present an unlovely sight: "The lecture
room was full of young women in short gowns, carrying
bulky handbags and enormous tattered bundles of notes;
they smelt inimitably of facepowder and (vaguely) Irish
stew, and they were dressed in woollen clothes."[18]
Women's behaviour in lecture rooms is unacceptably
different: "On the wooden benches about twenty
undergraduates sat, the women gowned, chattering
feverishly, the men ungowned, staring absently about
them."[19] No doubt the men were wondering how they
came to be in such unaccustomed circumstances, such
extraordinary company. We see more Dr Undertones in the
making.

Some forms of lunacy can be cured, or at least coaxed
into remission. "'Janet was one of our *most* successful
girls,'" gushes Miss Puncher, Mistress of St Helena's,
Oxford. "'Engaged in her second year, married in her
third. She never took Schools. An excellent career.'"[20]
Anthea Lambert's marriage means escape from the
fellowship of St Cecilia's, Oxford, where tea-drinking and
gossip replace the port-drinking and scholarship of the
men's colleges.[21] "After a time," says Nicolette Simney,

I didn't think much of Oxford. I was the wrong sex for what goes on

there. Young women who could get tense on cocoa and whose diet

[17] Robert Liddell, *The Last Enchantments* (London: Cape, 1948), p. 172.

[18] Philip Larkin, *Jill: A Novel* (London: Fortune Press, 1946), p. 70.

[19] Crispin, *The Moving Toyshop*, p. 158.

[20] J. P. V. D. Balsdon, *The Day They Burned Miss Termag* (London: Eyre & Spottiswoode, 1961), p. 68.

[21] J. I. M. Stewart, *Mark Lambert's Supper* (London: Gollancz, 1954).

was a muddied amalgam of precocious pedantry and belated crushes just didn't turn out to be my cup of tea any more than the little Emma Bovarys who were hopeful of careers on the London stage.[22]

Having achieved this rational insight Nicolette, like any cured lunatic, can be returned to normal society: like Janet and Anthea, she leaves. Oxford is no place for a sensible woman.

Wives confirm this uncharitable diagnosis. "Dons commonly marry fools," Vulliamy[23] tells us. Gavin Limbert is

A nice Cambridge boy, who had made squiggles in his notebooks between lectures on Julius Caesar and more lectures on Caesar Augustus. And held an exhibition above a tea-shop. And was told by all the wives of all the professors that he was a True Artist.[24]

We are invited to join in uttering a curse on "these self-satisfied dons' wives."[25] Whence the curse?

We are driven back to the monastic roots of Oxbridge. Until nineteenth-century reforms, only a college's head could be married. Other dons had to be celibate, or at least unmarried. Their modern descendants remain, says

---

[22] Michael Innes, *What Happened at Hazelwood* (London: Gollancz, 1946), p. 19.

[23] C. E. Vulliamy, *Don Among the Dead Men: A Satirical Thriller* (London: Michael Joseph, 1952), p. 25.

[24] Michael Innes, *A Private View* (1952; London: Gollancz, 1974), p. 38.

[25] D. Rees, *The Cambridge Murders* (1945; Harmondsworth: Penguin, 1952), pp. 218-19.

Michael Innes, "obstinately unconvinced of the necessity of the modern amenities either for themselves, their wives, or their children. Only recently, indeed, did they *discover* wives and children."[26] This discovery does not transform attitudes completely. "'When I first came to live in Oxford,'" says Arthur Aylwin, "'I thought High Table and common rooms and dining clubs and all the rest of it so many deplorable relics of a vanished celibate society. Now I'm inclined to see them as among the blessed alleviations of family life.'"[27] Balsdon's dystopia of twenty-first-century Oxford under a feminist onslaught imagines one men's college being sacrificed to the women. The notion that all colleges could become mixed he regards as too far-fetched to be credible even in a work of fantasy: "in a co-educational world, where could men escape to be alone?"[28] Little wonder, then, that one wife hated Cambridge "with much the same sort of jealousy as other wives hate their husbands' regiments or clubs."[29] Most particularly, wives threaten collegiate mateship. As the Master of Beaufort tells Ashe, his college's house radical,

It's always better having the Fellows in College. The undergraduates like us to be accessible, and it helps the College spirit if we're seen around. Half the trouble these days is that so many of us are married and submerged by families in North Oxford. There was a lot to be said for the old monastic ideal.[30]

---

[26] Michael Innes, *Death at the President's Lodging* (London: Gollancz, 1936), p. 123.

[27] J. I. M. Stewart, *The Bloody Wood* (London: Gollancz, 1966), p. 30.

[28] Balsdon, p. 14 [Ed.].

[29] Simon Raven, *Places Where They Sing* (London: Blond, 1970), p. 126.

[30] Howard Shaw, *Death of a Don* (London: Hodder & Stoughton, 1981), p. 16.

As a group dons' wives clearly are a Bad Thing. Treated individually the picture is rather more mixed. We are shown some admirable Oxford spouses. Mrs Vereker, wife of the President of St Thomas', is "a remarkable woman, not very artistic, not very clever, and yet, by virtue of character and a deep instinctive sympathy for others, a kind of natural leader."[31] Mary Aylwin is sensible, capable, and intelligent, a strong buttress for her husband's bid to gain election to his college's provostship.[32]   Janet McKechnie, wife of an Oxford classics professor and Duncan Pattullo's childhood sweetheart, is endowed with native Scots good sense.[33] Mabel Bedworth supports her Oxford senior tutor husband by surreptitiously mothering a succession of homesick undergraduates who fall safely in love with her.[34]   Alice Mannering, aristocratic wife of a humbly born Cambridge fellow, brings him family connections that greatly assist the smooth acceleration of his career.[35] To set against these positive accounts we are given less flattering portraits. In Oxford we are shown the foolish and snobbish Mrs Jobling, wife of a college's head.[36]   Gervase Fen's wife manages an appropriate answer to a question. "Fen gazed at her with something of the triumphant and sentimental pride of a dog owner whose pet has succeeded in balancing a biscuit on its

---

[31] J. C. Masterman, *An Oxford Tragedy* (1933; Harmondsworth: Penguin, 1939), p. 52.

[32] J. I. M. Stewart, *The Aylwins* (London: Gollancz, 1966), p. 155.

[33] J. I. M. Stewart, *The Gaudy* (London: Gollancz, 1974); *Young Pattullo* (London: Gollancz, 1975); *Full Term* (London: Gollancz, 1978).

[34] Stewart, *Full Term.*

[35] J. I. M. Stewart, *Our England is a Garden, and Other Stories* (London: Gollancz, 1979), p. 130.

[36] Stewart, *The Guardians.*

nose."[37] Cambridge novels give us cohorts of unappealling wives. Lady Muriel Royce is the aristocratic but graceless and tactless wife of a dying master.[38] Lady Mary Evans is Sir Godber's bigotted aristocratic Fabian spouse.[39] Mona Carrington is Lord Beyfus's *de facto* wife, threatening to withdraw her bizarre sexual favours in order to force him to lead the attack on Lancaster College's privilege.[40] Patricia Llewyllyn attacks her husband through calculated sexual promiscuity.[41] Alice Jago is "driven to inflict on him [her husband] the woes of a hypochondriac, the venom of a shrew, the faithlessness of one who had to find attention."[42] Her nature and conduct lose her husband support in a close election:

> It would be awkward if she spoke in that vein to others, I thought ....
> Nothing would give more offence, nothing was more against the
> rules of that society: I decided Brown, as manager of Jago's caucus,
> must know at once. As I was telling him, he flushed. "That woman's
> a confounded nuisance," he said.[43]

Since the novels' gaze is riveted so firmly on the men's colleges we see little of female Oxbridge academics. Stewart provides us with an unflattering view of the species in Diana Sandys's comment on Noel Gylby's plan for advertising Sappho chocolates as lesbian delights: "'I rather think you'll have female dons – all tense and arm in

---

[37] Crispin, *The Case of the Gilded Fly*, p. 70.

[38] C. P. Snow, *The Masters* (London: Macmillan, 1951).

[39] Sharpe.

[40] Raven.

[41] Raven.

[42] Snow, p. 279.

[43] Snow, p. 119.

arm, no doubt, as you want – going to their favourite sweet-shop and asking for *Sap-foh.'"*[44] Invited to watch the grace and culture of dinner in Warlock College's hall, we get an unpleasant close-up view of "Pearl Corker – the manly Corker of Walpurgis Hall. Beneath the table her knees were spread wide apart, and the elastic end of one woollen knicker-leg obtruded."[45] A policeman ruminates on a later encounter with this formidable Pearl: "'An educated woman. Thank God my girl's going in to be a stenographer.'"[46] We get distant views of Dame Helen Gardiner, emeritus Merton Professor of English Literature at Oxford;[47] of Professor Babcock – and of her college's Bursar, Cecilia Basket, a general's daughter who pulls a pistol on a drunken college servant when he threatens her with a cleaver.[48] We see (after her untimely death) Miss Termag, Mistress of Sapientia College. She wrote the stern Termag Commission report, which recommended that women should take over just one men's college after narrowly rejecting the attractive idea that all men should be thrown out of Oxford. Miss Puncher, her counterpart at St Helena's, is close to being elected vice-chancellor.[49] We see Mona Carrington refusing to speak to Beyfus until the door is closed, for "a life spent in a women's college had given her a horror of being overheard."[50] We see Helen Burns, who can decide whether Sefton Goldberg is elected to the coveted Disraeli Fellowship in a Cambridge college:

---

[44] Michael Innes, *Hamlet, Revenge!* (1937; Harmondsworth: Penguin, 1969), p. 157.

[45] Robinson, p. 26.

[46] Robinson, p. 56.

[47] Colin Dexter, *The Dead of Jericho* (London: Macmillan, 1981).

[48] J. I. M. Stewart, *A Memorial Service* (London: Gollancz, 1976).

[49] Balsdon.

[50] Raven, p. 68.

"Sefton watched in amazement as she moved her mouth and made real words and sentences .... Sefton felt as if he were listening to the rabbits talk."[51] We see Duncan Pattullo's niece (and, it is thought for a time, possibly his illegitimate daughter) Fiona Petrie, living with a female novelist in a hinted lesbian relationship.[52] We are shown two politically treacherous women: Mona Carrington, a left infantilist Girton anthropologist; and Emily Bryant, an able historian who is a fellow of a men's college that has opened its doors to women, and a Russian agent. Bryant is ugly.[53] Petrie may be lesbian. Anthea Lambert is attractive and heterosexual, but her inclination as well as the terms of her fellowship lead her to escape St Cecilia's. A normal, sensible woman should seek to leave Oxbridge. If she stays, then she has to avoid getting ideas above her station:

> Ruth is not what might be called a passionate supporter of women's lib; indeed, she seems to enjoy being feminine. But as Caval Professor of Mathematics at Oxford she is properly conscious of her identity and not at all disposed to think that her role in life is to cook for me .... "You've been very good, Peter, in not trying to stop me being a professor, but what's so difficult about being a woman is that only half of me really wants to be a professor – or rather I *do* want to be a professor, but another me wants to cook and make cushions and even knit socks for you."[54]

---

51 Howard Jacobson, *Coming from Behind* (1983; London: Black Swan, 1984), p. 96.

52 Stewart, *A Memorial Service; Full Term*.

53 Anthony Lejeune, *Professor in Peril* (London: Macmillan, 1987), p. 32.

54 J. R. L. Anderson, *Death in a High Latitude* (London: Gollancz, 1981), p. 9, p. 117.

Given the relatively small number of novels set in such places, women are much more evident in not-Oxbridge universities. Lacking sex-segregated colleges, these places display a promiscuous mixing of men and women. At Nesfield, a major redbrick, "girls hurried past, bespectacled, notebooked, serious; girls loitered past, nudging, giggling, powdering; men skylarked, shouted, bit into sandwiches."[55] But contact is less promiscuous, conduct less unconstrained, in the ghastly gentility of Nesfield's hall of residence for women:

In the gardens of St Cecilia's Hall young ladies, equipped with secateurs and suitable gloves, gathered flowers. On the terrace other young ladies walked with Miss Godkin's dogs. Under trees young ladies sketched. And through open windows and across the lawn floated the strains of violins and harps, pianos and cellos, discoursed by young ladies for whom, by the doom of Miss Godkin, musical accomplishment had been decreed. One could see at once that throughout the Hall refined cheerfulness and cultivated gaiety reigned. Indeed these qualities, together with unpunctuality, needlework, dips into *Country Life* and *The Queen*, unpainted fingernails, intelligent conversation, politeness to servants, and the use of Received Standard English, were required by Miss Godkin from eight fifteen in the morning to ten o'clock at night. Young ladies who so far wished to become girls again as to read film magazines, make bets on horses, discuss boys, discuss girls, toast bloaters before gas fires, consume grocer's port, fan dance, croon, pinch, weep, become deliciously sick on chocolate peppermint

---

[55] Michael Innes, *The Weight of the Evidence* (1944; Harmondsworth: Penguin, 1961), p. 7.

creams, tell each other about their homes and their neighbours, their mothers' troubles with hire-purchase and their fathers' triumphs with dogs: such recalcitrant elements could indulge their backslidings only in the nocturnal seclusion of the spare, but dainty and maiden-like, cubicles with which Miss Godkin provided them. By day life at St Cecilia's was elegant and controlled; it combined, Miss Godkin was accustomed to say, the variousness and verve of a noble household of the Renaissance with the dignity and repose of an English country seat. And some of the girls had to stay three whole years.[56]

Teachers' wives continue to be unsympathetic characters. The monied and socially ambitious wife of an ex-CAT's vice-chancellor is "almost Lady Macbeth."[57] Hilary Swallow makes trouble for the head of Rummidge's English department by seeking to resurrect her MA studies: "'it puts us in rather an awkward position. I mean, the wife of a colleague ....' If his colleagues had to have wives, he intimated, the least they could do was to keep them at home in decent obscurity."[58] Elsewhere, the wife of a classics lecturer maintains a ludicrous salon, unable to see that her pretension is pricked by her provincialism.[59] She is the literary ancestor of Neddy Welch's appalling wife, who keeps a similarly ludicrous salon. Happily she has not reckoned with Jim Dixon's incompetence at

---

[56] Innes, *The Weight of Evidence*, p. 181 [Ed.].

[57] J. B. Priestley, *Out of Town* (London: Heinemann, 1968), p. 18.

[58] David Lodge, *Changing Places* (1975; Harmondsworth: Penguin, 1978), p. 198.

[59] Innes, *The Weight of the Evidence*, pp. 91-4.

madrigal-singing and his penchant for smoking in bed.[60] Tom Cochrane is a senior lecturer in geography at Edinburgh. His wife is a professor of sociology.

> It didn't worry him unduly that Flora ranked higher in the university hierarchy than he did. But it did disturb him that Flora enjoyed incessant committee meetings, continual arranging of this or that, and endless entertaining of university personnel in whom Tom hadn't the slightest interest.[61]

Olivia Jory "was much too young and immeasurably too rare to be conceivably one of the considerable number of learned ladies on the staff" of a minor redbrick.[62] Elsewhere, too, learned ladies are not an impressive lot. Miss Godkin, Warden of St Cecilia's Hall at Nesfield, is "an assured and thoroughly illogical woman."[63] Margaret Peel is a lecturer in English, a neurotic leech bent on sucking Jim Dixon dry. Other women on the staff of Dixon's minor redbrick include the sexagenarian Professor of Philosophy and the fifteen-stone Senior Lecturer in Economics.[64] In an ex-CAT Dr Hazel Honeyfield, nicknamed Honeypot, is a sociologist whose research interests include the status implications of potted plants. Priestley describes her as "a rather small, delicious brunette, about thirty, midnight and cream when in repose, sparkling and dimpling as soon as

[60] Kingsley Amis, *Lucky Jim* (1954; Harmondworth: Penguin, 1961).
[61] Fred Hoyle and Geoffrey Hoyle, *The Monster of Loch Ness* (London: Heinemann, 1971), p. 143.
[62] Michael Innes, *Old Hall, New Hall* (1956; Harmondsworth: Penguin, 1961), p. 11.
[63] Innes, *The Weight of the Evidence*, p. 95.
[64] Amis, *Lucky Jim*, p. 107.

she talked or listened, no matter how idiotic the subject."[65]
This machine for generating sexual fantasies is balanced by
Dr Lois Terry:

> ... badly dressed, thinnish, with mousy and rather untidy hair, and
> would be generally considered quite plain, though Tuby, more
> perceptive than most men, decided it was because she had no
> excitement inside, no strong current of feeling, to light her up.[66]

Watermouth has the prim Annie Callendar, historically
programmed to be Howard Kirk's prey, and Flora
Beniform – a specialist on troilism in Walsall – who
sexually devours Howard along, it is implied, with many
other men.[67]

We need to notice one striking feature in the accounts of
women's place in British university life that we have
considered thus far: everything was written by men. What
sorts of accounts do women provide? Sometimes there are
strong continuities with what we have seen.

In a novel with a mid-nineteenth century setting Mary
Lamont waits to join the second cohort of students in
Oxford's embryo women's college. She gives us an account
of the embattled attitudes to be faced even from liberals
like her father, a painter:

> My father says that the coming of women has ruined Oxford. Before
> we came, he says, what a pleasant world it was, with women kept
> safely beyond Folly Bridge. He's joking, of course, because in the

---

[65] Priestley, p. 53.

[66] Priestley, p. 104 [Ed.].

[67] Bradbury, *The History Man* (1975; London: Arrow, 1977).

first place he likes women's company, and there are always plenty of wives and daughters about, but what he means is that none were students of the University. We might attend the lectures on Art by Professor Ruskin (and indeed I did), but until the last year or two we were not found at the lectures on Greek, Latin or Mathematics held in the Colleges for the young men undergraduates.[68]

The lively, vivacious and married Thea Sylvester is appointed to be the mock-Oxbridge not-Oxbridge Buriton University's professor of archaeology. "'I was very glad that they gave you the Chair,'" says Miss Eliot, a retired medieval historian soon to be murdered.

It seems extraordinary, fifty years on, that I should still be thinking that it's a boost for women .... I've sometimes wondered whether it wasn't the fault of people like myself – my generation of teachers, I mean. Perhaps our pupils were afraid of becoming like us.[69]

Students come to Rachel Ambrose [Cambridge], Sharon was thinking, sustained by visions of fountains in medieval courtyards and tendrils of creeper tawny-scarlet over grey stone walls: to get to this place they have to come past the warehouse and the gasworks, past the supermarkets and the Strict Ebenezer chapel [to] ... the tall Victorian houses, with their porches and flights of balustraded steps, crowned by stone urns pricked over with cacti, the sharp roofs with

---

[68] Gwendoline Butler, *A Coffin for Pandora* (1973; Harmondsworth: Penguin, 1978), p. 10.

[69] Jessica Mann, *The Only Security* (London: Macmillan, 1973), pp. 85-6.

their barge-boards and dormer windows, the pepperpot baronial tower.[70]

Meanings encoded in bricks and mortar tell us that this is a very marginal college indeed. The university does not permit Rachel Ambrose students to sit for its degrees. Ann Livingstone is enchanted by the architecture of Oxford's men's colleges. Then she arrives at her women's college. Her sensibilities are affronted. She is accommodated in a Victorian building, "that monstrous pile of red brick, with the small, arched, Gothic windows, crudely pointed in yellow brick."[71] She is horrified by her room in this pile. "Didn't they, in any case, always have 'rooms' at Oxford? They always had in the books she had read. Why should she, then, be consigned, like an underprivileged typist, to a sordid bed-sitting-room?"[72]

> On that first evening in College, dinner had been another insult to Ann's sensibilities and cherished preconceptions. Where were the cloistered calm, the low-voiced exchanges of wit, the erudite references? After the first meal, she did not think she could live through three years of them.
>
> The dining-hall was large and without character or beauty. Its rough plaster walls were finished off in white swirls, like cheap frosting, and the wooden beams that imitated rafters shone with yellow varnish. The refectory tables showed the same shoddiness.

---

[70] Valerie Grosvenor Myer, *Culture Shock* (London: Duckworth, 1988), pp. 13-14.

[71] Lois Day, *The Looker In* (London: Cape, 1961), p. 140.

[72] Day, p. 141 [Ed.].

The Academic Novel

There was nothing to relieve the eye, nothing moderately pretty to look at.[73]

Things do not mend when the other inmates appear.

The swarming girls coming in singly or in groups did nothing to improve the hall; Ann could not bear to look at them either. Many still wore their hairy sweaters and skirts, and their faces shone like the rafters. The noise they made was intolerable.[74]

Later, Ann reports to a man that

All the women at my place stand around in hairy, knee-length socks, drinking mugs of cocoa, and looking at the notice-board to see what jolly games they're going to play in the afternoon, or whose class they're in for Anglo-Saxon.[75]

Classes imply school, not Oxbridge university. The teachers – fake dons – confirm this impression. Their nature is summed up in the college's Principal with her grey, cropped hair, beaky nose and reserved manner. These suggest

the true academic, vowed to the life of the mind, medievally scholastic. Only gradually did it become obvious to Ann that behind this noble exterior cowered a vulgar and trivial mind; one without real learning, culture, or wisdom. As the months went by, the Principal disclosed herself as a woman obsessively concerned with

---

[73] Day, p. 156 [Ed.].
[74] Day, p. 156 [Ed.].

132

the rituals of good form, the preservation of law, the keeping of rules. Her guardedly formal manner was not a defence for the sensitive intellect, for she had no intellect. It was the defence of the frightened woman, charmless, neurotic, against any sort of human contact.[76]

An image of what an Oxford women's college should be like – gracious buildings, erudite dons – crashes against the awful reality. Female undergraduates should be feminine, but they clump around in hairy clothes. This is appropriate for a man: hairy tweeds hint at Augusts spent blasting birds from a Scottish sky. Hair on a woman is mannish, superfluous. Day measures her women's college against a feminine version of British university fiction's dominant discourse, and finds it grievously wanting. "The hierarchical character of a woman's college, with its petty disciplines, and its strict observance of protocol and rank, came to her as a shock."[77] Hierarchy and bed-sitters. The dreadful light breaks. Ann is in Oxford but not of it, immured in not-Oxbridge. On her new bicycle she pedals "the mile of suburban road that separated her from the 'real' and central Oxford."[78]

Margaret Forster shares Lois Day's structure of feeling. In *Dames' Delight* Morag, an undergraduate at a top Oxford women's college, tells us about her first dinner in hall: "I thought I'd never seen such a revolting sight than all those crowded tables full of jabbering, excited females. They were so ugly.... The sight of the high table distressed me even more."[79] The spectacle might be distressing in its

[75] Day, p. 187 [Ed.].

[76] Day, p. 137 [Ed.].

[77] Day, p. 137 [Ed.].

[78] Day, pp. 141-142 [Ed.].

[79] Margaret Forster, *Dames' Delight* (London: Cape, 1964), p. 18, p. 21.

own right, but it is rendered doubly so by the contrast which it provides with life in the men's colleges:

> I'd only been a witness to one college dinner before. It was at Ian's college when I'd sat on the hall stairs in the gallery above and listened to the riot below – glasses breaking, some crazy violin going, spontaneous obscene speeches, complete abandon. I'd felt quite moved by all the deep male roars and envied the tremendous camaraderie which was theirs. But this was a mockery.[80]

This is life in the women's colleges as men understand it: a pale imitation of the real Oxford. Like Day's *The Looker In, Dames' Delight* is a feminized novel of apparent Oxbridge undergraduate disillusion – a good male example is Wilfrid Sheed's *A Middle Class Education* (1960) – which reaffirms the discourse at a deeper level. A. S. Byatt[81] gives us a very different account of a Cambridge women's college. Returning to Newnham after a quarter of a century, Frederica "saw it as beautiful – graceful in scale, civilised in space, humane." At first glance this looks like the celebration of male Oxbridge, but some adjectives – beautiful, graceful – make it teeter on the edge of something else. Consider P. D. James's account of New Hall, Cambridge. She makes plain what Byatt hints at the college's feminine architecture:

> With its Byzantine air, its sunken court and its shining domed hall like a peeled orange, [it] reminded Cordelia of a harem; admittedly one owned by a sultan with liberal views and an odd predilection

---

[80] Forster, p. 108 [Ed.].
[81] A. S. Byatt, *Still Life* (London: Chatto & Windus, 1985).

for clever girls, but a harem nonetheless. The college was surely too distractingly pretty to be conducive to serious study.[82]

There are tensions in this passage. New Hall's buildings promote frivolity rather than scholarship; this is not a proper college. But the frivolity follows from its being a harem, an enclosure for women whose life's task is to give men sexual pleasure. The undergraduates and their teachers are to be seen as victims rather than predators.

Variations on this view underlie women novelists' accounts of wives as victims. Helen MacInnes[83] shows us the Junior Fellow of an Oxford men's college, a Labour voter who determinedly wears a tweed jacket at high table. As he feasts, he thinks guiltily of his wife dining at home on scrambled eggs and a baked apple. Margaret Yorke invites us to: "Think of all those poor lonely dons' wives with their tomato soup on their trays and the Sunday film on the box, while their husbands dine in hall. What a dreary life."[84]

These accounts support dons' wives; but they are kin to male authors' more ambiguous sympathy for wives abandoned to poached eggs (C. P. Snow), tinned salmon (Robert Robinson) and tinned spaghetti and sausages (Simon Raven).

Some other women's accounts of academic snares are more interesting. Celia Fremlin[85] gives us Lena, the mad first wife of Ivor, an Oxbridge classics professor. Lena was a brilliant Minoan scholar, herself a college fellow.

---

[82] P. D. James, *An Unsuitable Job for a Woman* (London: Faber & Faber, 1972), p. 76.

[83] Helen McInnes, *Friends and Lovers* (London: Harrap, 1948), p. 196.

[84] Margaret Yorke, *Grave Matters* (1973; Leicester: F. A. Thorpe, 1975), p. 138.

[85] Celia Fremlin, *The Long Shadow* (London: Gollancz, 1975).

Unmarried at 34, she was romanced by the devastatingly handsome 18-year-old Ivor, her pupil, who then used her work to build his own career. Gwendoline Butler[86] gives us Marion Manning, fellow of St Agatha's, Oxford. She is an anthropologist who turns to English literature after her husband dies, and develops a bizarre second – semi-Australian – personality. In her doomed, posthumously published campus novel Barbara Pym[87] gives us Caro Brimstone, married to an ethnohistorian in an ex-CAT. Caro is blackmailed by her husband into purloining a manuscript from the bedside of a dying anthropologist. What drives her to this action is fear that her husband is falling into the clutches of Iris Horniblow, a glamorously boring sociology lecturer.

Caro's dilemma is patterned on that in Barbara Pym's Oxford novel, published thirty-five years after it was written. Francis Cleveland is a fellow of Randolph College who falls for a female pupil but is much too timorous to carry through a successful elopement. His wife holds a deliciously wry attitude to the rigours of his academic life:

> Margaret Cleveland, who had at one time helped and encouraged her husband with his work, had now left him to do it alone, because she feared that with her help it might quite easily be finished before one of them died, and then where would they be? Francis was like a restless, difficult child if he had nothing to occupy him. This book meant that he spent long hours in his study, presumably working on it. It would not be at all convenient for Mrs Cleveland to have him

---

[86] Gwendoline Butler, *Death Lives Next Door* (London: Bles, 1960).

[87] Barbara Pym, *An Academic Question* (London: Macmillan, 1986).

hanging about the drawing-room, wanting to be amused.[88]

We see that women authors' accounts can give us a wife as minder as well as victim. A secretary is surrogate wife to the Warden of Pentecost, Oxford: "For the hundredth time, she wondered if the old man was as innocent as he looked. Did he realise how carefully she briefed him? Did he mind?"[89] Proper wives type their husbands' manuscripts. This skill is learnt early: some London University anthropology postgraduates

> had been fortunate enough to win the love of devoted women – women who might one day become their wives, but who, if they were thrown aside, would accept their fate cheerfully and without bitterness. They had learned early in life what it is to bear love's burdens, listening patiently to their men's troubles and ever ready at their typewriters, should a manuscript or even a short article get to the stage of being written down.[90]

"Newnham was in those days [1954] outside, but not far outside, Cambridge University proper," A. S. Byatt[91] tells us. Today it lies within the walls. Other recent novels show us women penetrating the Oxbridge citadel. The context is changing sexual mores. Duncan Pattullo muses on change in Oxford: "The dimensions of the sexual revolution which had come about in Junkin's time were to be among the

---

[88] Barbara Pym, *Crampton Hodnet* (London: Macmillan; New York: Dutton, 1985), pp. 14-15.

[89] Katharine Farrer, *Gownsman's Gallows* (London: Hodder and Stoughton, 1957), p. 15.

[90] Barbara Pym, *Less Than Angels* (1955; Bath: Chivers, 1971), p. 49.

[91] Byatt, p. 110 [Ed.].

more striking impressions of my middle years."[92] Fornication was not new. Of women in former men's colleges: "'They sleep in?' 'Some of them do. Still, some of them always did, didn't they?'"[93] Jemima Shore enjoys "agreeable memories of other sported oaks in her Cambridge days, doors in men's colleges shut not so much in her face as behind her back."[94] What is new is the treatment of fornication as routine[95], and the grudging opening of men's colleges to women (and, of course, the reverse). Grilling a potential witness, PC Walters misses a *double entendre* rooted in historical change:

"Where does Miss Edgeley work?"

"She's an undergraduate at Brasenose."

"Do they have women there?"

"They've always had women at Brasenose, haven't they?" said the brunette slowly.[96]

Entirely novel is "this new intelligent generation of women undergraduates, the post-Brideshead types, living in colleges in equal numbers and on equal terms with the men".[97] Inspector Morse contemplated the change as he

... watched the two young lovely ladies as they walked out through the Porter's Lodge. They must be members of the college – two

---

[92] Stewart, *Young Pattullo*, p. 139.

[93] Colin Dexter, *The Riddle of the Third Mile* (London: Macmillan, 1983), p. 44.

[94] Antonia Fraser, *Oxford Blood* (London: Weidenfeld and Nicolson, 1985), p. 52.

[95] Shaw, p. 4, p. 134, p.136.

[96] Dexter, *The Dead of Jericho*, p. 58.

outward and happily visible signs of the fundamental change of heart that had resulted in the admission of women to these erstwhile wholly-masculine precincts.[98]

This provides delicious possibilities:

"Do you know Serena of Christ Church?" He swept on: "Isn't it enjoyable hearing that? I'm old-fashioned enough to adore it. These days I only go out with girls from the best men's colleges, or rather the former men's colleges that were formerly the best. Rachel of Magdalen, Allegra of Trinity, I don't know anyone at Balliol yet unfortunately."[99]

We need to be clear about what has happened. Antonia Fraser's *Oxford Blood* celebrates not the fall of the citadel, but women's admission: their shift from being in Oxbridge to being of Oxbridge. Women appear at dinner in the hall of Duncan Pattullo's college, leading him to reflect that "this liberty, gained almost without a struggle after centuries in which the mere notion could scarcely have got into anybody's head, wasn't creating much of a revolution in Oxford life."[100] The underlying discourse is not disturbed. As in otherwise valuable feminist anthropological studies of Oxford and Cambridge academic wives' evaporating exclusion[101], the triumph

---

[97] Fraser, p. 49 [Ed.].

[98] Dexter, *The Riddle of the Third Mile*, p. 43.

[99] Fraser, p. 83 [Ed.].

[100] Stewart, *Full Term*, p. 153.

[101] Shirley Ardener, "Incorporation and exclusion: Oxford academic wives," and Lidia Sciama, "Ambivalence and dedication: academic

celebrated is not the denial of social closure through education but the inclusion of one group – middle-class women – hitherto excluded. This deserves applause, but no more than two cheers. The third cheer must be held back for a time when the dominant discourse is overthrown rather than circumvented. "'There's no lady here. I'm an Oxford professor,' Ruth objected. We laughed. 'There's no arguing with that,' I said."[102] How true. How very true. How sad.

wives in Cambridge University, 1870-1970," both in Hilary Callan and Shirley Ardener, Eds., *The Incorporated Wife* (London: Croom Helm, 1984).

[102] Anderson, p. 151.

THE DECLINE OF THE CAMPUS NOVEL[1]

Adam Begley

Think of it as a hopeful sign that the satirical campus novel is still with us. The bad patch is over, that awful moment a half dozen years ago when the ivory tower teetered under the combined weight of bad press and public disapproval, when the heavies from the audit firm of Kimball, Sykes, D'Souza & Bloom[2] did their best to topple it by force of sheer scorn. Though threats remain, mostly in the guise of the sinister legislator or the heartless provost brandishing the budget ax, the really scary interval – the public relations crisis – has passed. The novelist, attuned to both the mood on campus and the disposition of the lay reader, knows that it's safe now to poke a little fun.

Hence, Jane Smiley's *Moo* (Ballantine), a gentle, sprawling satire (first published two years ago[3]), and now Richard Russo's somewhat more frantic and narrow *Straight Man* (Random House). Even as they parcel out ridicule, these novels affirm the bedrock decency of university folk. Though campus denizens may be stressed, cramped in unattractive ways by budgetary constraints, their charm, their picturesque egghead absurdity, endures.

Moo and *Straight Man* are very similar, which at first

---

[1] Previously published in Lingua Franca (September 1997), pp. 39-46.

[2] Roger Kimball, *Tenured Radicals: How Politics Has Corrupted Higher Education* (New York: Harper & Row, 1990); Charles J. Sykes, *Profscam: Professors and the Demise of Higher Education* (Washington, DC: Regnery Gateway, 1988); Dinesh D'Souza, *Illiberal Education: The Politics of Race and Sex on Campus* (New York: Free Press, 1991); Allan Bloom, *The Closing of the American Mind: How Higher Education Has Failed Democracy and Impoverished the Souls of Today's Students* (New York: Simon & Schuster, 1987).

[3] i.e. 1995 [Ed.].

141

seems odd (surely Russo, a well-respected "serious" novelist, would want to avoid echoing Smiley, an even better respected "serious" novelist). But then, campus novels always cover the same turf. Even when you look back more than four decades to Mary McCarthy's *The Groves of Academe* (1952) and Randall Jarrell's *Pictures From an Institution* (1954), twinned classics of the genre, you're struck by how little has changed. The novelist's perspective shifts, but the place itself remains substantially the same. On every campus in every decade, there's the urgent need for new funds, issues of academic freedom, worries about hiring and admissions quotas, petty jealousies, endless inter- and intra-departmental squabbles. Descriptions of the scholarly temperament are amusingly constant. It seems they've been stamping out social scientists with the same cookie cutter for half a century. Ditto for English professors. The students are elemental, as unvarying as earth and fire.

The ever present, overriding question is tenure: Who will stay, who will go? The drama of inclusion and exclusion (or internment and escape) plays out against an absurdist comedy of eternal return. Students renew the cycle every year on "the day of the station wagons," as it's called in Don DeLillo's *White Noise* (1985), which begins as brilliant campus satire and winds up entirely elsewhere. In Randall Jarrell's novel, the narrator expresses amazement that undergraduates actually materialize at each summer's end:

> It's always seemed the most improbable thing in the world to me that they can fly out all over the country, all over the world, climb mountains and write books and get married and despair and go to Liechtenstein, and then every September the fifteenth all arrive here on the hour. It's stranger than the swallows. To come back *here*!

The Decline of the Campus Novel

Imagine *Waiting for Godot* strangely reversed, the faculty rooted to the spot like Vladimir and Estragon, yearning to leave, afraid to leave, and every fall, against all odds, these kids make their appearance.

But there is a difference between the campus novel of the Fifties and today's model. In the old days, the novelist typically had a greater degree of independence from the university, a critical distance. With the proliferation and expansion of writing programs, still few and tiny just after the war, the novelist has put down roots. Speculation about what the tenuring of writers has done and will do to American literature seems mostly a gassy enterprise, but one place to spot the consequences is the campus novel. The novelist is now part of the landscape, a fixture-writer in seemingly permanent residence. Smiley taught for thirteen years at Iowa State University. Russo spent three years at Penn State University, five years at Southern Illinois University, and, most recently, four years at Colby College. Will the author bite the hand that feeds, houses, insures? If Smiley and Russo constitute a trend, it's safe to say that the bite no longer breaks the skin.

In her day, Mary McCarthy dropped in on campus for visits of a "transient and picnicky character" (a phrase she fits to a young instructor); her *Groves of Academe*, a tangled faculty intrigue, is recklessly savage. Though he taught for much of his life, Randall Jarrell is nearly as nasty in *Pictures From an Institution* – he wrote with one foot out the door. His campus satire is about a lady novelist (based on Mary McCarthy) writing a vicious campus satire (*The Groves of Academe*). Both novels are about leaving campus – the action, if it doesn't involve swearing off academic life, leads at least to exodus from a specific college. The reverse is true of Smiley's *Moo* and Russo's *Straight Man*; these novels are about staying, looking on the bright side, laughing off misgivings, learning tolerance and accommodation.

The Academic Novel

Welcome to the era of the kinder, gentler campus satire. *Straight Man* looks at first like a bitter assault on university life. On the first page of chapter one, when an English professor driving a car makes a remark about the mechanics of his automobile, his voice sounds "academic, helpless." In that apposition is the short version of the novel. The long version runs to nearly four hundred pages, hurtling over a steeplechase plot, with unscheduled trips to jail and the hospital for its bounced and battered narrator-hero, William Henry Devereaux Jr. Hank Devereaux is the interim chair of the English department at West Central Pennsylvania University, where being promoted "was a little bit like being proclaimed the winner of a shit-eating contest."

The prospect of a 20 percent budget cut, threatened by a stingy state legislature, has roiled the campus. Even tenured ranks are at risk. Hank is being harassed by colleagues who think he's been asked to draw up a list of expendable faculty. An inveterate wiseass, he can't help musing aloud, "If we ever start cutting the deadwood in our department, we're not going to want to stop at twenty percent." Anxiety brings out the ugly in his friends and enemies, and soon Hank is facing a recall vote. Russo shows us campus politics in detail, at its turf-tending worst.

Hank's department colleagues are served up like circus freaks – strange yet familiar, ghouls from a recurring nightmare. There's the abusive drunk; the blowsy, perfumed poetess; the feminist hard at work on an article about "clitoral imagery in Emily Dickinson"; the pinched agitator for the politically correct, nicknamed Orshee because of his habit of correcting anyone who utters a masculine pronoun (Orshee teaches television sitcoms rather than "phallocentric, symbol-oriented texts"). Nostalgic for a golden age he's too skeptical to actually believe in, Hank notes that scholars no longer engage in reasoned argument; they're too busy "staking out territory and furthering agendas." These conditions obtain everywhere on campus. Hank asks how things are going over in the language department. "Silly, small, mean-spirited, lame," a Spanish professor replies. "Same as English."

Russo rags on the administration too. The "campus executive officer," or CEO, Dickie Pope, a bureaucrat at once unctuous and bland, says to Hank, "The colleges that survive the decade are going to be lean and mean. Efficient."

This sparks a brief duet:

"Efficient?" I say. "Education?"

"You bet."

"Higher education?"

"Lean and mean."

"Well, it's always been mean," I concede.

"And it's gonna get lean. Soon."

When the CEO expresses regret at the impending cuts, Hank has to admit that his "carefully calculated sincerity is almost indistinguishable from the real thing." Russo gets in a few good digs but nothing that compares with Randall Jarrell's college president and his "compromising voice" – "that voice did not sell itself to the highest bidder, it just gave itself away to everybody."

What is clever, sympathetic Hank doing in this dreadful place? A creative writing teacher who earned tenure after publishing his first and only novel twenty years ago, he knows that a move to a better institution would cost him "tenure or rank or salary, or some combination of the three." As for simply leaving the academy, going back to writing or taking up another line of work, the thought seems never to have crossed his mind. When the plot's slapstick gyrations are done, Hank tries to quit, to relinquish tenure, but can't: "True, I tendered my resignation ... but the letter got lost somehow."

In the final paragraph of *Straight Man* too many of Hank's colleagues crowd into a tiny room whose door opens inward, a metaphorical illustration of his plight:

> All at once we seemed to realize how close it was in there, and just as suddenly we all wanted out. Clearly, the only solution was for all of us to take one step backward so that the door could be pulled open. By this point a group of plumbers, a group of bricklayers, a group of hookers, a group of chimpanzees would have figured this out. But the room contained, unfortunately, a group of academics, and we couldn't quite believe what had happened to us.

Hank laughs at his colleagues – warm, embracing laughter; he knows full well he is one of them.

In fact, it's in his blood. He's the son of a famous critic, sometimes referred to as "the Father of American Literary Theory," who spent his life hopping from campus to campus, always honored with the title "distinguished visiting professor." Hank thinks of his father, a haughty, preening careerist and serial philanderer (imagine an unholy blend of David Lodge's Morris Zapp and Harold Bloom), as the embodiment of an "increasingly demoralized profession." This sorry paternal example teaches Hank that "one of the deepest purposes of intellectual sophistication is to provide distance between us and our most disturbing personal truths and gnawing fears."

The Decline of the Campus Novel

Is this chestnut the lesson of Russo's novel – that those who live the life of the mind are cut off from the promptings of the heart? The book splits more or less evenly, half budget-driven campus intrigue, half romantic complication. Hank suffers from a mild case of head-heart disjunction, which helps explain his attenuated relationship with a wife he professes to love without reservation. He's also half in love with his secretary. And with a colleague's daughter. "I try to tell myself it's nothing but decent affection," he waffles, "but the truth is, it doesn't feel entirely decent." Wondering what to call a state halfway between decency and indecency, he proposes "the Kingdom of Cowardice? The Fiefdom of Altruism? The Grove of Academe?" I prefer "academic, helpless."

John Irving, blurbing *Straight Man*, hails Russo's "compassion for his characters." Losers and burnouts abound, but there are no truly bad baddies in Russo's satire. Even the weak and the pathetic are endearing. The ax-wielding administrator, Dickie Pope, is merely small, "as diminutive as his name." Russo's compassion is hard to distinguish from kitsch as Milan Kundera memorably defined it: "the absolute denial of shit, in both the literal and figurative senses of the word." If promotion at Hank's university is, as he claims, like winning "a shit-eating contest," then some alchemy has made excrement palatable.

The crucial scene in the novel, a slapstick set piece, finds Hank in front of the cameras of a local television news crew. He's wearing a fake nose and eyeglasses, holding a live goose by the neck, threatening to kill a duck a day until he gets a budget to hire adjunct staff. The goose (which he calls a duck for alliterative effect - nice touch) comes from the pond by the student center; it carries a certain symbolic weight. "There was a time when these birds migrated," Hank tells us. Now they're "year-round

147

residents, tenured and content, squatting motionless on the bank, like abandoned decoys, subsisting on popcorn and other student junk food, too fat to fly and, as the saying goes, too ugly to love" – unless you've got loads of compassion.

Smiley, too, evinces open-armed tolerance. Her villains are figures of fun. A professor of economics, the highest-paid faculty member, likes to refer to matriculating students as "customers." Associate vice president Robert William Brown, the equivalent of Russo's Dickie Pope, calls himself "Just Plain Brown" and glides around campus "on a smear of eternal congeniality." The university president (flanked by "right-hand and left-hand men") is such a nonentity that Smiley doesn't bother to name him. This crew has brought corporate-think into the sacred precincts of the academy. They deal only in numbers. They're shallow, greedy, hypocritical buffoons, but they're not dangerous; their stratagems are defeated with ease.

Defeated, metaphorically speaking, by Earl Butz, a snow-white hog of Volkswagen dimensions whose sole occupation is to eat. Smuggled in his infancy into an abandoned building at the center of a Midwestern campus nicknamed Moo U. for its agricultural bent, Earl is part of a faculty member's secret experiment to see just how big a Landrace boar can grow. He's a champion eater; every day his bulk improves. Symbolically speaking, Smiley's great white hog is easier to read than his cetaceous Melvillean precursor: Earl stands for the ever expanding university, its boundless appetite. He represents a hidden truth, "the secret hog at the center of the university," busy at the trough even as fiscal crises come and go.

Moo U., of course, has been told to get lean and mean. At the state capitol, the cretinous governor O. T. Early has proposed budget reallocations; $10 million must be pared from the university's budget. This prompts panicked attempts to secure alternate funding and encourages the machinations of a slimy entrepreneur (a dead ringer for Ross Perot), who will gladly underwrite research of a potentially profitable but morally dubious nature – chicken feed made of chicken by-products, mining that entails rain forest exploitation, wholesale calf cloning. The main plotline (funding lost, false funding proffered, true funding found) is eclipsed by a proliferation of romantic subplots (love lost, false love proffered, true love found).

Thanks to Smiley's deft hand at characterization, what happens matters less than the people to whom it's happening. These are individuals not types, and a reader grows anxious about individual fates. Marly Hellmich works behind the food line at the commons and watches the university file past her pushing a tray. Magnificently self-centered Tim Monahan, who teaches creative writing, warns his students that "fiction writing will lead you into a number of socially unacceptable practices." Chairman X, the unreconstructed Marxist who runs the horticulture department, conceives of campus as "a passing micro climate." Mrs Lorraine Walker, the secretary to the provost, rigidly principled and correct in the office, passionate and kinky at home with her lesbian lover, runs the university behind her boss's back. Even the students are lovingly particularized.

Perhaps Smiley took a hint from Randall Jarrell, whose mouthpiece, the unnamed narrator of *Pictures From an Institution*, declares his campus "plotless" – nothing ever happens. Jarrell's novel is *ipso facto* plotless; Smiley's is half plotted in a jokey, slapdash way, as if to acknowledge that drama and suspense just aren't plausible at a place like Moo U. Her novel is a lark. Witness the fate of Earl Butz, recounted in a chapter titled "A Little Deconstruction."

Budget cuts require the destruction of the disused abattoir known on campus as Old Meats, the building where Earl, who now weighs 700 pounds, is covertly housed. Liberated by the accident of demolition from his snug basement pen on a frigid winter day, Earl streaks across the snowy campus (a hog on ice) and dies at the feet of a pretty undergraduate, Keri, whose only wish is that none of her classmates ever know she served a year as Warren County Pork Queen.

Does this event signal the end of an era for the university, the end of unchecked consumption, of seemingly inexorable growth? Not quite – a fresh allocation of state funds triggers a jubilant round of new spending some two dozen pages after Earl's demise. My guess is that Smiley couldn't resist the irony of a *pietà* starring Earl and Keri. You can tell she's enjoying herself. And she doesn't want to spoil her good time by digging up the worst about any of her characters; she prefers to touch lightly on their peccadilloes. Mixed in with the muffled satire, *Moo* has a slightly unreal, hedonistic quality, a wishful celebration of the pleasures of university life, pleasures that should go hand in land with security, a little money, and good company nearby.

"There was no end to the ways in which nice things are nicer than nasty ones" – that pearl of wisdom comes from the end of Kingsley Amis's *Lucky Jim* (1954), perhaps the funniest campus satire to come from either side of the Atlantic. Sadly, the nice things in *Lucky Jim* have nothing to do with the university. Campus is the province of the pretentious, the dangerously dull and self-absorbed, the militantly complacent, and the resolutely hypocritical. Amis's Jim Dixon is lucky mainly in that he is leaving it all behind.

McCarthy and Jarrell second the motion. In *The Groves of Academe*, McCarthy is too closely attentive to the nasty to spare a sentence for the nice. She tracks with single-minded intensity one teacher's successful struggle to stay on campus. Henry Mulcahy, a literature department instructor whose contract at Jocelyn College has not been renewed, wages a creepy, dishonest campaign to keep his job. The novel is hilarious and unremittingly brutal, Mulcahy fascinating and unremittingly awful. Though odious, he's "the cleverest man at Jocelyn and the victim ... of that ferocious envy of mediocrity for excellence that is the ruling passion of all systems of jobholders."

It's hard to imagine that other "systems of jobholders" could elicit similar contempt. McCarthy's professors aren't merely helpless – they're meant to be repulsive. Would you like to take an independent study with Ivy Legendre, the theater professor who argues in a "deep, bellicose, lesbian voice"? How about a tutorial with Mr Endicott, "the old man [who] smoked his pipe in comfort, with his hearing aid turned off"? Or Mrs Masterson of the psychology department, "a spinsterish, anxious little widow with a high, thin voice"? Turning the tables produces no more flattering results. Would you relish teaching one of "the conventional Allysons and Pattys whose favorite book was *Winnie-the-Pooh*"? A department meeting to decide Mulcahy's fate drags on for more than thirty pages of backbiting and crossed loyalties – all true to life but also hard to bear. Is there any horror more awful than boring horror? Who would fight for a place in this dismal purgatory? The novel ends with several of the more palatable characters resolved to quit Jocelyn.

If McCarthy's novel weren't psychologically precise, deadeye accurate in its estimation of everyday human hideousness, it could be dismissed as unkind exaggeration. And even so, her attacks trigger a protective reaction that's part pity for her victims, part denial in the face of bitter truth. There are surely many ways to be adequately mean about campus life without resorting to a scorched-earth policy. And surely Jarrell, who wrote *Pictures From an*

151

Institution about McCarthy's one-term teaching stint at Sarah Lawrence, found the very best way. Jarrell had also taught at Sarah Lawrence, and he had met McCarthy in New York. He concocted his satire combining the two elements. He paints, in acid, a portrait of Gertrude Johnson, a novelist "between novels," who ventures forth from Bleecker Street to teach creative writing at Benton College. Once arrived, she discovers a gold mine of "material" for a new book. Jarrell gets to echo Gertrude's cruel witticisms, rebuke them, and add some of his own. He gets to play a vigorous game of monkey in the middle. Sometimes the monkey is Gertrude, sometimes it's Benton.

The novelist engaged in research is a frightening spectacle: "Gertrude was never polite to anything but material: when she patted someone on the head you could be sure that the head was about to appear, smoked, in her next novel." But Jarrell manages to out-nasty her, even as he describes her nastiness: "Gertrude's bark was her bite; and many a bite has lain awake all night longing to be Gertrude's bark. Here's the fearsome bark in action: "When I first got here I said to myself, *How well all the animals get on together!* But then I saw they were vegetables." And here's her sharp-tongued Boswell: "Sometimes Gertrude was witty without even lying."

There are a handful of other "pictures," some of them tender, some even loving. Jarrell doesn't try to squeeze the entire college into the frame (a young woman, virtually the only student in the novel, hands in a short story about a bug that turns into a man – "It's influenced by Kafka," she shyly admits.) He allows a sense of the campus to emerge from bits and pieces of a loose-jointed narrative. It's *Moo* in concentrated form, with more than a dash of pepper. Smiley's novel ends with a flurry of weddings and reconciliations; the last chapter of *Pictures From an Institution*, aptly titled "They All Go," is full of farewells and capped with the news that our narrator has resigned from Benton.

Jarrell, at one point, arranges for an instructive comparison between Gertrude and Spinoza. The latter by his own account, "labored carefully not to mock, lament, and execrate, but to understand." Gertrude, says our narrator, "labored carefully to mock, lament, and execrate – to condemn utterly." This distinction seems an appropriate "gauge" for campus satires. Mary McCarthy is, of course, on the Gertrude side of the scale. She's so implacably mean that she dissipates in part the power of her wit. Over on the other side, where tolerance and compassion reign, Jane Smiley and Richard Russo are ready to understand and even forgive. Their campus, for all its quirks, is a nice neighborhood. So call it a good-neighbor policy: Smiley and Russo water down their wit with indulgent laughter. Poised in the middle, on a tightrope stretched between Gertrude and Spinoza, is Randall Jarrell, balancing delicately between execration and understanding. Where he mocks, it stings. And sometimes he refrains from mocking. It's unpopular work, in the age of Barney, recommending the nasty over the nice. And yet I can't help feeling that Russo and Smiley, by favoring the friendly, have consigned themselves to the crowded shelves of forgettable fiction. Although they're suffering some neglect, the campus satires of Amis, Jarrell, and McCarthy are still in print more than four decades later. I doubt whether the newer more comfortable models will wear so well.

WHO'S AFRAID OF THE CAMPUS NOVEL?[1]

Aida Edemariam

Ever since Vladimir Nabokov published his lovely, sad, ruthless and very funny novel *Pnin*, the beginning of term has been a staple scene in the campus novel.

The 1954 Fall term had begun .... Again in the margins of library books earnest freshmen inscribed such helpful glosses as 'Description of nature', or 'Irony'; and in a pretty edition of Mallarmé's poems an especially able scholiast had already underlined in violet ink the difficult word *oiseaux* and scrawled above it 'birds'.

The details of the scene change; the first paragraph of Don DeLillo's *White Noise*, for instance, is saturated with late 20th-century excess: "The station wagons arrived at noon, a long shining line that coursed through the West campus ... students sprang out and raced to the rear doors to begin removing the objects inside ...." Or, as Malcolm Bradbury put it in the first line of *The History Man*: "Now it is autumn again; the people are all coming back."

This academic year begins with Tom Wolfe's latest attempt to characterise an age. And despite those who believe that, while university life will continue, the novel of academia has had its day, Wolfe has chosen a campus novel – *I Am Charlotte Simmons*, 600 pages set at a moneyed college on the eastern seaboard – with which to do it.

From a practical point of view, of course, the attractions of the campus haven't changed much: it is a finite, enclosed space, like a boarding school, or like Agatha Christie's

---

[1] Previously published in *The Guardian* (2 October, 2004), p. 34.

country houses (the campus murder mystery being its own respectable sub-genre); academic terms, usefully, begin and end; there are clear power relationships (teacher/student; tenured professor/scrabbling lecturer) – and thus lots of scope for illicit affairs; circumscription forces a greater intensity – revolutions have been known to begin on campuses, though that doesn't seem to have happened for a while. And it's all set against the life of the mind.

"The high ideals of the university as an institution – the pursuit of knowledge and truth," says David Lodge, author of some of the more popular campus novels of the last century, "are set against the actual behaviour and motivations of the people who work in them, who are only human and subject to the same ignoble desires and selfish ambitions as anybody else. The contrast is perhaps more ironic, more marked, than it would be in any other professional milieu."

The campus novel began in America, with Mary McCarthy's *The Groves of Academe* (1952), Randall Jarrell's reply to it, *Pictures From an Institution* (1954), and *Pnin* (1955). (Nabokov's *Pale Fire* is, inter alia, a campus novel, and a murder mystery.) "Campus" is, of course, an American word, and Lodge makes the distinction between the campus novel and the varsity novel – the latter being set at Oxbridge, and usually among students, rather than teachers, thus disallowing the joys of *Zuleika Dobson*, or *Jill*, or *Brideshead Revisited*; he claims Kingsley Amis's *Lucky Jim* (1954) as the first British campus novel, and a template.

To all the standard elements, Lodge explains, Amis added "the English comic novel tradition, which goes back through Evelyn Waugh and Dickens to Fielding"; i.e. an element of robust farce later elaborated by Tom Sharpe in *Porterhouse Blue*, for example, or by Howard Jacobson.

"I don't see why the campus novel has to consist of

farce," says A. S. Byatt, who dislikes *Lucky Jim*, seeing it as both sexist and thoroughly anti-intellectual. "I find it baffling." She has much more time for what she calls true comedy, in Terry Pratchett's *Unseen University*, or in Lodge's *Nice Work* (1988), which she feels have more respect for a profession based on serious thought.

This is an older tradition, again. "I compare it to pastoral," says Lodge. "If you think of a comedy such as *As You Like It*, you get all these eccentric characters, all in one pastoral place, interacting in ways they wouldn't be able to do if they were part of a larger, more complex social scene. There's often an element of entertaining artifice, of escape from the everyday world, in the campus novel. Quite interesting issues are discussed, but not in a way which is terribly solemn or portentous."

The other, probably inevitable, addition was class. Much of the tension in *Lucky Jim* is between Jim Dixon and his socially superior boss; apart from the fact that she's simply prettier, the thing that binds Jim to his eventual girlfriend, Christine, is their mutual recognition of a kind of aggressive gaucheness, assumed to be more authentic than the baying, madrigal-singing Welches. But it's a fruitful collision nonetheless.

"If you're interested in the phenomenon of meritocracy, which transformed English society in the postwar period, then the university is – or was – a good place to observe it," says Lodge, who like many of his colleagues in the 60s and 70s was a first-generation university graduate. "The Kirks are, indeed, new people," wrote Bradbury in *The History Man*, which was published in the same year, 1975, as Lodge's *Changing Places*. "But where some people are born new people ... the Kirks arrived at that condition the harder way, by effort, mobility and harsh experience."

These two seminal English campus novels are set in and immediately after "the heroic period of student politics", to

Who's Afraid of the Campus Novel?

quote Lodge's *Nice Work*, when new universities seemed to be appearing all over the country, change seemed possible, social mobility achievable, and promiscuity mandatory – the necessary mixing and mating of comedy, or farce, meshing nicely with the burgeoning sexual revolution and women's lib. And even though Bradbury's novel especially has a great sense of darkness, pointing, among other things, to the inequalities of unfettered sexuality at that point in time, both now read as historical novels, imbued with a quixotic hope.

But in English higher education everything is set, even in celebration, against Oxbridge, says Ian Carter, author of *Ancient Cultures of Conceit: British University Fiction in the Post War Years* (1990), and a professor at the University of Auckland, citing those who made the conscious choice to go to Sussex, for example, instead. The American campus novel was, he feels, better able to avoid the trap of class, "perhaps because American universities are so highly differentiated, so recognisably placeable; novels could take on a larger variety of themes without automatically having to deal with class."

Though the oil crisis of 1973 was the beginning of the end of the boom in new universities, Thatcher prompted the next great satirical subject: Lodge cites Andrew Davies's *A Very Peculiar Practice*, and his own *Nice Work* transfers the contrapuntal, mutually illuminating UK university versus US university structure of *Changing Places* to UK university versus UK capitalist industry.

A concurrent subject was the rise of literary theory, gently skewered in Robyn Penrose, standing for the university side of *Nice Work* (she is a devotee of "semiotic materialism" who believes there is no such thing as the "self", though "in practice this doesn't seem to affect her very noticeably [so] I shall therefore take the liberty of treating her as a character"). John Mullan, lecturer in

157

English at University College London, who has written, in these pages[2], that the English campus novel is a fossil form, says "nobody notices, but A. S. Byatt's *Possession* [1990] is an extremely acid attack on feminist literary criticism."

So, as the university changed, British campus novels were changing in tone – angry, coruscating, debunking, or, in the case of Michael Frayn's haunting *The Trick of It* (1989), melancholy; and the younger generation of novelists – Martin Amis, Julian Barnes, Ian McEwan – weren't writing them. "It might be that the clutch of books that appeared in the 70s and 80s were to do with the fact that we were about to see a world vanish, maybe they were all elegies to an idea of the campus, says Howard Jacobson. "My novel [*Coming From Behind*, a "rotten poly" satire published in 1983] came towards the end of it – and was in a way a parody of what was already a parody, since my campus wasn't even a campus."

Jacobson argues that fear of elitism put paid to the campus novel.

> Although half the country goes to campuses ... everybody is embarrassed to talk about it. I think once democracy got going on the English novel, and we felt we didn't want to write anything that might upset anybody or make them feel out of it, that was the end of the campus novel. I miss it. And also, of course, campus novels were, by their very nature, funny, and funny is not in either. Campuses have become tragic places. Maybe that's all it is. They're pure wastelands, really.

"Universities are depressed," says Byatt. When

---

[2] i.e. *The Guardian* [Ed.].

institutions such as the University of East Anglia were built everything was "shiny, white and new," and because "in those days universities were intensely hopeful" you could afford farce, because "you had a solidity. Now they're terrified and cowering and underfinanced and over-examined and over-bureaucratised."

Not everyone shares this bleak view. Lodge, for one, published a new campus novel, *Thinks* ... in 2001, and says

> There's a tendency for people to sneer at the genre as if it's played out, while actually they take a good deal of interest in reading it. The fact is that universities change and societies change, and therefore there are always new fictional possibilities.

Laurie Taylor, who for 27 years has written a satirical column about universities for the *Times Higher Education Supplement* (and was rumoured to be the model for Howard Kirk in *The History Man*), concurs. This week he judged a competition for the *THES* that asked for the first chapter of a new campus novel. The entries were

> ... full of campuses in which management experts and management gurus and development leaders, all speaking management jargon, are locked in a battle with the few people left who still believe that there's something more to universities than providing people with degrees that enable them to get jobs.

For this is the major battle still being fought, first joined under Thatcher, and continued under Blair: "the campus is now a site for a clash between two pretty fundamental values": the instrumental and the intrinsic, auditors versus intellectuals. Taylor cites a novel he recently reviewed, *Academia Nuts*, by Michael Wilding (2002), "which is very clever, in the grand tradition of *Lucky Jim* – but all about the impossibility of writing campus novels any more."

> "This," said Henry. "All this." There it was, their world lay all before them. The deserted common room. The chipped cups. The worn, unfigured carpet. "There's not an awful lot here," said Pawley. "I think you need more than the common room." "The university as such," said Henry. "You'd better hurry," said Pawley. "It's all being out-sourced. There's hardly anything left. The virtual university. No tenured staff. No gross moral turpitude." "I shall write about the university in decline," said Henry. "I think you might have left it too late," said Dr Bee.

So "there are still plenty of laughs," says Taylor, "even though the laughter is now bitter instead of affectionate." But *Academia Nuts* is also Australian, and it is instructive to look away from England to see how the patient is really faring. Canada had Robertson Davies, now dead, and more recently Jeffrey Moore, who won the Commonwealth Best First Book award with a campus novel, *Red-Rose Chain*, in 2000; J. M. Coetzee's fierce, brilliant *Disgrace* (1999) is set in motion by the narrator's misdemeanors on a campus in Cape Town.

Europe never had very many, though *All Souls*, by Javier Marias, is "wonderful", says Byatt; in order to write a good campus novel you have to have been a university teacher, says Lodge, and in Europe that would be a betrayal of professional dignity. But in America the genre seems to have grown in stature, mutating into something important, and relevant. The increasing ubiquity of the university education is as true there as it is here (as David Mamet put it in *Oleanna*, "college education, since the war, has become so much a matter of course, and such a fashionable necessity ... that we espouse it as a matter of right, and have ceased to ask 'What is it good for'?") and ensures a large audience less hamstrung than the British by class-consciousness.

The English department continues to provide great fodder (for Richard Russo, for example) but one of the more obvious trends has been the rise of novels satirising creative writing courses, such as *Wonder Boys*, by Michael Chabon. "It's like shooting fish in a barrel," laughs Francine Prose, whose National Book Award-nominated *Blue Angel* updates the Marlene Dietrich movie, placing it in a creative writing course in a tiny college in northern Vermont. "The minute they started allowing writers on campus they were in trouble"; of course they were going to start mocking the day job.

"Where is the novel we ought to have, about science departments?" wonders Byatt, who frankly wishes that English departments, wallowing in self-referentiality, could be discontinued; Lodge's *Thinks* ... again of contrapuntal, bipartite structure, plays a novelist teaching a creative writing course off against a cognitive scientist; the usual farcical bed-hopping ensues, but it's a knowing nod to the genre in what is mainly a serious exploration of the nature of consciousness and the limits of AI.

This, too, is a trend established in the US, by writers such as Jonathan Lethem, whose *As She Climbed Across the Table* is about a physicist who discovers a hole in the universe, and a sociologist who studies academic environments; or by Richard Powers, who in *Galatea 2.2* has a cognitive neurologist train a neural net to pass a course on Great Books.

Francine Prose set out to write a novel of obsessive love and ambition, "and somehow the campus seemed the perfect way to talk about those things." This seems a general discovery: *White Noise*, 20 years old now, is, as well as a study of the threats, and the seductive promises of science, and a celebration of family, a sustained and darkly funny engagement with the idea of death; Donna Tartt's bestseller *The Secret History* (also a campus thriller) takes the influence tutors have over their nubile charges to violent extremes. Power is so clearly demarcated on campus, and, increasingly, so easy to lose.

The great novel about this – though it is great about nearly everything – is Philip Roth's *The Human Stain*. Coleman Silk, professor of classics, is also dean when he utters one inadvisable word, "spooks"; the tumbrils of politically correct outrage roll, and he loses his job. (One of the central ironies of the book is that he is African-American, passing as white.) In the controlled space of the campus he has been king, overhauling departments, sweeping them clean, but in a word he has been forced into exile.

Exile is, in the late 20th century, itself almost a fossilised concept: where, centuries ago, you might be forced to leave a village as punishment, how many communities now are close-knit enough to function in this way? The campus, especially highly differentiated, self-sufficient American campuses such as Coleman Silk's in sleepy New England, is our alternative; banishment is no less keenly felt. And it nearly drives Silk mad.

Political correctness never made much headway on British campuses, and in fact, says Alexander Star, who edited *Lingua Franca*, the magazine of American academia, until it folded three years ago, the worst has been over in the US for a while now. The animating anger of *The Human Stain* is, therefore, dated. But it doesn't matter. For in pc, and in literary theory, and on a modern campus, Roth found a way to address some of the big cultural questions of the later 20th century.

Silk's nemesis is a young French academic called

Delphine, bright, ambitious, a mistress of theory. She is also far from home, and lonely, and increasingly "destabilised to the point of shame by the discrepancy between how she must deal with literature in order to succeed professionally and why she first came to literature": that instrumental *v* intrinsic argument rearing its head again.

The dichotomy, for Roth, is clear: ideology is the enemy of humanism, of the human; ideology is fascism, communism – is political correctness. And so, in America at least, the campus novel has become a way to measure the state of the nation. It has taken on the elements of classical tragedy, but it is still amusing, albeit often bleakly so. No wonder Tom Wolfe wants to join in the fun.

II

Examples

"I MAY TURN UP YET, ON ANOTHER CAMPUS": VLADIMIR NABOKOV AND THE ACADEMY

Samuel Schuman

By all accounts, except perhaps his own, Vladimir Nabokov was a brilliant and eccentric teacher. And, certainly, both brilliance and eccentricity characterize the pedagogues of his fiction. Two of his English novels – *Pnin* (1957) and *Pale Fire* (1962) – are set in academe and have college professors as their central characters. Although the novels, and their protagonists, are clearly and importantly related, they are also wildly dissimilar. There is much to be learned from both the resemblances and the differences.

I

Nabokov himself had a grandly international academic career. He attended an enlightened private academy in his Russian youth, the Tenishev School in St Petersburg, was graduated in 1923 from Cambridge University and taught at Wellesley College and Cornell University (with brief stints at Harvard and Stanford) from the time of his emigration in 1940 until the success of *Lolita* at the end of the '50s freed him to move to Switzerland and devote himself to full-time labors as a novelist. He taught both literature and Russian language courses; his most notorious class was in "Masters of European Fiction," taught at Cornell through most of the 1950s. This course is the basis for most of the material in *Lectures on Literature*,

The Academic Novel

Lectures on Don Quixote, and *Lectures on Russian Literature*.[1] There are several eye-witness accounts of Nabokov's pedagogical methods. These are universally reported to be both captivating and rigidly formal. He prepared lectures before the beginning of the term. Those lectures were read with animation and humor. They "focused on specific details of literary works and rejected consideration of 'general ideas.'"[2] Some sample of his technique is offered in a video production of Nabokov's lecture on Kafka's "Metamorphosis," produced for Public Television, and starring Christopher Plummer.[3] He obviously made a memorable impression on his students. Alfred Appel, a student at Cornell, remembers: "As a lecturer, Nabokov was on occasion an excellent actor, making full use of his expressive face and rich, accented baritone voice. Certain performances remain firmly in one's mind."[4]

Another former pupil, Hannah Green who enrolled in Nabokov's Russian Literature in translation course at Wellesley recalls: "... to us he was Mister Nabokov, he was our teacher, and we found him dashing and extraordinary. He dazzled our minds and instilled in us feelings of the most exalted romance – not with him, but with Russian

---

[1] See Vladimir Nabokov, *Speak, Memory* (1947; New York: Vintage, 1989), pp. 180-93, 259-73; Samuel Schuman, *Vladimir Nabokov: A Reference Guide* (Boston: G. K. Hall, 1979), pp. 1-5; Brian Boyd, *Vladimir Nabokov* (Princeton: Princeton University Press, 1990, 1991), Vol. 1, pp. 86-109, 163-95; Vol. 2, pp. 11-389.

[2] Charles Nicol, "Teaching," from *The Garland Companion to Vladimir Nabokov*, Ed. Vladimir Alexandrov (New York: Garland, 1995), p. 708.

[3] Dmitri Nabokov, in conversation with the author, praises Plummer's skills as an actor, but expresses dissatisfaction with this particular depiction of his father (Schuman, p. 3, p. 95).

[4] Alfred Appel, "Remembering Nabokov," from *Vladimir Nabokov: His Life, His World, His Work: A Tribute*, Ed. Peter Quennell (London: Weidenfeld and Nicolson, 1979; New York: Morrow, 1980), p. 16.

"I May Turn Up Yet, On Another Campus"
Literature ..."[5]

Nabokov himself describes his teaching in rather uncharacteristic modest tones:

> My method of teaching precluded genuine contact with my students .... Every lecture I delivered had been carefully, lovingly handwritten and typed out, and I leisurely read it out in class, sometimes stopping to rewrite a sentence and sometimes repeating a paragraph.... Vainly I tried to replace my appearances at the lectern by taped records to be played over the college radio.[6]

It is evident that Nabokov taught with a kind of unconventional genius; that college teaching gave him the tremendously important gifts of time, a livelihood, a congenial home, during his first years in the United States; and that he never felt the stirrings of a professorial vocation.

II

Teachers pop in and out of many of Nabokov's works, early and late. Krug, the hero of *Bend Sinister* (1947), is a University Professor of Philosophy "of international reputation in a small unidentified country of middle-European flavour."[7] Even infamous Humbert is the author of a French textbook, who chooses to settle in Beardsley, a woman's college-town, where his most amiable

[5] Hannah Green, "Mister Nabokov," from Quennell, pp. 34-5.

[6] Vladimir Nabokov, *Strong Opinions* (New York: McGraw-Hill, 1973; London: Weidenfeld and Nicolson, 1974), p. 104.

[7] Tony Sharpe, *Vladimir Nabokov* (London: Edward Arnold, 1991), p. 26.

relationship is with the lethargically homosexual Professor of Foreign Languages, Gaston Godin.[8] In *Pnin* and *Pale Fire*, though, academe and academics are not peripheral details (if there *are* peripheral details in Nabokov), but matters of central concern.

Timofey Pnin is surely Nabokov's most lovable character, just as *Pnin* is his sweetest novel. The work consists of seven quite free-standing chapters (four of which initially appeared independently in *The New Yorker*). Each concerns some aspect of Pnin's evolving personal and professional life as a teacher of Russian at Waindell College. Pnin is an odd specimen: physically, mentally, historically. His spindly legs support a broad torso, and a shiny, large bald head. He is an exile from the Russia of communism, whose academic degree is in sociology and political economy,[9] but whose teaching load consists of instructing a pathetic few students in elementary Russian grammar and literature in translation. He is famous, and beloved by the more perceptive of his students, and most of Nabokov's readers, for his asides, his anecdotes, for the exuberant passion he lavishes upon a dead past:

> ... Pnin would get drunk on his private wines as he produced sample after sample of what his listeners politely surmised was Russian humor. Presently the fun would become too much for him: pear-shaped tears would trickle down his tanned cheeks ... his complete surrender to his own merriment would prove irresistible. By the time he was helpless with it he would have his students in

---

[8] Vladimir Nabokov, *Lolita* (1955; rpt. New York: Vintage, 1989), pp. 177ff.

[9] Vladimir Nabokov, *Pnin* (1953; rpt. New York: Vintage, 1989), p. 10.

stitches.[10]

Pnin's most endearing characteristic, perhaps, is his slavically mangled English:

> I will now speak to you about sport. The first description of box in Russian literature we find in a poem by Mihail Lermontov, born 1814, killed 1841 – easy to remember. The first description of tennis, on the other hand, is found in *Anna Karenina* ....[11]

Pnin is funny, and we, like the novel's rather cruel narrator, laugh at him, but we also recognize the tragedies of his life. His first beloved, Mira, was brutally killed by the Nazis, and Pnin's enduring pain overwhelms him, and us:

> One had to forget – because one could not live with the thought that this graceful, fragile, tender young woman with those eyes, that smile, those gardens and snows in the background, had been brought in a cattle car to an extermination camp and killed by an injection of phenol into the heart, into the gentle heart one had heard beating under one's lips in the dusk of the past.[12]

Surely it is no surprise that this eccentric, ill-spoken, un-American tender pedagogue will not fare well at Waindell College:

---

[10] Nabokov, *Pnin*, p. 12.

[11] Nabokov, *Pnin*, p. 104.

[12] Nabokov, *Pnin*, p. 104.

The Academic Novel

... a somewhat provincial institution characterized by an artificial lake in the middle of a landscaped campus, by ivied galleries connecting the various halls, by murals displaying recognizable members of the faculty in the act of passing on the torch of knowledge from Aristotle, Shakespeare, and Pasteur to a lot of monstrously built farm boys and farm girls, and by a huge, active, buoyantly thriving German Department which its Head, Dr Hagen, smugly called (pronouncing every syllable very distinctly) "a university within a university."[13]

(That mural, and Dr Hagen's pronunciational habits, seem to me quintessentially Nabokovian.) Waindell's provinciality seeps from nearly every page of the novel. It seems a kind of American academic variant of Nabokov's *poshlust*: a kind of unknowing, simple and often cruel vulgarity, with its own kind of tasteless, crude energy. There is Professor Clements (Pnin's temporary landlord), "whose only popular course was the Philosophy of Gesture."[14] There are quaint local traditions: "The 1954 Fall Term had begun. Again the marble neck of a homely Venus in the vestibule of Humanities Hall received the vermilion imprint, in applied lipstick, of a mimicked kiss."[15]

And there is what passes for scholarship:

... the renowned Waindell psychiatrist, Dr Rudolph Aura, [applied] to ten thousand elementary school pupils the so-called Fingerbowl Test, in which the child is asked to dip his index finger in cups of

---

[13] Nabokov, *Pnin* , p. 9.
[14] Nabokov, *Pnin*, p. 29.
[15] Nabokov, *Pnin*, p. 137.

colored fluids whereupon the proportion between length of digit and wetted part is measured and plotted in all kinds of fascinating graphs.[16]

Perhaps most memorable is the description (Chapter 6, sections 7-13, pp. 152-172) of a stultifying faculty party chez Pnin:

> By ten o'clock, Pnin's Punch and Betty's Scotch were causing some of the guests to talk louder than they thought they did .... Roy Thayer was weakly twinkling to himself as he looked into his punch, down his gray porous nose, and politely listened to Joan Clements .... "But don't you think – haw – that what he is trying to do – haw – practically in all his novels – haw – is – haw – to express the fantastic recurrence of certain situations?" ... In a corner of the davenport, bored Clements was flipping through an album of Flemish Masterpieces .... [17]

Not everything about Waindell is funny, however: much is cruel. Pnin is an object of scorn and active derision of some of his insensitive colleagues, one of whom, it turns out, is the narrator of *Pnin*. And, despite his naive charm, he is finally fired by the College, as a consequence of a rather Byzantine series of moves involving the Department of German (which includes

---

[16] Nabokov, *Pnin*, p. 137.

[17] Nabokov, *Pnin*, pp. 158-9.

Russian), the Department of French (headed by an enemy of Pnin's) and the Department of English. As the novel concludes, Pnin bravely, but sadly, leaves the college town in his tiny used car, and the work fades out as another professor prepares to tell, as a joke, his favorite Pnin story. It turns out to be the very story that began the novel.

III

Nabokov's other "academic novel" is a considerably more challenging work than *Pnin*. (Although, happily, Pnin himself defies all odds, and turns up, a prospering Department Chair, in *Pale Fire!*[18]) The plot and structure of *Pale Fire* are initially bewildering, and finally enigmatic. The characters are elusive (one group is called "The Shadows," and a central figure is another "shadow," John Shade). Ostensibly the novel is to be a scholarly edition of the poem "Pale Fire" by Shade, a sort of lesser Robert Frost, edited by a colleague of the recently deceased poet, one Charles Kinbote. Both teach at Wordsmith University, located in "New Wye, Appalachia, USA."[19] Shade teaches English Literature (he has written a book on Alexander Pope); Kinbote teaches the language and literature of "Zembla," his native land. Kinbote's notes to Shade's "Pale Fire" quickly veer wildly from the "scholarly," and it becomes apparent that he is using the apparatus of a scholarly edition to tell his own story, which is that of the exiled monarch of Zembla, "Charles the Beloved," who, we discover toward the end of the novel, is in fact Kinbote

---

[18] Vladimir Nabokov, *Pale Fire* (New York: Berkley; London: Weidenfeld and Nicolson, 1962), p. 112.

[19] Nabokov, *Pale Fire*, p. 7.

174

himself.

Or is he? Several readers have found another mask behind the first. Kinbote, they argue, is not Charles the Beloved of Zembla in disguise, but a lunatic professor of Russian at Wordsmith named "Botkin."[20] There is evidence in the text to support this reading, but not to prove it. For example, Shade's death, Kinbote maintains, is the failed act of a Zemblan regicide, who is actually seeking to slay Kinbote. The evidence of the book suggests, though, that the "real" murderer is an escaped homicidal maniac, who mistakes Shade for the judge who sentenced him to the Institute for the Criminally Insane ("ICI", in an icy little word game!)

An opposite theory, proposed very seriously in Brian Boyd's authoritative biography of Nabokov, is that Shade himself is the author of both poem *and* commentary (and "index" and "foreword").[21]

Most of the "action" of this wonderfully bizarre novel takes place either at Wordsmith University, or in the fantastic, vaguely Slavic kingdom of Zembla.

Based on the evidence of his own descriptions, Kinbote is a flamboyantly eccentric professor. He is extravagantly homosexual ... in an era when gay teachers inhabited either the closet or the jail cell: "I explained that I could not stay long as I was about to have a kind of little seminar at home followed by some table tennis, with two charming identical twins and another boy, another boy."[22]

He is pathetically paranoid: "The sound of a rapid car or a groaning truck would come as a strange mixture of friendly life's relief and death's fearful shadow: would that shadow pull up at my door? Were those phantom

---

[20] see, e.g. Nabokov, *Pale Fire*, p. 112.

[21] Boyd, Vol. 2, p. 445.

[22] Nabokov, *Pale Fire* , p. 14.

thugs coming for me?"[23]

Kinbote's English is far from perfect, and he constantly stumbles into linguistic errors which he himself rarely detects. For example, he confuses an anonymous note which suggests he suffers from "halitosis" for an accusation of "hallucinations." When Shade, speaking of his unathletic youth, remarks, "I never bounced a ball or swung a bat," Kinbote confuses American basketball and baseball for his Zemblan recreations, and comments "Frankly I too never excelled in soccer and cricket."[24] Kinbote also has a kind of gigantic, monstrous arrogance, which makes most of his other eccentricities unpleasant. His attitude to Sybil, the wife of John Shade, can only be described as "bitchy." He is incapable of understanding other people, except in the ways they relate to himself. A fairly typical sampling of self-absorbed Kinbote utterances:

> ... the amenities of my habitation. The charming, charmingly vague lady (see note to line 691), who secured it for me, sight unseen, meant well, no doubt.... Actually, it was an old, dismal, white-and-black, half-timbered house, of the type termed *wodnaggen* in my country, with carved gables, drafty bow windows and a so-called "semi-noble" porch, surmounted by a hideous veranda.[25]

> I should add that, despite my protests, at all three meals my vegetarian limitations of fare were not taken into account, and I was exposed to animal matter in, or around, the contaminated greens I

---

[23] Nabokov, *Pale Fire*, p. 70.

[24] Nabokov, *Pale Fire*, p. 26, p. 85.

[25] Nabokov, *Pale Fire*, p. 60.

might have deigned to taste.[26]

Let me state that without my notes Shade's text simply has no human reality at all since the human reality of a poem such as his ... has to depend entirely on the reality of its author and his surroundings, attachments and so forth, a reality that only my notes can provide.[27]

Kinbote's colleagues recognize and, for the most part, do not tolerate his eccentricities: he himself reports as early as the novel's preface that one calls him (for his huge beard) "the great beaver"[28]; another says (accurately), "What's more, you are insane."[29]

If many readers initially react to Kinbote with derision and repulsion, for most, a careful reading of the novel brings a strange Nabokovian metamorphosis. There is a note of pathos and desperation which transforms our scorn to pity and even affection. Kinbote, like several other Nabokovian madmen, grows into a kind of exotic flower. Nabokov suggests that, in his wild starts of self-invention, he becomes, finally, a poet: "a person who deliberately peels off a drab and unhappy past and replaces it with a brilliant invention."[30]

Even as we move towards acceptance and understanding of this weird and wild academic, our sense of the academy in which he has been placed veers towards contempt. Nabokov's satiric view of American university

---

[26] Nabokov, *Pale Fire*, p. 163.

[27] Nabokov, *Pale Fire*, p. 19.

[28] Nabokov, *Pale Fire*, p. 15.

[29] Nabokov, *Pale Fire*, p. 16.

[30] Nabokov, *Pale Fire*, p. 169.

life has never been given freer rein than in *Pale Fire*. Wordsmith University itself manifests some of the same sorts of institutional academic foibles that characterized *Pnin*'s Waindell. In Kinbote's rather idiosyncratic description:

> ... the campus. Here are the great mansions of madness, the impeccably planned dormitories – bedlams of jungle music – the magnificent palace of the Administration, the brick walls ... the prisonlike edifice containing our classrooms and offices ... the famous avenue of all the trees mentioned by Shakespeare ..... [31]

Faculty politics are familiarly and realistically venal. Feuds within and between Departments take on the tones of Jihad: "The manuscript fell into the hands of a person who not only is unqualified for the job of editing it, belonging as he does to another department, but is known to have a deranged mind." [32]

Nabokov dwells with some glee on foibles of the pedagogical life: discussing student papers, Shade announces that he downgrades essays severely for such unforgivable sins as:

> looking ... for symbols; example: "The author uses the striking image *green leaves* because green is the symbol of happiness and frustration." I am also in the habit of lowering a student's mark catastrophically if he uses "simple" and "sincere" in a commendatory sense. [33]

---

[31] Nabokov, *Pale Fire*, p. 67.

[32] Nabokov, *Pale Fire*, p. 139.

[33] Nabokov, *Pale Fire*, p. 112.

(This sounds rather like Nabokov himself: "I endeavored to provide students of literature with exact information about details ... general ideas are of no importance ...."[34])

As in *Pnin*, some of the idiocies of scholarship are parodied. Freudian psychology, again, is an easy and common target: "The little cap of red velvet in the German version of Little Red Riding Hood is a symbol of menstruation .... Do these clowns really *believe* what they teach?"[35]

Literary scholarship is also parodied, in the person of Conmal, the Zemblan translator of Shakespeare. This kindly, but wholly inept, linguist so mangles the text of *Timon of Athens*, for example, that the title of Shade's poem, and Nabokov's novel, becomes a mystery, rather than a straightforward Shakespearean citation. ("Pale fire" becomes "silvery light"[36]). Conmal's "beautiful and touching end" is surely the last word on incompetent Shakespearean (and other) translation: "his last words in his last delirium being 'Comment dit-on *mourir* en anglais?'"[37]

An even deeper level of absurdity is reached in Shade's depiction of another post-secondary institution, the "Institute of Preparation for the Hereafter," or "IPH" or, as Shade jokes, "big if."[38] This appears to be one of those "think tanks" where an interdisciplinary collection of important thinkers mull together some overwhelming topic, in this case, getting ready for being dead. Any serious implications of IPH disappear when the actual

---

[34] Nabokov, *Strong Opinions*, p. 156.

[35] Nabokov, *Pale Fire*, p. 191.

[36] Nabokov, *Pale Fire*, p. 58.

[37] Nabokov, *Pale Fire*, p. 201.

[38] Nabokov, *Pale Fire*, p. 36.

trivia of its concerns are revealed: such esoterica as what to do when, in the afterlife, a twice-married man meets *both* his former wives, or what to do if reincarnated as a "young and vulnerable toad / Plump in the middle of a busy road."[39]

IV

It is evident that Kinbote and Pnin are both reflections and parodies of Nabokov, the academic. Indeed, it is interesting to think of the three characters, one "real," two "fictional" as speaking to each other in the complex, interweaving pattern of a piece of chamber music: first one speaks, then another, then two together, then all three go off in different directions, only to converge at a surprising conclusion.

Some of Nabokov's perennial themes and preoccupations seem especially stimulated by the academic settings of *Pnin* and *Pale Fire*. Perhaps because the academy gave Nabokov his first and most comfortable resting places after he and his family fled Russia, we are especially conscious of Pnin and Kinbote as exiles, emigrés, outsiders. Pnin, like Nabokov, is a Russian teaching Slavic language and literature, to American college students; Kinbote seems a kind of fantastic parody of that figure. He has fled a drab, totalitarian revolution in "Zembla," a cold Northern land which "re-sembles" a remembered Russia. Both teachers are seen as oddities by their students, but viewed with varying degrees of tolerance because their very exile brings with it the credentials to profess the

---

[39] Nabokov, *Pale Fire*, p. 38.

foreign language and culture from which they fled.

Another recurrent topic which is emphasised in these "academic novels" is the relationship between true, exact, factual scholarship, and vague, unsupported and insupportable pseudo-learning. As we have seen, Freudian psychology is the most obvious target of Nabokov's (and Pnin's and Kinbote's and Shade's) contempt for intellectual fraud. Rather less obviously, we should note that Nabokov seems to have a genuine admiration for the sort of arcane researches undertaken in the fertile isolation of college libraries by his protagonists. Pnin's efforts to restore the concrete physical underpinnings of his favorite Russian writings, and even Kinbote's Zemblan lore are presented quite sympathetically, especially when contrasted with what Nabokov saw as the windy and empty pomposity of the psychologists.

Of course, the entire structure of *Pale Fire* is an academic joke about "scholarly editions." And the punch line is that, for all the apparatus of a poem and commentary, Kinbote's "edition" of Shade's "Pale Fire" is about the commentator himself more than the poet or the poem. We must remember when chuckling at this joke, though, that *Pale Fire* was published in 1962, just as Nabokov was finally nearing the completion of a decade-and-a-half of work on *his* scholarly edition of Pushkin's *Eugene Onegin*, an edition in which the scholarly apparatus outweighs the poem to which it is appended in a most Kinbotian manner. *Eugene Onegin* fills four large volumes, of which only a fraction of the first is the actual translation of the poem, and the remaining 1,200 pages are *extremely* detailed and rather idiosyncratic commentary. Several readers have seen in *Pale Fire* the novelist's wry look at his own scholarly labors/excesses. When, in the concluding lines of *Pale Fire* Charles Kinbote suggests that "I may turn up yet, on another campus, as an old, happy healthy heterosexual Russian, a writer in exile,"[40] it is difficult not to see the novelist peeking out from behind the mask of his crazed character.

Nabokov believed in the literal validity of Shakespeare's equation of lunatic, lover and poet. "You can always count on a murderer for a fancy prose style," comments Humbert Humbert in *Lolita*.[41] At least in Nabokov's novels, as Humbert himself so richly proves, you can indeed. Kinbote and Pnin (and their creator) represent a particular sub-species of the type: the lunatic as eccentric academic, the lover of both ladies and learning, the poets of pedantry.

Finally, the odd relationship of these three academics, one of whom created the other two, reflects Nabokov's preoccupation with the indistinct border between fiction and life, between the "real" and the "created." Pnin, Nabokov's character, outlives his own novel, and surfaces in *Pale Fire*. So, too, does "Hurricane Lolita" in both poem[42] and commentary: "Why our poet chose to give his 1958 hurricane a little-used Spanish name ... is not clear."[43] Kinbote threatens to turn up on another campus as a happy, healthy heterosexual Russian; that is, to metamorphose into Vladimir Nabokov. And Nabokov also makes a cameo appearance in *Pnin*: "'Pity Vladimir Vladimirovich is not here,' remarked Chateau. 'He could have told us all about these enchanting insects.'"[44]

In this dizzying self-reflexivity, Nabokov is making a speculative point, not simply playing a cute literary game. He is affirming, as he does over and over, that the "real

---

[40] Nabokov, *Pale Fire*, p. 212.
[41] Nabokov, *Lolita*, p. 9.
[42] Nabokov, *Pale Fire*, p. 41.
[43] Nabokov, *Pale Fire*, p. 172.
[44] Nabokov, *Pnin*, p. 128.

world" is a created work of art, just as the work of fiction partakes, almost parasitically, of reality. One of Nabokov's final works is the novel *Transparent Things*,[45] and one of those "transparent things" is the borderline between fact and fantasy. This is the final lesson we learn in the classroom of Nabokov's academic novels.

---

[45] Vladimir Nabokov, *Transparent Things* (New York: McGraw-Hill, 1972; London: Weidenfeld and Nicolson, 1973).

RANDALL JARRELL, MARY McCARTHY, AND FIFTIES LIBERALISM

Merritt Moseley

It is something of a commonplace to link Mary McCarthy's academic novel, *The Groves of Academe* (1952), the only academic novel among her many books of prose, and Randall Jarrell's *Pictures from an Institution* (1954), the only novel by this distinguished poet and critic. There are many telling linkages between the two, including the settings, the targets of satire, and certain important themes. But the most important one is the somewhat vexed question of a biographical/historical linkage. Doris Grumbach writes:

> The world at large knows what Mary McCarthy thought of Vassar, of Bard and, most explicitly, is aware of her lack of respect for the students, faculty, curriculum and general climate of Sarah Lawrence. What she was like on the campus of Sarah Lawrence, what her colleagues thought of her, can only be surmised from the one piece of possible evidence, this a novel by the late Randall Jarrell published in 1960 [actually 1954] and called *Pictures from an Institution*. Jarrell – poet, critic, and novelist – taught at Sarah Lawrence, Mary McCarthy knew him, although he was not at Sarah Lawrence at the same time she was. Yet her detractors are united in their view that Gertrude in that novel is the spit and image of Mary McCarthy.[1]

---

[1] Doris Grumbach, *The Company She Kept* (New York: Coward, McCann; London: Bodley Head, 1967), p. 123.

Randall Jarrell, Mary McCarthy, and Fifties Liberalism

Though Grumbach goes on to argue that the identification is less simple than it may seem, she ends by quoting a page of comments about Gertrude from *Pictures* and summing up:

> Her propensity for the fact in fiction, her affection for catalogues, her wit and sharpness of attack when she feels the need to attack, her customary resort to the people she knows well for her characters: all these ring true.[2]

Sister Bernetta Quinn explains that Benton, Jarrell's fictional college, is "a school similar to but not identical with Sarah Lawrence College, where Jarrell taught after coming out of the Army Air Force, just as Gertrude is similar to but different from Mary McCarthy, whose earlier satire of campus life, *The Groves of Academe*, immediately suggests her as candidate for Jarrell's artist-in-residence."[3]

Let us consider the evidence in the case followed by some reflections on what the importance of the identification might be. Jarrell's Gertrude Johnson is a moderately well-known novelist teaching creative writing on a short-term basis in a progressive women's college. She is nearly indifferent to the girls she teaches – the narrator explains that she has no interest in anyone who is not a writer[4] – and her teaching is elegantly slack. One nice but not very bright girl named Sylvia Moomaw comments on Gertrude's methods (teaching is supposed to be done in conferences at Benton): "She reads *awfully* fast. Sometimes when she's reading one of my stories – she just glances them over again so they'll be fresh in her mind – she reads

[2] Grumbach, p. 126.
[3] Sister Bernetta Quinn, *Randall Jarrell* (Boston: Twayne, 1981), p. 127.
[4] Randall Jarrell, *Pictures from an Institution: A Comedy* (New York: Alfred A. Knopf; London: Faber & Faber, 1954), p. 22.

them a page at a look."[5] Gertrude is malicious and witty, thinks the worst of everyone, and is reckless with the truth; at one point she enjoys spreading a scandalous rumor about an affair between Constance Morgan, the novel's ingenue, and Gottfried Rosenbaum, old, married, a European refugee, and the novel's moral exemplar.

Mary McCarthy was a published and well-regarded novelist who taught for short periods at Bard College (1947-48) and Sarah Lawrence College (one semester in 1948). She is on record as enjoying her experience at Bard but not at Sarah Lawrence, where she found the students shockingly poor.[6] Unlike Gertrude Johnson, though, she was beautiful, unmarried, stylish; it could never be said of her, as Jarrell does of Gertrude, "Nothing nice had ever happened to Gertrude in bed."[7]

Moreover, Mary McCarthy did not teach creative writing (though Randall Jarrell did); she taught ordinary literature courses, and worked very hard: "meeting her tutorial responsibilities, preparing lectures on both Russian literature and the novels of Jane Austen, George Eliot and Henry James, she worked alone late into the nights."[8]

Finally, for what it is worth, both Jarrell and McCarthy denied that Gertrude was a portrait of her. Doris Grumbach relates that McCarthy, in a letter to Jarrell on another subject (they were acquaintances, both contributed to *Partisan Review*, he is even mentioned in her novel as a major poet overlooked in the invitations to a literary conference), "said she had heard 'that Gertrude was supposed to be me, and that I didn't think so. He wrote

---

[5] Mary McCarthy, *The Groves of Academe* (New York: Harcourt, Brace & World, 1952; London: Heinemann, 1953), p. 199.

[6] Grumbach, p. 122.

[7] Jarrell, *Pictures from an Institution*, p. 213.

[8] Carol Brightman, *Writing Dangerously: Mary McCarthy and Her World* (New York: Clarkson Potter, 1992; London: Lime Tree, 1993), p. 284.

back and said, No, it's me, – you know, like Flaubert.'"[9] In a letter regarding periodical publication, Jarrell comments at some length on the real-life originals of the characters in *Pictures*, more or less acknowledging his President Robbins' origins in Harold Taylor, president of Sarah Lawrence, worrying a little bit about libel, and going on to write:

> This is the only section of the book that would raise any Problems of this Nature. My lady writer, Gertrude, reminds people violently of five or six lady writers, whichever one they happen to know, but there are many deplorable writers of the sort, just as, alas, there's only one young president of a progressive college.[10]

Among other candidates for the original of Gertrude, Jean Stafford, wife of Jarrell's friend Robert Lowell, is sometimes nominated.

Whether Jarrell meant Mary McCarthy by Gertrude Johnson is unlikely to be settled. If he did, it was surely an unfair portrait, and small-minded as well; perhaps McCarthy could be cold and cruelly witty, but why go to the trouble of portraying her as ugly, dowdy, sexless, a bad homemaker and a lazy teacher?

If we assume, for a little longer, that the character of Gertrude Johnson is the most important in *Pictures from an Institution*, we must raise the question of what Jarrell intended by this characterization. *Pictures* is told by an unnamed and somewhat shadowy narrator, another

---

[9] Grumbach, p. 124.

[10] Randall Jarrell, *Randall Jarrell's Letters: An Autobiographical and Literary Selection*, Ed. Mary Jarrell (Boston: Houghton Mifflin, 1985; London: Faber, 1986), p. 367.

faculty member at Benton, also a writer (a poet); this man is an old friend of Gertrude's from Greenwich Village who, like her, is dubious about the kind of education offered at Benton. He tells us a great deal about Gertrude, even giving us copious accounts of her thought processes, her deepest unexpressed fears, and the motivations she does not admit even to herself. It is his moral relationship to her which is of greater interest.

Jarrell is on record as thinking of Gertrude as a "deplorable" writer. The novel offers many reasons to deplore her. She seems callously using Benton and its occupants as mere material for a novel. She thinks the worst of everyone. She is egocentric. Most of all, though, the narrator seems to deplore her caustic wit.

And yet the narrator is always the conduit for it. *Pictures from an Institution* is one of the wittiest novels ever written - sometimes the wit becomes too effortful. Here the narrator is describing Mrs Robbins, the wife of the college president:

For Mrs Robbins understanding anybody, having a fellow-feeling for anybody, admitting anybody else exists, were incomprehensible vices of Americans, Negroes, continentals, cats, dogs, parrots. She was "half British phlegm and half perfidious Albion," according to Gertrude Johnson, who loved to refer to Pamela [originally South African] as the Black Man's Burden; any future work on Mrs Robbins will have to be based on Gertrude's. This *half ... half* formula was Gertrude's favorite. She said that the President was "half *jeune fille*, half *faux bonhomme*." I hadn't liked her formula for Pamela, so I accepted her description of the President with bored matter-of-factness, as if she'd told me that he was half H_2 and half SO_4, but then I thought, "It's so; it's so." Sometimes Gertrude was witty

Randall Jarrell, Mary McCarthy, and Fifties Liberalism

without even lying.[11]

As this passage illustrates, there is a complicity between the narrator and Gertrude which greatly qualifies the moral satire against her. Many of the wittiest lines in the novel are approving quotations from Gertrude. Others might as well be.[12]

It is true that the novel moves toward a redemption of Gertrude, a humanizing of her, when two events – her husband's illness, and the death of a former teacher whom she has never known – cause her to think of other people as more than material for her fiction. As the novel ends, the narrator learns, she may *not* write her novel about Benton; she may write about a writer instead.[13] The narrator is leaving, too, and the ending of the novel has him wondering if he has not been unfair to Benton. His change is analogous to Gertrude's, then, and a careful reader may not find enough distance between the narrator and Gertrude to permit an easy judgment on her. And if there is little distance between Gertrude and the narrator, there is even less between her and Randall Jarrell; after all, he imagined and wrote down all the wickedly witty things Gertrude thinks and says; and, despite *her* late change of

---

[11] Jarrell, *Pictures from an Institution*, pp. 11-12.

[12] William Pritchard attributes to Jarrell's friend Peter Taylor the idea that *Pictures* is "a catalogue of Jarrell's witty talk, often - especially in the book's earlier parts - of a malicious, at least satiric bent." (William Pritchard, *Randall Jarrell: A Literary Life* [New York: Farrar, Straus and Giroux, 1990], p. 236).

[13] See John Crowe Ransom, "The Rugged Way of Genius," in Robert Lowell, Peter Taylor and Robert Penn Warren, Eds. *Randall Jarrell, 1914-1965* (New York: Farrar, Straus and Giroux, 1967) and J. A. Bryant, Jr., *Understanding Randall Jarrell* (Columbia: University of South Carolina Press, 1986), both of whom discuss this change in Gertrude.

heart, he went ahead and wrote a novel about Benton, though his has noble and admirable people in it as well as the rogues and fools who exclusively inhabit Gertrude's fictional universe.

A minor, if indirect, biographical connection between the two novelists is far more important, finally, than whether Gertrude Johnson is like Mary McCarthy: the influence on both writers of Hannah Arendt. Arendt was one of the exciting refugee intellectuals in postwar New York. Brightman points to:

> ... [Nicola] Chiaromonte, Arthur Koestler, Hannah Arendt and her husband, Heinrich Blucher; along with others who traveled in wider orbits – among them, Paul Tillich, Thomas Mann, Bertolt Brecht, Albert Einstein, Arnold Schoenberg, Fernand Leger, and Marc Chagall. The Europeans had "a certain wisdom," McCarthy thought, which was lacking in the "crude society" of American intellectuals ...[14]

Alfred Kazin calls Hannah Arendt Mary McCarthy's "first love": "with Hannah she was almost humble, deferential."[15] Their friendship lasted until Hannah Arendt's death; their letters, published in 1994, are a testament to the depth and importance of this relationship.

Jarrell, too, came under Hannah Arendt's spell. They met frequently in New York in the late 1940s. She has testified to his importance to her in opening up English poetry for her; in his turn, he claimed that he had been moved to write *Pictures from an Institution* by her book *The Origins of Totalitarianism*; writing in May, 1951, he said

---

14 Brightman, p. 198.
15 Brightman, p. 299.

"You can imagine how delighted I was to see your chubby girlish face on the front of the *Saturday Review*. Inspired by your example, I too have written a prose book, and I'll bring it along for you to read. I'm not joking, I really have."[16]

In one sense this is an absurd claim, as his short novel and her major treatise on totalitarianism have in common only that each is a prose book. But in another it is exactly correct. Jarrell has acknowledged that the characters of Gottfried and Irene Rosenbaum, the embodiments of wisdom and culture at Benton, are based on Hannah Arendt and her husband.[17] More broadly, his friendship with Arendt helped to strengthen the belief which becomes a major theme in *Pictures*: the superiority of European intellectual and cultural life to that of America. If knowing Hannah Arendt helped Mary McCarthy to conclude that the Europeans had a wisdom that contrasted sharply with American crudity, the same diagnosis, derived from the same woman, and embodied in a character based on her, is at the heart of *Pictures*. In a more muted way this same contrast exists in *The Groves of Academe*, where the most intense, most principled, most idealistic and most honest faculty member is a Russian, Domna Rejnev, described as "a smoldering anachronism, a throwback to one of those ardent young women of the Sixties, Turgenev's heroines, who cut their curls short, studied Hegel, crossed their mammas and papas, reproved their suitors, and dreamed resolutely of 'a new day' for peasants, workers, and technicians."[18] Domna is hardly Hannah Arendt, but her culture, her impressive learning (she is only twenty-three)

---

[16] Jarrell, *Randall Jarrell's Letters*, p. 250.
[17] Bryant, p. 107.
[18] McCarthy, p. 37.

and her complete lack of crudity are, the reader may well feel, a quality of her Europeanness.

Thus one characteristic which links *The Groves of Academe* and *Pictures from an Institution* is a general conviction of the superior culture of Europe: made quite explicit by Jarrell, somewhat less so by McCarthy, and, in both cases, undoubtedly indebted to the example of Hannah Arendt.[19]

Another is the character of the college president. Though McCarthy's Jocelyn College and Jarrell's Benton are both generalized so that they are more generic pictures of mid-century progressive colleges than specific accounts of Sarah Lawrence (McCarthy going so far as to make Jocelyn co-educational), the two novelists each provide a fictional portrait of Harold Taylor, the president of Sarah Lawrence.[20]

McCarthy and Jarrell agree that the President is

---

[19] David Lehman in *Signs of the Times: Deconstruction and the Fall of Paul de Man* (New York: Poseidon Press; London: Deutsch, 1992) contributes some interesting information about another European member of the Jocelyn College faculty. This is Aristide Poncy, the head of the foreign languages department of the division of Literature and Language, based on Artine Artinian, who filled the same position at Bard when McCarthy taught there. In September, 1949, Artinian hired the young Paul de Man in a temporary appointment to teach French. They soon fell out and de Man was, like Henry Mulcahy, not reappointed. Mary McCarthy, who had recommended de Man to Artinian, seems to have left a "trace" of the future celebrated literary theorist in the comment that Poncy, who had a prejudice against the French of France, had hired a number of odd persons, including one Belgian - like de Man (McCarthy, pp. 85-6). Lehman (pp. 269 ff) has a full account of de Man's short career at Bard during which he stole, vandalized, refused to pay his debts, and entered into a bigamous marriage.

[20] Taylor recognized his portrayal in both novels and later said that we would "think twice before appointing visiting 'novelist-teachers with a predisposition to carve people up.'" (Pritchard, p. 153).

Randall Jarrell, Mary McCarthy, and Fifties Liberalism

vigorous, good-looking and youthful, at least in attitude: Jocelyn's President Maynard Hoar:

> ... was one of those rugged men who looked exactly like their photographs – dark, resilient, keen-eyed, buoyant, yet thoughtful.... He was much preoccupied with youth, with America as a young country; he tried to have up-to-date opinions which were as sound as grandpa's digestion. He had a strong true voice and liked to sing folk songs, especially work songs and prison chants.[21]

Benton's President Dwight Robbins is portrayed at much more length, in static descriptions, though he plays little role in *Pictures from an Institution*. Jarrell is hard on him. He has been a diver in the Olympics and remains boyish, the implication being that this is the result of much hard work. Further, "President Robbins, judge him as you please, was not human. He had not had time to be; besides, his own gift was for seeming human."[22] He has shaky educational credentials; despite an MA from Oxford, his only doctorate is an honorary one, granted by Menuire (pronounced "manure"?), a college in Florida.

Though McCarthy's Hoar has an earned PhD from a good university, the major way he differs from Dwight Robbins is that he is a man of honor and principle. The plot of *The Groves of Academe* concerns a plan not to renew a temporary instructor's contract because there is no position for him and he is no good. The instructor thwarts the plan by claiming past Communist party membership and painting himself as the victim of a political firing. His well-meaning supporters call on Hoar, who listens carefully to them, quite willing to see the other side, and

---

[21] McCarthy, p. 172.
[22] Jarrell, *Pictures from an Institution*, p. 22.

eventually agrees so far as to renew the contract. At the end of the novel he resigns from the presidency on principle.

Compare Dwight Robbins, whose moral and intellectual fixity is described by Jarrell thus:

> About anything, anything at all, Dwight Robbins believed what Reason and Virtue and Tolerance and a Comprehensively Organic Synthesis of Values would have him believe. And about anything, anything at all, he believed what it was expedient for the President of Benton College to believe. You looked at the two beliefs and lo! the two were one.... President Robbins was so well adjusted to his environment that sometimes you could not tell which was the environment and which was President Robbins.[23]

In case this characterization is too oblique, the narrator returns to Dr Robbins some chapters later and explains that "morality, to him, was making a good impression on everybody, selling himself (that accurately ambiguous phrase) to everybody."[24]

***

More important than the character of the college president, of course, is the character of the college – in these two novels, the character of the progressive private liberal arts college in America. Benton and Jocelyn are both examples of this twentieth-century phenomenon. Both Jarrell and

---

[23] Jarrell, *Pictures from an Institution*, pp. 10-11.
[24] Jarrell, *Pictures from an Institution*, pp. 72-3.

Randall Jarrell, Mary McCarthy, and Fifties Liberalism

McCarthy had been educated at more traditional institutions, with an elite system of restrictive admissions and a more conventional and rigorous curriculum: Jarrell at Vanderbilt and McCarthy at Vassar. And both found much to deplore and satirize in the progressive college.

Mary McCarthy directs her most serious criticism at the progressive philosophy itself and at the curriculum, pedagogy, student body and faculty which it has engendered at Jocelyn. In the chapter ironically entitled "Ancient History" (Jocelyn is twelve years old), she sets out its claims to progressive status, beginning by contrasting it with its sister institutions (note the studied reference to Sarah Lawrence, usually taken to be Jocelyn's original, as a different college):

> Jocelyn College ... had a faculty of forty-one persons and a student-body of two hundred and eighty-three – a ratio of one teacher to every 6.9 students, which made possible the practice of "individual instruction" as carried on at Bennington (6:1), Sarah Lawrence (6.4:1), Bard (6.9:1), and St John's (7.7:1). It had been founded in the late Thirties by an experimental educator and lecturer, backed by a group of society-women in Cleveland, Pittsburgh, and Cincinnati who wished to strike a middle course between the existing extremes, between Aquinas and Dewey, the modern dance and the labor movement. Its students were neither to till the soil as at Antioch nor weave on looms as at Black Mountain; they were to be grounded neither in the grass-roots present as at Sarah Lawrence nor in the great-books past as at St John's or Chicago; they were to specialize neither in verse-writing, nor in the poetic theatre, nor in the techniques of co-operative living – they were simply to be free,

spontaneous, and coeducational.[25]

The two distinctive features of the educational program – both subjects of controversy at the time during which the novel is set – are the "field period" and individualized instruction. Borrowed from Bennington, the field period,

> the four weeks spent by the student *away* from the college in factory, laboratory, newspaper plant, publishing firm or settlement house were the test of his self-reliance and his ability to learn through *doing*: the measure of the success of the field-period was the measure of the success of the college.[26]

The widespread recognition that the field-period has not actually succeeded as advertised conflicts with the self-interest of the faculty, for whom it is a four-week vacation from teaching. Individualized instruction through a "major project" is similarly problematic:

> In brief, the system was this: the student was supposed to spend one hour a week with a tutor in his major field, this tutorial hour being the center of his education, accounting, theoretically, for one-fourth of his academic work and requiring a minimum of eight hours of preparation.[27]

Beautiful in theory, the major project and individual tutoring have all sorts of real-world problems, including disparity of workload and expectations (students in the sciences and performing arts actually do a great deal of

---

[25] McCarthy, p. 60.
[26] McCarthy, p. 72.
[27] McCarthy, p. 75.

work; those in English and other "reading subjects" do not) and a realistic accommodation to the abilities of the faculty; in principle a student can choose any project at all, but this proves impossible for the limited number of faculty with their limited knowledge base to supervise, so in fact the choice is much narrower and keyed to recognized faculty interests. Individualized instruction survives, though, because of a combination of genuine dedication to progressive educational idealism and something colder and more practical: "it was obvious that only individual instruction could justify the high tuition, which alone kept the college going."[28]

The progressive characteristics – and aspirations and perhaps pretensions – of Jocelyn lead to a certain amount of fudging and trimming; to strenuous competition for, and manipulation of, tutees; and, combined with a liberal admissions policy, to a peculiar human selection. McCarthy is quite severe on the students, particularly the boys:

the male part of the college included an unusual number of child prodigies, mathematical wizards of fourteen, as well as some spastics and paraplegics, cripples of various sorts, boys with tics, polio victims. There were a deaf boy, a dumb boy, boys with several kinds of speech-defects; there were two boys who had fits, boys with unusual skin diseases, with ordinary acne, with glasses, with poor teeth, a boy with a religious complex, boys who had grown too fast, with long, chickeny necks and quivering Adam's apples. The girls, by comparison, were blooming, healthy, often pretty specimens,

---

28 McCarthy, p. 80.

with the usual desires and values, daughters of commercial artists, commercial writers, radio-singers, insurance-salesmen, dermatologists, girls who had failed to get into Smith or nearby Swarthmore, girls from the surrounding region, narcissistic, indolent girls wanting a good time and not choosey, girls who sculpted or did ceramics of animals or fashion-drawing, hard-driving, liverish girls, older than the rest, on scholarships.[29]

This cruelly specific anatomy arises in a discussion of the college dances, in which the contrast between boys and girls would naturally be most strongly felt – especially by the girls.

As for the instructors, the significant salary scale and the attractions of progressive education have enabled Jocelyn

... to recruit a faculty of poets, sculptors, critics, composers, painters, scene-designers, and so on, without academic experience and without, also, academic ambitions of the careerist sort – as well as beginners in history, science, or philosophy fired with the love of a subject and impatient of graduate-school norms; plus a certain number of seasoned non-conformists and dissenters, sexual deviants, feather-bedders, alcoholics, impostors.[30]

Mary McCarthy shows an amused tolerance for much of this, and the faculty members who play important roles in the plot, with the exception of the repellent and conniving Henry Mulcahy, the main character and villain, are engaging, thoughtful, well-intentioned and well-educated

___

29 McCarthy, p. 26-7.
30 McCarthy, p. 84.

intellectuals, though some more marginal figures are stupid or malign.[31]

By contrast the faculty members of Jarrell's Benton College are mostly unsatisfactory or preposterous. The shining exceptions are Dr Rosenbaum, almost every one of whose actions or utterances is a standing reproach to American higher education; Gertrude Johnson, who is intelligent, creative, witty and well-read, but not really interested in teaching or in her students; and the narrator, whose perspicacity is mostly shown by his awareness that Gertrude Johnson and Gottfried Rosenbaum are superior to the rest of the faculty, not to mention the President. The rest of the faculty are nearly faceless, with the exception of a retired teacher of writing, now dead, who was a kind and good lady even if not a good teacher, and a sociologist who is "almost famous"[32] but leaden and dull. Where Mary McCarthy is specific and creates many different faculty members, most of them vivid, Randall Jarrell hardly goes beyond the three or four already mentioned, preferring instead to generalize about the Benton faculty.

One of the generalizations illustrates what George

---

[31] Elaine Showalter probably goes too far, though, in her summary: "*The Groves of Academe* is bracingly cynical and worldly-wise without condemning higher education, liberals, or intellectuals. With the exception of the repellent and unctuous Mulcahy, the faculty are motivated by the highest ideals, and they share a genuine community of learning." (*Faculty Towers: the Academic Novel and its Discontents* [Philadelphia: University of Pennsylvania Press; Oxford: Oxford University Press, 2005], p. 29). Compare Adam Begley's "The Decline of the Campus Novel," (*Lingua Franca*, [September 1997], pp. 39-46), reprinted elsewhere in this volume, which sees McCarthy's novel as full of contempt, brutality, and meanness, and her professors uniformly despicable.

[32] Jarrell, *Pictures from an Institution*, p. 40.

The Academic Novel

Watson[33] calls the sin of Pygmalion:

> the faculty – insofar as they were real Benton faculty, and not just
> nomadic barbarians – reasoned with the students, "appreciated their
> point of view," used Socratic methods on them, made allowances for
> them, kept looking into the oven to see if they were done; but there
> was just one allowance they never under any circumstances made –
> that the students might be right about something and they wrong....
> According to [one Benton student], a professor at an ordinary school
> tells you "what's so," you admit that it is on examination, and what
> you really believe or come to believe has "that obscurity which is the
> privilege of young things." But at Benton, where education was as
> democratic as in "that book about America by that French writer –
> de, de – you know the one I mean"; she meant de Tocqueville; there
> at Benton they wanted you really to believe everything that they did,
> especially if they hadn't told you what it was. You gave them the
> facts, the opinions of authorities, what you hoped was their own
> opinion; but they replied, "That's not the point. What do *you yourself*
> *really believe?*" If it wasn't what your professors believed, you and
> they could go on searching for your real belief forever – unless you
> stumbled at last upon that primal scene which is, by definition, at
> the root of everything....[34]

The faculty are, with the exception of skeptics like
Gertrude and the narrator and foreigners like Dr
Rosenbaum, "committed" to Benton, in a smug and
complacent way: "The people who weren't contented got

---

[33] See his essay, "Fictions of Academe: Dons and Realities," (*Encounter,*
51 [November, 1978], pp. 42-5), reprinted elsewhere in this volume.
[34] Jarrell, *Pictures from an Institution*, pp. 81-2.

jobs elsewhere – as did, usually, any very exceptional people – and the others stayed. They didn't need to be exceptional: they were at Benton."[35] Their complacency and feeling of superiority (they look down on Oxford) derive from the educational theory according to which Benton is run: if the extramural reading and talking are the most important part of an ordinary college education, why not redefine college education to make them the curriculum, lest students be bored.

> So the students' conversation and reading and 'extra-curricular cultural activities' and decisions about Life were made, as much as possible, the curriculum through which the teachers of Benton shepherded the students of Benton ... they called this 'allowing the student to use his own individual initiative.'[36]

As at Jocelyn, teachers have a weekly conference with each student, though Jarrell indicates, as McCarthy does not, the almost psychoanalytical nature of these encounters. The students often find the prying of the faculty troubling; though the intellectual demands of the college are light, the emotional ones are harrowing.

Both Randall Jarrell and Mary McCarthy depict colleges which, though expensive to attend, are not selective on ordinary academic grounds; which work through "progressive" methods – that is, a regime of sentimental, educationally misguided (though often sincere and certainly, when done properly, labor-intensive) education; and which, for various reasons, attract to themselves an

---

[35] Jarrell, *Pictures from an Institution*, p. 105.
[36] Jarrell, *Pictures from an Institution*, p. 84.

odd group of students and faculty.

That the students are not very well-prepared (Jarrell insists that in the early, *really* progressive days of Benton, several of the students would have had difficulty writing "cat") and do not learn very much while they are undergraduates is, from what Jarrell and McCarthy suggest, true, but a truth not to be acknowledged. And this is because of the tolerance, the reluctance to make judgements, the essential *liberalism* of both institutions. This is the final great topic which preoccupies both novelists – the liberalism of the American 1950s, especially as found in a quintessentially liberal place like the progressive college. Another of Jarrell's waspish observations on the Benton faculty claims that:

> Most of the people of Benton would have swallowed a porcupine, if you had dyed its quills and called it Modern Art; they longed for men to be discovered on the moon, so they could show that *they* weren't prejudiced towards moon men; and they were so liberal and selfless, politically, that – but what words of men, or tongue of man or angel, can I find adequate to this great theme?[37]

McCarthy's analysis of her liberals is more probing, ultimately more intelligent. She was the more politically concerned of the two writers (having been active in Communist, then left anti-Stalinist, politics in New York for many years). Henry Mulcahy, the faculty thorn in the flesh of Jocelyn College, raises more vexing political problems than Gertrude Johnson can ever do at Benton. When Mulcahy's temporary contract is not renewed (for excellent reasons, it appears), he constructs an elaborate and mendacious political psychodrama, the theme of

---

[37] Jarrell, *Pictures from an Institution*, p. 104.

which is that he is the victim of political intolerance because of his (falsely claimed) past membership in the Communist Party. He turns the tables on the administration and the rest of the faculty, making them, the liberals, his victims.

The novel is full of observations on the predicaments associated with liberalism: Mulcahy's colleagues, though aware of his misfeasances, "felt that reluctance to intervene that characterized them as true liberals."[38] Mulcahy reflects on Domna Rejnev, his staunchest supporter:

> ... she was a true liberal, as he had always suspected, who could not
> tolerate in her well-modulated heart that others should be wickeder
> than she, any more than she could bear that she should be richer,
> better born, better looking than some statistical median.[39]

And a true outsider, a visiting poet who actually *has* been a Communist, reflects on the milieu:

> Possibly they were all very nice, high-minded, scrupulous people
> with only an occupational tendency toward backbiting and a
> nervous habit of self-correction, always emending, penciling,
> erasing; but he did not care to catch the bug, which seemed to be
> endemic in these ivied haunts.[40]

Though Jarrell uses the term "liberal" less often, he depicts the same state of mind. His President, for instance:

> ... was as informal and democratic with [his young secretary] as

---

[38] McCarthy, p. 248.
[39] McCarthy, p. 52.
[40] McCarthy, p. 295.

though the United Nations were going to give him an award for it;
but he was that way with everybody, and was proud that he was:
the sun shines on the just and unjust, and on secretaries.[41]

Both novels suggest, though this is more strongly
marked out in *The Groves of Academe*, that liberals are
defenseless in the face of the illiberal – either extremists
like Gertrude or unscrupulous careerists like Henry
Mulcahy. The best lack all conviction, while the worst are
full of passionate intensity.

It is a very American concern – this liberalism under
attack – in the 1950s, in the aftermath of McCarthyism, the
investigations of the House Committee on UnAmerican
Activities, and the broad assault on universities. Jocelyn's
President Maynard Hoar is famous as a defender of free
thought in colleges and an enemy of political persecution;
as he tells the Communist poet, "We're all liberals, believe
me ... and there's not one of us who isn't shocked and
sickened by the reign of terror in our colleges."[42] Of course,
this carefully and bravely earned reputation as a defender
of faculty liberties makes Hoar almost helpless against
Mulcahy's claim to be a former Communist.

The thematic interest in liberalism relates *The Groves of
Academe* and *Pictures From an Institution* to a nearly
contemporary novel by the English author Malcolm
Bradbury, *Eating People is Wrong*, begun in the early 1950s
when he was a student and published in 1959. It is a study
of an ineffectual lecturer in English at a nondescript
provincial university, Stuart Treece, and his inability to
cope with life, particularly with women and with students
who appeal to his liberal tolerance, notably a Nigerian and

---

[41] Jarrell, *Pictures from an Institution*, p. 146.
[42] McCarthy, p. 289.

Louis Bates, an older student who is ugly, obnoxious, inept and emotionally needy.

Though Treece's university college is very different from Benton and Jocelyn, the liberal arts college playing no role in British higher education, Treece is a familiar figure because of his baffled liberalism: "The trouble with me is, Treece thought, that I'm a liberal humanist who believes in original sin."[43] Trying to cajole the African Mr Eborabelosa into conforming a bit more (by not bringing animals into his rooms):

> ... as for Professor Treece, who had tried to be nice to people, and was going to go on trying to be nice to people, even though all they were was people, and as such things tremendously difficult to be nice to – as for the good and liberal Treece, even he found himself cracking a little under the strain.... It is well I am a liberal, and can love all men, thought Treece; for if I were not, I doubt if I could.[44]

Treece's is a troubled liberalism; not under threat, as with his American counterparts facing real or imagined reigns of terror, but belated. He thinks back to when liberalism really *stood for* something – at the time of the Spanish Civil War – and contrasts his own amorphous and smudged condition:

> Being a liberal, after all *that* [the Thirties] meant something special; one was a messenger from somewhere. One was, now, a humanist, neither Christian nor communist any more, but in some vague, unstable central place, a humanist, yes, but not one of those who

[43] Malcolm Bradbury, *Eating People Is Wrong* (1959; Chicago: Academy Chicago Publishers, 1986), p. 15.
[44] Bradbury, *Eating People is Wrong*, p. 34

supposes that man is good or progress attractive. One has no firm affiliations, political, religious or moral, but lies outside it all.[45]

Recognizing the moral paralysis which comes from his liberal convictions, or his liberal convictionlessness, he is nevertheless powerless to change. He ends by failing to do anything meaningful about Louis Bates or the women in his life, and finally retreats into a hospital.

In his afterword added to the novel in 1986 Bradbury comments on the centrality of liberalism to the novel; the book, he explains, is "about the tensions and contradictions and comedies of the liberal life": further, Treece's problem is that the "liberalism that makes Treece virtuous also makes him inert; it is a latter-day philosophy; finally he fails of his own inertia ...."[46]

***

One of the attractions of the academic novel is that it offers to outsiders an insiders' view. When readers see Jim Dixon, in Amis's *Lucky Jim*, scheming, changing the curriculum and reading list of his proposed special study, in order to attract the three prettiest girls in the History department into it while repelling the smartest and thus most intimidating male student, one of the small secrets of the university teaching profession is being humorously revealed. Likewise McCarthy and Jarrell, and Bradbury, provide insiders' views: not only of the kind of education

---

[45] Bradbury, *Eating People is Wrong*, p. 56.
[46] Bradbury, *Eating People is Wrong*, p. 291-6. For a much more serious examination of the failures of liberalism, this time in the face of real evil, not troublesome students and a perplexing romantic life, see Bradbury's *The History Man* (London: Secker & Warburg, 1975; Boston: Houghton Mifflin, 1976).

provided by their institutions, as seen by those who are paid to provide it, but more importantly of 1950s liberalism as it flourished – if flourished is the correct term for a growth still querulous and self-doubting – on college and university campuses. Both Jarrell and McCarthy are themselves liberals; both are clearly committed to an idea of liberal education (though not necessarily as pursued at Benton or Jocelyn); but both *The Groves of Academe* and *Pictures From An Institution* seem to be suggesting that liberal education is not ideally entrusted to liberals.

ACADEMIC LIFE IN *LUCKY JIM* AND *JAKE'S THING*

Dale Salwak

The origin of Kingsley Amis's interest in the "academic novel" goes back to at least the spring of 1946, when he visited his old friend Philip Larkin, an assistant librarian at University College in Leicester. On Saturday morning Larkin had to go to the campus for a few minutes, and so he left his friend behind to wait in the Common Room, where the lecturers and masters gathered for a quick coffee.

Amis was fascinated to find himself pushed into a unique community, into new territory full of potential for a writer's sensibilities: "Professors and lecturers sitting, standing, talking, laughing, reading, drifting in and out, drinking coffee." Here, he thought, was "a whole mode of existence no one had got on to; ... somebody ought to do something about *this*."[1]

Out of that morning visit an idea dawned in the novelist's mind, a notion about "being bored by powerful people,"[2] about situations where one must deal with the mundane and the monotonous – in short, with the minutiae of a society one is trying to win entry into. Years later he recalled his thoughts at the time in note form:

---

[1] Dennis Chambers, "Kingsley Amis Interviewed" (*The Writer*, February 1973), pp. 3-8; see also Kingsley Amis, "Real and Made-up People", from *The Amis Collection* (London: Hutchinson; New York: Summit, 1990), pp. 5-6.

[2] Clive James, "Profile 4: Kingsley Amis" (*The New Review* 1 [July 1974]), p. 22.

Academic Life in *Lucky Jim* and *Jake's Thing*

University Shags, Provincial. Probably keen on Culture. Crappy culture. Fellow who doesn't fit in. Seems anti-culture. Non-U. Non-Oxbridge. Beer. Girls. Can't say what he really thinks. Boss trouble. Given chores. Disasters. Boring boss (a) so boring girl (b). Nice girl comes but someone else's property. Whose? Etc.[3]

In other words, for a moment Amis had glimpsed university life from "the other side," the lecturer's side – a rich vein of material that he would return to often during his career, most notably in *Lucky Jim* (1954) and *Jake's Thing* (1978).

***

Lucky Jim, to begin with, is not only an enchanting and original novel but a remarkable performance by a young writer who has something serious to say and who says it with great humor. Its hero, James Dixon, is a man battling an almost terminal case of galloping ennui. A history instructor mired in the traditions and politics of a provincial British university, he spins his wheels in various ill-fated attempts to extricate himself from the stifling boredom of the work he must do and the people he must befriend in order to advance his career. In the process the muck flies, bespattering Jim and those around him, with hilarious results. Throughout, Jim remains the *naif,* an innocent and fundamentally decent chap whose contention that the Emperor isn't wearing any clothes endears him to us at the same time it endangers his professional life and muddies up his personal one. By surviving despite an unrewarding job, pretentious associates, and a predatory

---

[3] Amis, "Real and Made-Up People," p. 5.

female colleague, Jim becomes the first in a long line of Amisian heroes who stand for common sense, authenticity, honesty, spontaneity, and decency; for the belief that life is to be lived happily now; for the notion that, as Dixon puts it, "nice things are nicer than nasty things."

To develop his moral stance in *Lucky Jim*, Amis divides his characters in the novel into two easily recognizable groups: generally praiseworthy figures, the ones who gain the greatest share of our sympathy; and evil or at best worldly and corrupt characters who obstruct the fortunes of the good ones. Jim (the awkward outsider), Julius Gore-Urquhart (his benefactor or saviour), and Christine Callaghan (the decent girl who accepts Jim despite his faults) are distinguished by moral honesty, personal sincerity, and a lack of pretense. Among the antagonists are Professor Ned Welch (Jim's principal tormentor), Bertrand Welch (the defeated boaster), and the neurotic Margaret Peel (the thwarted "witch"), all of whom disguise their motives and present a false appearance. Gore-Urquhart functions as a mediator between common sense (Jim) and excess (the Welches), providing the norm by which to judge other frequently unstable personalities.

Lucky Jim is a journey toward self-awareness, in which Amis uses connections between locale and experience to lay bare a society and to reveal the moral fiber of his hero. Jim's character is established immediately with the description of his dual predicaments: he has a job he does not want but for financial reasons is trying hard to keep; and he has become involved, without quite knowing why, with Margaret, a younger but better-established colleague. It becomes immediately apparent that academic life for Jim is little more than a running duel with his superior, a never-ending speculation as to whether he will be dropped at the term's end or continued on probation for another year. In response to this perpetual potential for disaster,

Jim has become the adaptable antihero who tries to control his fate – as a jack-of-all-trades, a skilled manipulator, an adept deceiver, a fashioner of disguises. Amis emphasizes Jim's ingenuity in this struggle for survival. Jim's entry upon the fictional stage in this particular fashion reveals the role in which he will be cast throughout the story – that of an out-of-place young man engaged in an attempt to cope with and ultimately outwit the social and academic world of the Welches.

In many respects, Amis's work emulates the spirit of the picaresque novel with its episodic lurchings, its opportunistic hero, and its emphasis on satirizing various English character types. Although resourceful, the *picaro* is by tradition simple, a *naif* who reveals, by his simplicity, the tattered moral fabric of a society based on pretension. It is Amis's great achievement in *Lucky Jim* that he has taken the ramshackle form of the traditional picaresque novel, centralized his moral theme (the firm value of being one's own person), and added the conventional plot element of lovers separated by evil forces. Like Tom Jones, Amis's hero is a well-intentioned, authentic, honest young man who compromises just enough to live comfortably. Like Tom he is essentially good-hearted: he is genuinely concerned for Margaret's welfare, at least until he learns she is a fraud; he wants to do well at his job in spite of the chairman's unreasonable demands; and he is troubled to learn that Bertrand is carrying on with a married woman while dating Christine.

But unlike Tom Jones or Joseph Andrews – who are good enough fellows but lack the ability for self-examination, often judging others but not themselves – Jim is a thinker. The single most endearing feature about him is that under no circumstances does he take himself seriously, a quality that both helps him to oppose the most unpleasant people in the novel and adds to *Lucky Jim's* comic tone. Jim is both realistic and reasonable, and his reasonableness makes up for his many shortcomings. Expedient, manipulative, cynical, lazy though he sometimes is (he specialized in medieval studies at college because "the medieval papers were a soft option"), Jim has the merit of looking at everyone, including himself, with a sane, critical good sense, devoid of pretense or self-delusion. After all, he is in some respects as much a hypocrite as the hypocrites he opposes. Jim refuses to align himself with those characters who deny their own hypocrisies and whose perceptions of reality are distorted by various degrees of egotism. As a "rogue" occupying a marginal position in society, he is eminently qualified to be an astute observer of human foibles; and as the outsider bucking the system he both amuses us and wins our sympathies, the proverbial mouse wreaking havoc among the elephants.

The picaresque novel is commonly a novel of quest, and Jim's standby and salvation through his own journey is a strong sense of humor that enables him to make light of much very real distress and disaster. Although he hates the Welch family, he knows that deference to them is essential if he is to retain his job. In order to maintain self-respect, however, he resorts to a comic fantasy world in which he can express rage or loathing toward certain imbecilities of the social group the Welch set represents. His rude faces and clever pranks serve a therapeutic function – a means by which Jim can express token resistance that will not seriously endanger his always tenuous position. He is, in his own way, shadow boxing. While engaging in a typically frustrating conversation with the professor, for example, Jim internally diverts it, mentally debunking his superior's effetism: "Look here, you old cockchafer," he tells himself, "what makes you think you can run a history department?" At other times his fantasies become more aggressive: stuffing the professor down a toilet, dashing his fist into Welch's face, beating him about the head and shoulders with a bottle, or "picking up the spanner he could see in the dashboard pocket and hitting him on the back of the neck with it." Jim is practicing defiance in the only way possible for a man in his position.

Yet another of Jim's methods for purging rage and loathing is to assume a dazzling variety of faces. His repertoire includes a Martian invader face, a sex life in ancient Rome face, an Eskimo face and a tragic mask, among others. Jim's use of masquerade conceals his inner self, placing one more layer of disguise between the vulnerable young man and the external antagonists that threaten him. The bed-burning, the stolen taxi cab and the drunken Merrie England lecture are additional dramatic, albeit comic, expressions of Jim's pent-up loathing and rage against the Welch's academic life and values; by them he assumes the roles of destroyer, plunderer and debunker, each a means of acting out, if only temporarily, positions of power that are otherwise closed to him or beyond his reach. Jim's other role changes – from madrigal singer to keen medieval scholar to university lecturer to romantic to dancer – exemplify his versatility and adaptability. In that respect they permit him to shift his ground quickly, another defense; a moving target is always harder to hit.

On the other hand, Jim can also behave instinctively and constructively when he is threatened. The first explicitly rebellious deed Jim commits is to rescue Christine from Bertrand's clutches at a dance and flee with her in a stolen taxi. Later in the novel Jim again acts constructively when he punches Bertrand. The immediate provocation is Bertrand's warning Jim not to curry favor with Christine, coupled with an offensive reference to Jim himself. When

Bertrand hits him, Jim reacts and strikes out against his persecutor, a blow that wins our respect and admiration. Jim may panic and behave foolishly, as when he flees the Welches' party or hides the damaged bedclothes, but when his fundamental humanity is at stake he falls back upon high moral values and does what we see as "the right thing." Beneath the horseplay and high spirits Amis rhetorically manipulates our judgment so that we believe Jim's fundamental moral stance is in keeping with our own.

Although several Amis characters in *Lucky Jim* could be more accurately called caricatures, the author has sketched them with precision and economy, calling upon comic elements both to instruct and to entertain. In the tradition of Smollett and Dickens, Amis gives life to his grotesque figures by emphasizing details of their eccentricity and indicates his attitude towards them by dwelling on specific bodily and facial characteristics. Like Roderick Random or Peregrine Pickle, for example, Professor Welch is clearly a man to be neither admired nor trusted. Although Amis does not label these characters as detestable, the language with which they are described makes that inference inescapable. These fictional miscreants are reminiscent of Dickens's rogues, whose physical deformities are intended to signify their inner corruption. The use of such characterizing details occurs from the first page, when Jim and Professor Welch are strolling through the university grounds, with Welch holding forth about the differences between a flute and a recorder. The contrast between what the professor seems to be (a scholar discussing weighty issues of history) and what he is (a harlequin splitting hairs in an inconsequential and labored discussion of musical instruments) establishes the farcical picture of life which Amis will later elaborate. The reference to a variety act, with Jim portrayed as Welch's unwilling but doggedly resigned sidekick, makes it clear that Welch is not to be taken seriously. Like the Henry Fielding who buttonholes his readers, guiding them through *Tom Jones* or *Joseph Andrews* accompanied by good-natured but nonetheless moral commentary, here Amis takes control of his story through the vehicle of an informed, tongue-in-cheek, almost conspiratorial narrator who tells us the facts but winks knowingly at the same time. And like Fielding, too, Amis is primarily interested in the *moral* nature of his characters as it is revealed against the backdrop of a corrupt social system. In this technique he recalls Thackeray's narrator in *Vanity Fair*, a knowing and moral consciousness who reveals to us, without ever telling us, *exactly* what we should think of Becky Sharp and company – and of the social structure she systematically infiltrates and subsequently dismantles.

The presence of the narrator is important to the humor throughout the novel and serves to heighten the clarity of Amis's characterizations and, concomitantly, his moral stance. The active role of this narrating impresario, with his exaggerations, jokes, and philosophizing, establishes the moral tone but also creates the distance necessary to make us view Jim's exploits with the proper detachment. In *Lucky Jim* such commentary by the narrator invites the reader to stop, step back, consider, judge. This informed, often bemused voice encourages the reader to examine details, to take descriptions of persons and events with a grain of salt. The effect is a subtle irony. When we are told, "No other professor in Great Britain ... set such store by being called Professor," we can't help but be amused even as we see the truth in the narrator's words.

While we are able to see things as Jim sees them – and he is an acute and discerning observer – the narrator's distance from him insures that we view Jim from the narrator's vantage point, a dual relationship that gives the book its moral center. The moral and philosophical interests that suffuse the book are the author's rather than Jim's. Because this sensible storyteller is obviously for the most part good-humored and rather fond of Jim, we are never allowed to take the events so seriously that they become pathetic or tragic. In *Jake's Thing*, however, this attitude will change as indeed Amis's vision darkens.

Succeeding physical description underscores Welch's superficiality and strengthens his role as the archetype of an amoral or at least corrupt social class: we are told that he resembles "an old boxer," "an African savage," "a broken robot." He is violent, uncivilized, inhuman. We see both Welch and his wife, Celia, as eccentric, absent-minded sham artists who engage in *ersatz* intellectual chatter and hide behind a facade of specious culture to preserve their supposed high status. This almost whimsical picture of the real Welch comes via a narrator who not only sees through Jim's eyes but also comments humorously on what he is describing. The comedy arises from the discrepancy between the character's interpretation of his situation and the narrator's (and, consequently, the reader's) perception of it. Jim believes that what is lacking is luck; what we see, through the narrator's gentle proddings, is that Jim's gaffes have more to do with his perverse nature than with misfortune, just as the happy solutions to his problems are based on his positive qualities and decent actions. Welch, on the other hand, believes that he is a conscientious department chairman, while the narrator makes it clear – ("The old man was well known for an incurable evader") – that he is a pompous ass. Welch's pretension is even worse because he is at a redbrick university, not Oxford or Cambridge. Appearance and reality, then, are two very different things, and the narrator's wise moderating helps us discern them for what they are, even if the characters themselves do not.

Amis uses another kind of incongruity to dehumanize his antagonists, so that they are rendered even less sympathetic in our eyes. Welch's state of mind, for example, is characterized by disrupted, disjointed communication. He muddles his way through his sentences, frequently failing to finish them. Hesitations, interruptions and false starts are, of course, incongruous coming from such a supposedly "learned" and cogent source, inappropriate and therefore revealing. Further, we learn that Welch professes to worship "integrated village-type community life" and to oppose anything mechanical. In fact, he is himself a virtual automaton whose behavior at work and in various social settings seems programmed.

One of the funniest scenes in the novel occurs when Welch, an ill-made human machine, mismanages another machine, his automobile. Oftentimes the jerky movements of Welch's car are compared to his conversational habits; the inability to *get* anywhere whether in thought or in deed creates a linkage of the human and the mechanical that is significant in this and later Amis novels. In this case, the union of man and machine jeopardizes Welch's passengers because he allows the course of his conversation to dictate the actual direction of the car. The machine, not the man, predominates. By using such imagery drawn from mechanisms, Amis suggests his characters' lack of humanity, their repetition of programmed motions and emotions. For example, as practiced and imposed by Welch, music, which should be a free-flowing, liberating art form, is instead stifling, and at worst, even dehumanizing. The dissertation on the differences between the flute and the recorder, for instance, pushes the music itself right out of existence. Not only Welch but also his wife exhibits these mechanistic characteristics, and as a result they are reduced to the level of unfeeling objects that take on a malevolent life of their own. The image signifies a person not in control of himself – an impression reinforced, particularly in the later novels, by the comparison of characters to mechanisms or automata.

The professor's son, Bertrand, is a good study in the techniques Amis calls upon to establish his narrative commentary and focus his moral views. Another exponent of the art of fine living whose life is an exemplar of wrong behavior, Bertrand demonstrates his true and uncomplimentary colors through the shallowness of his ideas, through his mode of speech, and his mannerisms. Affectation of accent and vocabulary in Bertrand's comments on painting clearly makes him an object of ridicule rather than admiration. The epitome of affectation, "a refined gracious-liver and arty-rubbish-talker," according to Dixon, Bertrand is, much like his father, "a bore, … the only thing that interests him is him"; he is "a twister and a snob and a bully and a fool…. Touchy and vain, yes, but not sensitive." Even his French name and the silly little beret he wears suggest his assumed status, further indications of the superficiality of the Welches' affectation of continental refinement. The assumption here – and elsewhere in the Amis canon – is that a certain amount of ego, or pride, or selfishness, or a moderate amount of acquisitiveness, is normal in every human being; such foibles are to be expected in less than perfect organisms. Jim, our hero, certainly has his faults. But any human quality taken to extreme becomes absurd; the Welches and the crowd they represent are an absurd lot because of their excesses, not just their weaknesses. Jim's faults make him more human; their extremes dehumanize them in the end.

Amis's physical description of Bertrand adds weight to our judgment of him as fundamentally ridiculous. His beard hangs down further on one side than on the other. His eyes lack "the convexity of the normal eyeball" and resemble "polished glass." His ears are strangely mismatched. Even the effect of his clothes – the "lemon-yellow" coat and "vine-patterned" tie – labels him as purely oddball; what *he* perceives in his style is, of course, avant-garde, and Henry Fielding's comments on the role of vanity and hypocrisy in the comic come quickly to mind. The fact is, Bertrand is a fake, and fakes are boring – like most people in the novel whose favorite topic is their own idiosyncracies.

To add to Amis's indictment of Bertrand, not only is he having an affair with the wife of one of his father's subordinates but he is also courting Christine for the purpose of winning her rich uncle's favor. A person of no scruples or sensibility, he manipulates by flattery, dishonesty – even ruthlessness, as when he warns Jim to stay away from Christine. He compares himself to the rich set because, in his view, they keep the arts going, are charming and generous, appreciate the things he likes, and fill their homes with beautiful *objets d'art*. The irony is that for readers, Bertrand clearly is *not* charming, generous, or rich, and does nothing to help advance the arts.

In the end, the Welches and the boastful, self-deceived pedantry they represent are defeated, so that the comic values of life and humanity are affirmed. The Welches are, in Jim's eyes as in our own, "bloody old fool[s]." Such a wholesale damnation in itself might seem to be only the petulant commentary of an uncharitable young writer, a cheap comic shot at a social class taken by a resentful outsider. In *Lucky Jim*, however, the depiction of a corrupt class serves a calculated narrative purpose; it provides a gauge upon which we may read the author's moral temperature. Amis's approach to traditional culture is to attack its snobbery and exclusivity; none the less, he does not demean society's traditions themselves. He is an iconoclast, not an anarchist.

A further extension of Amis's rather complex moral structure in the novel is a series of evaluative contrasts to affect our judgment of Margaret Peel and Christine Callaghan. Margaret is everything Jim does not want in a woman: unattractive, predictable, tedious and neurotic. Jim, though caught in her tricks until quite late in the novel, does observe early on that she is like an actress planning her effects. We learn that she feigns sexual avidity to entice, then denounce Jim; that she shows no sympathy when he is in trouble with the Welches and uses her knowledge of his plight to coerce him; and that she exploits him by manipulating him into paying for everything when they go out, even though he cannot afford it and she can. Jim's amiability and insecurity make him vulnerable to the likes of Margaret, whose bad qualities contrast sharply with his own basically good ones; he is "drawn into the Margaret business," the narrator observes, "by a combination of virtues he hadn't known he'd possessed: politeness, friendly interest, ordinary concern, a good-natured willingness to be imposed upon, a desire for unequivocal friendship." The neurotic spinster has none of these qualities, and a good many worse ones.

Margaret's moral opposite is Christine Callaghan – a picture of serious health. In Christine there is indeed much more to like, both physically and emotionally, than there will ever be in Margaret. She is attractive: "Christine's aim, he imagined, had been to show off the emphasis of her natural coloring and skin texture. The result was painfully successful, making everybody else look like an assemblage of granulated half tones." She is also clear-headed and stable, and that stability serves to contrast her with the grotesque and quixotic characters of the Welch world. Her natural good sense and keen intuition allow her to see Jim's struggle against that world, further validation of the rightness of his moral stance, and she allies herself with it. She helps him camouflage the burns in the Welch's bedclothes, for example, and she laughs as they share this joke played on Celia. Jim finds her intoxicatingly refreshing because she is free of phoniness, and he falls almost immediately in love with her. Christine quickly comes to represent the goal of respectability towards which Jim eventually strives, and as a result she helps Jim define his identity. The two share a view of the world – one that Amis, through his reward of them and his condemnation of the Welches, clearly wants us to accept.

Any discussion of *Lucky Jim* inevitably brings us to the novel's climax: the comic Merrie Olde England speech. Aided by a number of stiff drinks and sporting a black eye from his fight with Bertrand, Jim turns the lecture, planned as an encomium to Welch's accomplishments, into a condemnation of them. In a hilarious dismantling of all that infuriates Jim about his superior, he finds himself imitating Welch's "preludial blaring sound" and inserting into his address a number of Welch's speech idiosyncracies and tag lines – "you see," "as you might call it," "integration of the social consciousness." He tries to gain control of himself, but again parodies Welch as he trips up on one or two phrases, hesitates and repeats words, even loses his place and seems to have forgotten how to speak normally.

None of this behavior is lost on the audience, whose murmurs and restlessness grows as Jim loses control. "What's the matter with you, Dixon?" Welch hisses. "Sorry, sir," Jim says, "bit nervous ... all right in a minute." But the absurdity builds as he is overcome by sadness (at the thought of losing Christine), then by horror (at the thought of what he feels about Margaret), then by anger and fear (as he thinks of Bertrand, Mrs Welch, Welch, the principal, the registrar, the college council, the college).

Noting that Christine, the only one he cares about, has left the room, he decides that if this is to be his last public appearance, he would do "some good, however small, to some of those present, however few." Finally speaking for himself, he attacks Welch's values directly with tones of "a sarcastic, wounding bitterness." He punctuates his discourse with "smothered snorts of derision" and spits out syllables "like curses." Then he concludes: "The point about Merrie England is that it was about the most un-Merrie period in our history." Jim has fired his final salvos, debunking the historian's greatest myth of all. He falls into a stupor, overcome by "the heat, the drink, the nervousness, the guilt." The next day he receives word that he will be fired.

But the disaster is short-lived, for Jim's luck has turned, at a crucial moment; the old song, "Oh, lucky Jim/How I envy him" is appropriate indeed. With Dixon's winning Christine, the novel ends on a note of celebration – an appropriate ending because it is clear from the beginning that, in the eighteenth-century tradition, this is a comic novel that depends upon unrealistic exaggeration. Many of the incidents are overt parodies of what university life is supposed to be like, with people who are grotesquely unrepresentative of those who teach and learn in such places. Jim does not object to the academic system; he just does not like some facets of that system. We laugh at Jim as he blunders along in error, but rejoice in his charity and dignity when he celebrates his new opportunity. And this comic spirit, which is founded on the rejection of one society and the joining of a new one, is carried through to the final page, where Jim has won the girl and the Welch family appears. He notices that they have one another's hats on: "Dixon drew in breath to denounce them both, then blew it all out again in a howl of laughter." Jim has finally come to terms with his persecutors; no longer must he remain on outwardly cordial terms with them in order to keep his job. More important, the scene points to Jim's moral growth. Instead of flinging himself against them through denunciation, he chooses here to let go of that resentment and respond to them in a more appropriate fashion; instead of berating these pathetic and absurd people, he laughs at them. He has known all along that they are ridiculous; forced to submit, he chafes at that necessity and gets a little raw as a result. When he is freed from their control, he can give up some of his own nastiness.

Jim Dixon's adventures allow us to indulge our own compulsion to break free from well-ordered, sensible lives. We can revel vicariously in his haphazard and improbable experiences. For all the buffoonery, self-indulgence and self-interest in Amis's first published novel, Jim emerges fundamentally, if vaguely, decent, one of the "nice" rather than the "nasty" people between whom he is careful to discriminate. He deserves to survive.

But Jim is not magically transformed into a rich and idle young man as the conventional Cinderella formula has it. His final success is modest. He has won Christine, that is true, but his job offers a salary of only 500 pounds sterling, the same amount he would receive with – and without the security of – tenure. Although the odds are better, once again he is taking a risk. But if his past experiences are any sign, that is exactly what he must do to succeed. You make your own luck, it seems, through kindness, decency, and good humor in the face of great distress.

The imaginative core of the novel, then, is not the fact that Jim rebels or that he wins, but in the *way* he rebels and wins. The ending is a satisfying conclusion to all of the comic injustices that have gone on before. This happy ending is not contrived; it comes about naturally and can be explained in part as a convention of the novel, in part as the protagonist's wish-fulfillment, in part as his final nose-thumbing at the spiteful and the malicious people whom Amis brings to life. The ending is based on the affirmation of a moral order, and as such it is both acceptable and laudable to us. In dealing with those others so successfully, Jim wins both our hearts and our sanction.

What is most memorable about *Lucky Jim* is the comic moments. Most of the time, Jim is not an angry young man. Rather, he is a funny, bumbling, confused young man for whom a joke makes life bearable. Jim is reasonably confident in his world, secure in his relationship with it, made self-reliant by a sanity-preserving sense of humor. His story is a fairy tale – and Jim is the Cinderella rescued from the tyranny of the ugly and the mean-spirited.

***

"Ugly" and "mean-spirited" clearly apply to the hero's perspective on academe and life generally in another of Amis's novels, *Jake's Thing*, published twenty-five years later. Jake Richardson *is* an angry man who holds a grudge against the world, a world of change and instability that is reflected on a personal level in his impotence – that is, an inability to control even something so personal as his own "thing." In the past that "thing" has been both active and reliable; Jake boasts of having "more than a hundred affairs" and is currently involved with his third wife, Brenda, with whom he attends various humiliating and on the surface silly therapies in order to reactivate his flagging libido. But much more is going on with Jake than his loss of sexual control; the society in which he lives, the London and the Oxford of 1978, has also moved, subtly but surely, out of his range of understanding and/or desire, and Jake has responded by becoming bitter and cynical. Neither his career nor his other activities stimulate much interest in this 59-year-old Oxford don, so that his social, professional and emotional desires have become as stultified as his sexual ones.

Perhaps it is not coincidental that Jake's impotence comes at a time when Comyns College is debating the question of admitting women to its hallowed, previously all-male inhabited, halls. Jake, who is fighting for his psychic life on several fronts, inadvertently exposes his deep hostility to the project during a college meeting, where his colleagues had expected him to "speak for the ladies." Confronted by a personal and cultural sexual revolution, faced with the loss of his wife to a man he despises, surrounded by a society whose basic make-up has turned foreign and threatening, Jake is the male chauvinist as victim. At the end of his travail, and after nearly three hundred pages of unrelenting exposure to the incompetence and stupidity of professional therapists and the institutions that sustain them, Jake's desire for sex is gone, his dislike for women has intensified, and he decides that he would just as soon remain impotent. Offered a physical cure on the last page of the novel, he looks back on all the women he has known – "their never listening and lots of other things like that" – and decides, "No thanks." On that note the novel ends.

Despite the twenty-five years that have lapsed between the two novels, certain likenesses are apparent. Both Jim Dixon and Jake Richardson are academic misfits who like to drink, have a keen eye for hypocrites and phoneys, write articles that bore even themselves (Jake's are about early settlers in Asia Minor), cope with ferocious inner monologues on their own prejudices and irrational likes and dislikes, have rollicking senses of fun, play practical jokes, enjoy puns and wordplay, and talk a lot to themselves in voices that parody types they have encountered in books, television, movies, the army and academe. Both characters also suffer from the undesired attentions of a neurotic woman who stages a fake suicide attempt. And both characters manage to reconcile what Keith Wilson calls "inner thoughts and outer statements"[4] in a public denunciation of a cause, delivered while they are drunk.

Many of the comic set pieces in *Jake's Thing* are reminiscent of some of the classic scenes in *Lucky Jim* in that they serve to set the protagonist's role as an outsider to the contemporary world. That alienation often serves to parody the protagonist himself. Early in the story, for example, Jake treats himself to an expensive bottle of claret. He brings it home and finds his wife entertaining a friend whom he loathes, but etiquette forces him against his will to offer to share the wine. To avoid actually giving her any of it, he takes the bottle into the kitchen where he frantically drains a bottle of cheap "Tunisian red," pours the claret into the empty bottle, and fills the fancy bottle with the cheap wine. The loathsome friend enters the kitchen as this operation is being concluded, spots the "Tunisian red" bottle and insists that the cheap wine is good enough for her, thus defeating his scheme. Like Jim Dixon, Jake is caught in a snare of his own devising; his readiness to do battle with his foes and his gift for running into squabbles, fights and embarrassments increases the chaos in a life that is already frustratingly out of control.

Those frustrations are many, as they were for Jim, and signify the social and cultural impotence Jake feels. The world around him is no longer to his liking, and everyday incidents painfully amplify that effect. His Harley Street

---

[4] Keith Wilson, "Jim, Jake and the Years Between," from *Kingsley Amis, In Life and Letters,* Ed. Dale Salwak (Basingstoke: Macmillan, 1990; New York: St. Martin's Press, 1991), p. 77.

doctor shortens a consultation so that he can see another patient, not coincidentally an Arab sheikh. Jake cannot take a taxi because "no sooner had one black, brown or yellow person, or group of such, been set down on the pavement than Americans, Germans, Spaniards were taken up and vice versa." He has trouble making his way through London traffic. He is charged an insultingly high train fare to Oxford. English place names have been changed and are now unfamiliar to him. The telephone fails to work. On another occasion he makes a purchase at a liquor store, expecting to benefit from a discount, but the one item he wants – chocolates – is omitted from the parcel. Jake is no longer at home on his own turf, and that sense of foreignness compels him to withdraw further and further from the contemporary world. Jim's problems with his department chairman, with some of his students, and with a potential publisher for his essay on shipbuilding techniques are, of course, similar sources of frustration and outward signs that he is a man out of sync, immersed in the wrong culture for his personality.

Also, as in *Lucky Jim,* one of the great sources of entertainment in this novel is Amis's parody of posturing fools – in this case quack sexologists and fake psychologists. As part of his treatment Jake is ordered to plug himself into a "nocturnal mensurator" designed to register and record signs of arousal during his sleep. He is also told to buy and study "pictorial pornographic material" and write out a sexual fantasy of his own imagining in no fewer than 600 words; he comes up 73 words short, despite much padding. He and Brenda engage in sessions of "non-genital sensate focusing" and embarrassing group workshops. Jake even allows himself to be tested, his trousers down, before a group of attentive medical students. When Brenda asks Jake what's wrong with the workshop, his response reinforces the connection between his sexual dysfunction and the "dysfunction" he believes has overtaken his society: "*Wrong* with it? If there's one word that sums up everything that's gone wrong since the war, it's 'Workshop.'" Like Jim's parody of Professor Welch, his wife Celia and his son Bertrand, Jake's view points to the essential phoniness of these so-called experts who are testing him. These experts could not exist, of course, were not society itself "sick" enough to allow their rise to influence.

In spite of the resemblances between the two novels, however, there is in fact a great conceptual jump from one to the other. Suffering from a general weariness of which his loss of libido is but one indication, Jake has definite feelings about the modern world: he doesn't like it. There is no equivocation, no attempt to be "fair," to look at things from other angles as Jim was inclined to do. Here, the world is going from bad to worse, changes that infuriate and baffle Jake. At one point he sees "the world in its true light, as a place where nothing had ever been any good and nothing of significance done." Included on his list of personal dislikes are airplanes, American tourists, psychologists, the working-class, the young, strangers, sloppy language, wealthy Arabs, cocky youngsters, advertisements, telephones, architecture, cuisine – in other words, all facets of present-day England. Above all, he discovers that he despises women because "they don't mean what they say ... they take all disagreement as opposition" and are concerned only with the "surface of things." These days sex and romance are a chore to him; even his lectures and research have become perfunctory. Other than doing as little work as possible and watching television, his only real pleasure is in finding his expectations of dirt, decay, inefficiency, and boring and stupid behavior fulfilled.

The inner and outer tirades are increasingly vituperative. Jake's seething narration, his scathing internal commentary and his sometimes vicious dialogue are instrumental in creating the universe of misogyny, prejudice and dissatisfaction. By viewing Jake both in his own mind and in relation to others, we come to see him as he really is: a man with a mind that is prejudicial, set wrong.

While *Lucky Jim* ends with what Keith Wilson calls "a triumphant opening up" to Jim of a new life, a new world, *Jake's Thing* ends with "a jaded closing down, a closeted spurning of the world"[5] for which Jake feels at best indifferent – a retreat into TV dinners and TV movies. By the end of the novel he has arrived at a stage of rejecting everything. Evidence points to a deepening misanthropy in Jake as he anguishes over his spiritual isolation, vainly attempts to recover his interest in sex, and learns to come to terms with impotence and acedia, the deathlike condition of not caring. In the end we see in Jake a gesture of impotence, puzzlement, anger, and eventual retreat from the contemporary world. All of this gives to the novel an overall mood of defeat and confusion far removed from the light comedy so much in evidence in *Lucky Jim*.

---

[5] Wilson, p. 78.

"WOMEN AND WIVES MUSTN'T GO NEAR IT": ACADEMIA, LANGUAGE AND GENDER IN THE NOVELS OF ALISON LURIE[1]

Susan Watkins

In her introduction to the only monograph on the work of Alison Lurie, Judie Newman describes the critical consensus about her writing as follows: "Lurie writes comedies about the three M's – marriage, the middle classes and morality."[2] Her fiction is therefore commonly linked with the English and Anglo-American nineteenth-century realist tradition, with novelists like Jane Austen and Henry James, who write about the manners and mores of confined upper-middle class social spheres. Horst Kruse (1993), for example, sets her work firmly in the context of the "novel of manners" and notes the similarities between her writing and James's.[3] John Stark suggests that "her territory resembles Austen's" in its narrow social range and use of satire.[4]

Generally, then, Lurie's work is perceived to be unaffected by the scepticism about the relationship between the textual and the material that characterises

---

[1] Previously published in *Revista Canaria de Estudios Ingleses 48* (April 2004), pp. 29-46; online at http://webpages.ull.es/users/rceing/
(I would like to thank Mary Eagleton for her detailed comments on an earlier version of this article. It was also given as a paper in the Autumn 2002 Cultural Studies Seminar Series at Leeds Metropolitan University where it provoked extremely helpful comments from Louise Jackson, Tom Herron, Jago Morrison and Christine Bousfield.)
[2] Judie Newman, *Alison Lurie: A Critical Study* (Amsterdam: Rodopi, 2000), p. 26.
[3] Horst Kruse, "Museums and Manners: The Novels of Alison Lurie" (*Anglia: Zeitschrift für Englische Philologie, 3-4*, 1993), p. 411.
[4] John Stark, "Alison Lurie's Career" (*The Hollins Critic, 26*, 1989), p. 2.

much of the fiction and philosophy of the later twentieth century. If present at all, consciousness of debate about this relationship seems to be generated merely by the fact that her work is set in academic contexts where the characters *discuss* these issues. In other words, what might broadly be termed poststructuralist insights (about the materiality of language and the textuality of the "real world") appear to impact only at the most superficial level, as a consequence of the fact that Lurie is a "campus novelist" or practitioner of "academic" fiction. Newman argues that Lurie's work is also frequently interpreted as that of "a campus novelist working within a narrow palette and a restricted range of character types."[5]   Therefore, it might seem inevitable that, like many other writers of university fiction, for example David Lodge and Malcolm Bradbury, Lurie incorporates aspects of current literary theoretical/philosophical debate.   For a Professor of English at Cornell, a "stronghold of structuralism and deconstruction,"[6] this is hardly surprising.   However, some have seen the interpolation of "theory" in this genre as an attempt to dress straightforward realism in borrowed clothes. Discussing David Lodge, Tom Shone writes:

> Lodge has spent most of it [his career] putting off having to choose between two mutually exclusive modes of writing: safe but dull English realism and exciting but dangerous post-modern experimentation. His gloriously muddle-browed solution was the campus novel: in which, if you don't have any of your post-modern experimentation as such, you still ship in characters who can talk

---

[5] Newman, *Alison Lurie: A Critical Study* (2000), p. 26 [Ed.].
[6] Malcolm Bradbury, "The Paleface Professor" (*The Times*, 19 January 1985), p. 6.

about maybe one day getting down to a spot of post-modern experimentation, all things permitting, perhaps.[7]

Whether or not this is fair to Lodge, whose work does contain some characteristically postmodern elements, I want to argue that Lurie's fiction certainly does ask searching questions about the "discursivity" or "textuality" of the world around us. Her fiction engages seriously with developments in philosophy and literary theory that can broadly be termed poststructuralist: Lurie is interested in the way that language appears to operate in terms of stable governing oppositions but always finally eludes fixed meanings. Her fiction establishes hierarchies of meaning only to invert, exceed or destabilise them. Her novels demonstrate the insights that language always *mediates* our perceptions and experiences and that power is controlled and wielded discursively.

Discussing her book *The Language of Clothes* Lurie commented:

> The idea is the language of clothes: it will explain to you what your clothes mean. It's based on the premise that we are speaking to each other continually through what we wear and how our hair is done ... As many people have pointed out before, clothing is a language. Well, if it is a language it must have a vocabulary and a grammar and the rules that apply to a language may apply to it.[8]

Lurie's understanding of clothing as a language clearly suggests that it can be interpreted and read like a spoken

---

[7] Tom Shone, "Textual Intercourse" (*The Modern Review*, October-November, 1992), p. 6.
[8] David Jackson, "An Interview with Alison Lurie" (*Shenandoah: The Washington and Lee University Review*, 31, 1980), pp. 20-1.

or written text. In other words, Lurie understands clothing *discursively*, as a sign system that operates according to certain linguistic or "textual" practices. Newman also notes Lurie's interest in the interaction between art and life. She comments on her use of intertextuality and suggests that "her readers gain a sense of real life as being structured according to patterns familiar from literary culture, just as literary culture may be structured according to patterns from real life."[9]

In addition, however, I argue that, whereas most male writers of university fiction play with poststructuralist ideas to some degree, Lurie's texts interrogate these issues from a specifically gendered perspective. Throughout her fiction, it is her interest in the point of view of women characters, often contrasted to great effect with those of their academic male partners or other significant male characters, which allows her to compare clearly the different ways in which language and power intersect for men and women. Her texts foreground but also question the gendered assumptions that provide the basis for poststructuralist theories of language. In this respect some of the work of Hélène Cixous and Luce Irigaray, which I have elsewhere characterised under the umbrella term "poststructuralist feminism,"[10] offers an analysis of femininity and its relation to language and power that resembles Lurie's fictional exploration of women's position in academia.

My analysis will be confined to three of Lurie's novels: *Love and Friendship* (1962), *The War Between the Tates* (1974), and *Foreign Affairs* (1984) This choice is the consequence of a number of factors: first, *Love and Friendship* and *The War Between the Tates* are campus novels whose action is

---

[9] Newman, *Alison Lurie: A Critical Study* (2000), p. 6 [Ed.].

[10] Susan Watkins, *Twentieth-Century Women Novelists: Feminist Theory into Practice* (Basingstoke: Palgrave, 2001), pp. 96-121.

explicitly centred on the world of academia; second, although a number of Lurie's novels concern academics placed in unfamiliar and alternative settings (*Nowhere City* [1965], *Imaginary Friends* [1967] and *Foreign Affairs*), *Foreign Affairs* retains the strongest connection with the world of academia through its device of having the central characters on sabbatical, researching in the UK. In addition, these three novels were published in the 1960s, 1970s and 1980s respectively, providing an interesting overview of Lurie's development as a writer, and allowing comparison of the impact on her work of three crucial decades of twentieth-century American history. Despite a clear focus on class, age and nationality respectively, the three novels here examined all share a common emphasis on gender as a key discourse in the construction of subjectivity and access to power. Lurie's texts represent the world of academia as a Lacanian symbolic order from which women are excluded as other or admitted only on the same terms as men. However, in each novel serious challenges to this "double-bind" take place. I argue that these challenges strikingly resemble, in both their risks and their rewards, the interventions made by poststructuralist feminist writers such as Cixous and Irigaray.

That's just the way she talks?

Lurie's novels demonstrate that differences of gender, class, age and nationality are mediated in language, or discursively produced. In her first, *Love and Friendship*, it is class differences that are initially most apparent. The heroine, Emily Stockwell Turner, has married "beneath" her. Independently wealthy, privately educated, and privileged in every sense apart from her gender, Emily has, in the opinion of her socially inferior husband, Holman, acquired a "finishing school" voice. He has persuaded her to avoid certain expressions, but admits "he could do nothing about the tone."[11] Lurie cleverly suggests the impact of Emmy's superior class position through the way the niceties of her particular linguistic habits affect her relationship with her husband and others around her. Lucy Green, a peripheral character struggling to exist on her husband's junior academic salary, resents Emmy's wealth and class and the advantages these can buy. This resentment is expressed in the form of critical comments about Emmy's "stage English" accent and her expensive Saks Fifth Avenue coat.[12] Lucy "reads" the language of Emmy's clothes in the most basic way, by assessing their price, and she also interprets Emmy's accent as indicative of her privileged background and patronising personality. Her husband Charley, however, resists the idea that language can be interpreted at all by saying "that's just the way she talks."[13]

In *The War Between the Tates* language differences between the characters are less a consequence of class than of age. Erica Tate finds that her children no longer speak her language; indeed they often refuse to communicate with her at all. The opening scene of the novel shows her teenage son and daughter ignoring her remark about the beginning of Spring. Wendy Gahaghan, the graduate student with whom her husband Brian is having an affair, is defined by the language of seventies "alternative" youth culture. When discussing Brian's book on American foreign policy with Erica, Wendy remarks:

"... if The Book is published in time, and the right people in Washington read it, it's going to really zap them. And that could have a fantastic effect, you know? Like once they realise what

---

[11] Alison Lurie, *Love and Friendship* (1962; London: Abacus, 1993), p. 12.
[12] Lurie, *Love and Friendship*, p. 132 [Ed.].

happened before, they could reverse their strategy, and stop trashing the rest of the world."[14]

Wendy's discourse is cleverly juxtaposed with that of the "people in Washington". The linguistic "age gap" in the novel is made concrete by the contrast between the university and the Krishna bookshop, where the book titles represent to Brian the recurrence of "lies, superstition, fear."[15] In contrast, Brian relies on rationality, logic and sequential rather than lateral thinking and argument.

In *Foreign Affairs* Lurie's focus shifts to the linguistic differences between American and English cultures. Her two central characters, Vinnie Miner and Fred Turner, whose intersected narratives occupy the novel, are American academics on sabbatical in London. Vinnie, the Anglophile relishing the chance to spend time in England, encounters Chuck Mumpson, a florid middle-American sanitary engineer who dresses like a cowboy, on the plane. "Misled by her New England accent and academic intonation" he (flatteringly in Vinnie's estimation) thinks she is English.[16] This initial linguistic misjudgement, reluctantly corrected by Vinnie, prompts the conversation that begins their subsequent relationship. Vinnie's judgements of Chuck are based similarly on language use: hailed in Fortnums by "a much less refined, – in fact, blaringly mid-American" voice,[17] Vinnie terms Chuck "a person without inner resources who splits infinitives."[18]

---

13 Lurie, *Love and Friendship*, p. 132 [Ed.].
14 Alison Lurie, *The War Between the Tates* (1974; London: Abacus, 1993), p. 107.
15 Lurie, *The War Between the Tates*, p. 92 [Ed.].
16 Alison Lurie, *Foreign Affairs* (1984; London: Abacus, 1993), p.17.
17 Lurie, *Foreign Affairs*, p. 65 [Ed.].
18 Lurie, *Foreign Affairs*, p. 68 [Ed.].

Clearly, the contrast between these two characters is established initially in terms of their superficial judgements about national characteristics as perceived in language: Chuck thinks Vinnie is typically English and she thinks he is typically American. It is not surprising that such judgements have to be reassessed as the novel progresses.

The other plot in the novel, concerning Fred Turner and his relationship with Lady Rosemary Radley, a television actress, confirms more conventional English and American stereotypes. Lady Rosemary's typically English appearance, television roles, and linguistic tics such as extravagant compliments and tinkling laughter are contrasted with Fred Turner's stolid American sincerity, reliability and straightforwardness, epitomised by the phrase "brave handsome yankee lad,"[19] which a doctor used to describe him as a boy. Fred's opinion of England and London fluctuates, although at bottom it can be summarised in his comparison of the game of charades as it is played in England and America. The American version "rewards speed and individual achievement, and encourages frantic attempts to communicate with compatriots who literally or metaphorically don't speak your language"; the traditional English version "combines verbal ingenuity, in-group loyalty and co-operation, love of elaborate public performance, and private childishness."[20] What alters in the novel is Fred's relative estimation of these sets of qualities.

In these three novels, then, the most immediate way of identifying language differences shifts from class, to age, to nationality. This development constructs a particular version of the *Zeitgeist* of the specific decades in which the novels were written and published. Malcolm Bradbury remarks of her novels that they "collectively form a biting

[19] Lurie, *Foreign Affairs*, p. 28 [Ed.].
[20] Lurie, *Foreign Affairs*, p. 93 [Ed.].

record of American social, moral and sexual mores from the early 1960s ... to the present."[21] One obvious gap or absence is the issue of race, which suggests the ways in which the white and middle-class world represented in her texts has traditionally perceived itself as racially "unmarked". However, it can be clearly established that gender difference remains the most consistent factor in all three novels' discussion of the relationship between language and power. The academic world represents, for Lurie, what might be understood in Lacanian terms as a "symbolic order", which is hierarchical, competitive and most obviously patriarchal: "It is in the *name of the father* that we must recognize the support of the symbolic function which, from the dawn of history, has identified his person with the figure of the law."[22]

Essential exclusion

For Lacan, entering into the symbolic order is a necessity for the acquisition of subjectivity, language and the creation of desire.

> No one is supposed to be ignorant of the law; this somewhat humorous formula taken direct from our Code of Justice nevertheless expresses the truth in which our experience is grounded, and which our experience confirms. No man is actually ignorant of it, since the law of man has been the law of language since the first words of recognition presided over the first gifts.[23]

---

[21] Bradbury, p. 6 [Ed.].
[22] Jacques Lacan, *Écrits: A Selection*, Trans. Alan Sheridan (London: Tavistock/Routledge, 1977), p. 67.
[23] Lacan, p. 61 [Ed.].

"Women and Wives Musn't Go Near It"

Women do enter the symbolic order, but they do so only by losing their *difference* from men. In poststructuralist feminist terms women's difference is excluded from the symbolic order because their otherness is essential to its maintenance: in other words, the rejection of the (m)other is what allows the subject to assume his privileged place in the symbolic. As Cixous suggests: "writing has been run by a libidinal and cultural – hence political, typically masculine – economy ... this locus has grossly exaggerated all the signs of sexual opposition (and not sexual difference), where woman has never *her* turn to speak."[24]

What could be termed woman's "essential exclusion"[25] is most apparent in academia in its specialist language. As Newman suggests, *Love and Friendship* "emphasizes the mythic substructures and archaic practices of the academic community, and by extension of society at large."[26] This is most apparent in Emmy's battle to understand the Humanities course that her husband teaches. John Stark, writing about this aspect of the novel, comments:

> The third perspective on the action, a humanities course required of
> all freshman [sic] does not quite come off. It has something to do
> with dissolving preconceptions and forcing students to construct
> their own ethics, but its goals, and their relations to the novel's plots
> and themes, never become totally clear.[27]

---

[24] Hélène Cixous, "The Laugh Of The Medusa," from *New French Feminisms: An Anthology*, Ed. Elaine Marks and Isabelle De Courtivron (Hemel Hempstead: Harvester Wheatsheaf, 1981), p. 249.
[25] Watkins, p. 99 [Ed.].
[26] Newman, *Alison Lurie: A Critical Study* (2000), p. 36 [Ed.].
[27] Stark, p. 3 [Ed.].

I would argue that the Hum C course is clearly at the centre of the novel. When explained to the reader, it is described as "a course in semantics based on positivist and operationalist principles." However, the narrator makes clear that the methods used when teaching the course are intended to obscure in order to distinguish and exclude. The Socratic method is termed "mean"; no one is allowed to tell students the basic principles of the course: "it was believed that the students had to learn the truth themselves in terms of their own experience."[28] Freshmen are "compelled" to take it; instructors "compelled" to teach it; their academic futures depending on "how quickly they caught on." Holman Turner enjoys teaching the course because it allows him to ask the questions instead of answering them. However, he is unable to discover the power politics operating around the Hum C course and the Literature division in which he works, which is indicative of the fact that the obfuscation operates at all levels. At a low point in the hierarchy himself, he takes the weekly Hum C assignments home for Emmy, thus reassuring himself that he is at least on the inside of the symbolic order with the possibility of progression, even if he is currently rather insignificant in it. Emmy is not, as Holman thinks, unable to understand the abstract ideas in the assignment, but instead *unwilling* to do so. She is reluctant to accept that all that the course consists of is a "stupid word game."[29] Holman's definitions of femininity are reassured by the experience of teaching Emmy the Hum C course:

---

28 Lurie, *Love and Friendship*, p. 14 [Ed.].
29 Lurie, *Love and Friendship*, p. 16 [Ed.].

"Women and Wives Musn't Go Near It"

She would always want to see every idea from an emotional point of
view, if possible, as an emotion; the class of things that had no
connection with feeling did not interest her. He did not mind -
women should be that way.[30]

Emmy's exclusion from the academic world is also
made apparent when she tries unsuccessfully to interfere
in it. When a colleague of Holman's, whose wife is a friend
of Emmy's, is in danger of losing his position, Emmy
decides to ask her father, a college trustee, to intervene.
She asks him to have a quiet word with the relevant
person. Emmy is here using her class privileges to try and
affect events. What she has not realized is that gender is in
this instance a more important factor. Her father replies:
"Convers College can take care of itself" and later "I let
Charley King [the College president] run his business and
he lets me run mine."[31] It is impossible for her father to
intervene in college power politics for merely personal
reasons. Emmy has failed to understand the point that it is
crucial to the operation of the symbolic order that
femininity be excluded from it. This is apparent to the
reader when Emmy resists Holman's attempt to prevent
her from speaking to her father:

"You want me to leave Convers alone, even if the Fenns' life is
ruined, because it all belongs to you, and women and wives mustn't
go near it, or know anything about it, they must just stay in their
place outside."[32]

---

[30] Lurie, *Love and Friendship*, p. 49 [Ed.].
[31] Lurie, *Love and Friendship*, p. 98 [Ed.].
[32] Lurie, *Love and Friendship*, p. 91 [Ed.].

Emmy learns by bitter experience the truth and wider application of these remarks: even her father will not contravene this unwritten rule. Provoked by her incapacity to affect the world of academia, Emmy embarks on an affair. Clearly because she has no power to act as a woman within the symbolic order or public sphere she determines instead to act within the private sphere of emotion assigned to her. The affair thus provides the illusion of the power to act subversively when in fact it does little more than confirm Emmy's position in the domestic and personal realm.

In *The War Between the Tates* Lurie focuses more closely on the ways in which the symbolic order functions and maintains itself at particular historical moments. She considers the question of the value and purpose of domestic labour, demonstrating that by operating in the domestic, feminised environment women actually maintain the fabric of the public sphere.[33] She traces Brian's views about different "spheres of operation" for men and women back to nineteenth-century discourses about the sanctity of the feminised private sphere and its "angel in the house,"[34] which were derived, as Barrett argues, from distinctions between work in and outside the home that developed much earlier alongside capitalism and industrialisation.[35] She also echoes the influential work of Betty Friedan in her demonstration of how these ideologies were being recapitulated in mid-twentieth-

---

[33] See the chapters in the section entitled "Towards Marxist Feminism" in Roberta Hamilton and Michele Barrett, *The Politics of Diversity: Feminism, Marxism and Nationalism* (London: Verso, 1986), which all consider the domestic labour debate.

[34] See Coventry Patmore's 1854-62 poem of the same name.

[35] Michele Barrett, *Women's Oppression Today: The Marxist Feminist Encounter*, Rev. Ed. (London: Verso, 1988), pp. 176-86.

century US culture.[36] Brian Tate believes in "the doctrine of separate spheres, both in national and domestic matters ... he would not question her [Erica's] management of the home, nor would she ever try to intervene in his professional life."[37] As in *Love and Friendship* Brian resists Erica's involvement with the university. He discourages her from accepting a part-time research post by invoking the "honorific or divine title" of "The Children" and Erica's responsibilities to them.[38] Throughout the novel we see examples of the language of warfare between opposing "sides" or "areas" used to explain the way that Brian and Erica think of their relationship. To choose only the most striking examples, at one point their sex life is described in terms of Brian's "invasion" and "occupation" of Erica, with the occasional "victory" for Erica when "she was able to hold back the invading troops for so long that ... they discharged all their artillery at the frontier."[39] Elsewhere in the novel Brian draws an explicit and lengthy parallel between events in his own house and the Vietnam War.[40] Judie Newman has discussed the interpenetration in the novel of the marital conflict between Brian and Erica and the Vietnam War.[41] Although such language is most frequently associated with Brian it is obvious that these warlike figures of speech have "rubbed off" on Erica. When Brian tells Erica that Wendy is not her concern she

---

[36] See Watkins, pp. 31-54, for a consideration of *The War Between the Tates* in relation to Friedan's work.
[37] Lurie, *The War Between the Tates*, p. 5 [Ed.].
[38] Lurie, *The War Between the Tates*, p. 63 [Ed.].
[39] Lurie, *The War Between the Tates*, p. 57 [Ed.].
[40] Lurie, *The War Between the Tates*, pp. 78-80 [Ed.].
[41] Judie Newman, "Sexual and Civil Conflicts: *The War Between The Tates*," from *University Fiction*, Ed. David Bevan (Amsterdam: Rodopi, 1990), pp. 103-23, and Newman, *Alison Lurie: A Critical Study*, 2000.

replies: "'I don't agree that it's not my concern.... That's what the 'Good Germans' said.'"[42]

The logic of the same

In *Foreign Affairs*, the heroine is no longer the wife of an academic but an academic herself. This is obviously an extremely significant development. Professor Vinnie Miner appears to be the first of Lurie's heroines who is not excluded from academia. However, this assertion has to be qualified. As the narrator tells us:

> the truth is that children's literature is a poor relation in her department ... a step-daughter grudgingly tolerated because, as in the old tales, her words are glittering jewels of a sort that attract large, if not equally brilliant masses of undergraduates. Within the departmental family she sits in the chimney-corner, while her idle, ugly siblings dine at the chairman's table.[43]

Vinnie is the Cinderella of her department. This is an appropriate metaphor for her specialism's lack of prestige, which arises from its association with women and children. In contrast, Fred's specialism is an advantage, because, as we are told "good candidates are scarce" in eighteenth-century literature.[44] Fred's particular interest in the work of John Gay is also associated with patriarchal power. At one point he wonders if he could be compared with Macheath in *The Beggar's Opera*, who seduces and then deserts both his wife and mistress, but is finally saved

---

[42] Lurie, *The War Between the Tates*, p. 141 [Ed.].
[43] Lurie, *Foreign Affairs*, p. 4 [Ed.].
[44] Lurie, *Foreign Affairs*, p. 61 [Ed.].

by a happy ending.[45] The "poor relation" metaphor for children's literature also suggests the elderly spinster of Jane Austen's novels who must be tolerated and endured and who never marries the handsome hero. Indeed, Vinnie's academic career is seen to be, to some degree, a compensatory one. Unattractive and unloved, Vinnie dreams of academic recognition in place of romance:

> It annoys Vinnie that she is enough a woman of her generation to be rather ashamed of these imaginings when fully awake.... But Vinnie has been brought up to believe that though a man may work for wealth or fame, a woman must labor for love – if not that of a husband or children, at least that of a profession.[46]

Vinnie's career must be a vocation if she has one at all. In these ways Lurie implies that Vinnie is only a part of academia on sufferance or as a substitite for more conventionally feminine pursuits.

Lurie's analysis of Vinnie's position suggests, therefore, that women have to occupy the symbolic order in ways that are patriarchally defined. In other words, if repudiation of the feminised "other" maintains the symbolic, women have to become the "same" as men to occupy the symbolic order at all. Her thinking here echoes Luce Irigaray's analysis of the "logic of the same." By positioning woman as the inferior copy or opposite of man she is actually constructed in the same terms: the same because always centred on the presence or absence of the phallus: "Listen: all round us, men and women sound just the same. The same discussions, the same arguments, the

---

[45] Lurie, *Foreign Affairs*, p. 256 [Ed.].
[46] Lurie, *Foreign Affairs*, p. 111 [Ed.].

same scenes. The same attractions and separations. The same difficulties, the same impossibility of making connections. The same ... Same ... Always the same."[47]

It is the extent of Vinnie's lack of "sameness" that is used to distinguish her from her male peers. Lurie clearly indicates the degree to which moves to discredit Vinnie's academic reputation are made in patriarchal language. On the plane to London, Vinnie reads in the *Atlantic* magazine "a scornful and disparaging reference to her life's work" asking "Do we really need a scholarly study of playground doggerel?"[48] The attack, by L. D. Zimmern (unknown to Vinnie but known to any reader of Lurie's novels) rejects the notion that there could be anything of value in the sayings of children. It is particularly disturbing to Vinnie because the *Atlantic* is one of her favourite magazines, where she has fantasised that her work will be lauded. She imagines (in a somewhat paranoid manner), the magazine and its negative review being read by friends and colleagues and designs a reply in her head which will never be sent because "in academic life it was considered weak and undignified to complain of your reviews."[49] However, Vinnie's research grant is not renewed. In a letter from an acquaintance on the committee Vinnie hears that Zimmern was another member, and that "'lots of people consider his remarks about you in the *Atlantic* most unfair.'"[50] While it may seem preposterous to imply that a review in a magazine like the *Atlantic* could affect the outcome of a research committee's deliberations, Lurie makes the broader point that academic reputations can

---

[47] Luce Irigaray, *This Sex Which Is Not One* (Ithaca: Cornell UP, 1985), p. 205.
[48] Lurie, *Foreign Affairs*, p. 3 [Ed.].
[49] Lurie, *Foreign Affairs*, p. 6 [Ed.].
[50] Lurie, *Foreign Affairs*, pp. 152-3 [Ed.].

depend on reviews (usually in more scholarly contexts) and therefore, on patriarchal language.

Is there nothing outside the text?

The three Lurie novels examined here, therefore, all suggest the complex ways in which language and gender intersect to exclude women from the symbolic order, as it is embodied, in her fiction, by the Academy. The simultaneous "othering" and "saming" of woman is clearly seen to operate through language. This is apparent in the Hum C course in *Love and Friendship*, the language of warfare and separate spheres in *The War Between the Tates*, and the vitriolic review, circulating around the community of scholars, in *Foreign Affairs*. Do Lurie's novels therefore suggest, like Derrida, that "there is nothing outside the text?"[51] In *Love and Friendship* the basic principle of the Hum C course might *appear* to endorse this view: "'The meaning of this word (or line) depends on the other words (or lines) which surround it at the time I use it.'"[52] Later Emmy summarises the course as follows: "After all, in Hum C terms, an experience or emotion which could not be communicated to anyone was meaningless."[53] Language constructs and shapes reality. The central tenets of the Hum C course, then, could be read as an endorsement of a Derridean principle of *difference*.

In *The War Between the Tates* Lurie also demonstrates clearly the textual or discursive construction of subjectivity. Erica experiences intense fluctuations in her conception of her own identity as a consequence of her

---

[51] Jacques Derrida, *Of Grammatology*, Gayatri Chakravorty Spivak, Trans. (Baltimore: Johns Hopkins University Press, 1976), p.163.

[52] Lurie, *Love and Friendship*, p. 14 [Ed.].

[53] Lurie, *Love and Friendship*, p. 209 [Ed.].

discovery of Brian's affair. When she initially finds the letter from Wendy and tackles Brian, he denies that the relationship meant anything, which is, to Erica, the "wrong excuse ... the wife who is betrayed for a grand passion retains some of her dignity. Pale-faced and silent, or even storming and wailing as in classical drama, she has a tragic authority."[54] Instead of taking a place in the discourse of tragic drama queen, Erica is forced to occupy the comic role of "typical wife of a casually unfaithful husband: jealous and shrewish and unforgiving."[55] That both are merely roles, suggesting what Newman had termed "dramaturgical" concepts of identity[56] is underlined by the dramatic simile that follows: "It was like being on stage ... the scenery alters behind the actors ... the villagers have not moved, but now they appear awkward, small, and overdressed against the new backdrop of mountains and ruins."[57] Positioned by clichés about adultery, Erica realises that "identity is at the mercy of circumstances, of other people's actions,"[58] but it is also at the mercy of the discourses by which those actions are interpreted. This "reading" of Erica continues throughout the novel: she figures as a bad mother, a deserted wife, a woman who becomes sexually available to men because of this desertion. None of these discourses finally fits or persists until the most enduring one – the wife of Brian – is restored. Other characters fluctuate similarly in the novel. Wendy coalesces into one figure after appearing to be three to Erica. Brian occupies the positions of radical supporter of women's causes and typical misogynist (in the pages of the *New York Times*) simultaneously.

---

54 Lurie, *The War Between the Tates*, p. 45 [Ed.].
55 Lurie, *The War Between the Tates*, p. 45 [Ed.].
56 Newman, *Alison Lurie: A Critical Study*, p. 143.
57 Lurie, *The War Between the Tates*, p. 45 [Ed.].
58 Lurie, *The War Between the Tates*, p. 45 [Ed.].

"Women and Wives Musn't Go Near It"

Foreign Affairs equally appears to imply the inescapability of textuality. Vinnie and Fred initially interpret Chuck and Rosemary, the people with whom they become romantically involved intertextually, in terms of literary characters associated with their own research specialisms. It is Vinnie's interest in folklore that provokes her involvement with Chuck, who tells her the story of his ancestor, the Hermit of Southley. Vinnie advises him on how to research this figure, but Chuck's desire to uncover aristocratic relations to compete with his wife's Waspish family background proves fruitless. Fred Turner's attraction to Rosemary Radley is also literary: specifically, she reminds him of the heroines of eighteenth-century novels as well as women in eighteenth-century paintings. Later she begins to seem like "one of James' beautiful, worldly, corrupt European villainesses."[59] Allusions to the novels of Henry James are important in establishing the transatlantic or "international" theme of the differences between American and English or European cultures. They also demonstrate the extent to which the two central characters are steeped in the language of their respective fields of study. Not only does this language affect their perceptions of the people around them and the relationships they form, it "scripts" them in patriarchal terms, suggesting, as Julia Kristeva would argue, the inevitability of the novel genre's (and the subject's) formation by mutiple systems of pre-existing signs.[60]

---

[59] Lurie, *Foreign Affairs*, p. 194 [Ed.].
[60] Julia Kristeva, *Revolution in Poetic Language*; Margaret Waller, Trans.; Leon S. Roudiez, Introd. (New York: Columbia University Press, 1984), pp. 59-60, and Julia Kristeva, *Desire In Language: A Semiotic Approach To Literature And Art*; Leon S. Roudiez, Ed.; Thomas Gora, Alice Jardine, Leon S. Roudiez, Trans. (Oxford: Basil Blackwell, 1980), p. 37.

Textuality is material: Writing the body

However, Lurie's texts resemble those of poststructuralist feminism more than poststructuralism *per se*. While she clearly suggests that materiality is textually or discursively constructed and uses deconstructive strategies to attack patriarchal discourses, her work also offers a *reconstructive* strategy, which moves beyond these insights. Like Cixous, Irigaray and, to a more qualified extent, Julia Kristeva, Lurie suggests the importance of the related (if opposed) insight that textuality is material. "Writing the body" is an important strategy for inscribing women's real difference into culture: "Woman must write her self: must write about women and bring women to writing.... Woman must put herself into the text."[61] Both Cixous and Irigaray use the risky strategy of deploying essentialist language about the female body in order to remind us of the physicality of language: "There is no need for blood shed, between us. No need for a wound to remind us that blood exists. It flows within us, from us. Blood is familiar, close. You are all red. And so very white. Both at once."[62] They attempt to write a language of the female body that genuinely acknowledges female difference, even though they are aware of that project's near impossibility, given (to twist Dale Spender) the "man made" nature of language in the symbolic order.[63] The "utopian" aspects of this project are referred to by Whitford in her discussion of Irigaray as valuable ways of discussing and diagnosing patriarchy.[64] Similarly, Newman also situates Lurie in a

---

61 Cixous, p. 244 [Ed.].
62 Irigaray, *This Sex Which Is Not One*, pp. 206-7.
63 Dale Spender, *Man Made Language* (London: Routledge, 2nd ed., 1985).
64 Margaret Whitford, *Luce Irigaray: Philosophy In The Feminine* (London: Routledge, 1991), pp. 15-17.

partial, ironic relation to American utopianism.[65]

In a number of key scenes involving women characters, Lurie allows the female body insistently and insidiously to attempt a rewriting of patriarchal language. In the first scene, from *Love and Friendship*, the male members of the Literature division debate the Hum C course and its principles at a party. While they get to grips with philosophical and theoretical issues, Lucy Green, the wife of one of the group, exhausted by her late pregnancy, demands to be taken home, interrupting the conversation by leaning her heavy stomach against her husband. In the second scene Emmy, who has just made love with Will, feels as if "'No one knows about this but me, so maybe it isn't really happening ... like Hum C, if you don't express it, does it exist?'"[66] The discussion pauses temporarily while Emmy touches Will and remarks that he feels warm. They make love again. As Newman remarks, the novel "exposes the male language game, with its pretensions to privileged truth, and idealistic moral content, to experience – and finds it decidedly wanting."[67]

In *The War between the Tates* Brian's affair with Wendy causes a blurring (albeit temporary) of the distinctions between their separate spheres. The affair directly impinges on both Brian's professional and personal lives; in fact (in deconstructive terms) Wendy appears to be the "supplement,"[68] which causes the distinction between them to collapse. Brian is forced to move out of the family home temporarily and live with Wendy, becoming informal adviser to her friends and recommending courses of political protest and action against one of his own blatantly chauvinist colleagues that lead to the final

[65] Newman, *Alison Lurie: A Critical Study*, pp. 7-8.
[66] Lurie, *Love and Friendship*, p. 157 [Ed.].
[67] Newman, *Alison Lurie: A Critical Study*, pp. 35-6.
[68] Derrida, pp. 141-64 [Ed.].

The Academic Novel

debacle of the novel. It is certainly significant, in terms of a poststructuralist feminist analysis, that it is Wendy's pregnancy with Brian's child that threatens his marriage, when Erica decides to support and help Wendy in a gesture of female solidarity. In a lengthy extended metaphor, the frying eggs Erica cooks for Wendy become her unborn child: "the golden, nourishing domed yolks, quiver against each other and come to rest, surrounded by the thin, gluey, viscous whites, like semen;"[69] "the eggs are swelling and congealing in the frying pan; Wendy is pregnant."[70] That there is something fundamental about pregnancy and maternity is suggested in the way that Erica joins with Wendy against Brian to protect the child. This is also apparent in Wendy's understanding, later in the novel, that in comparison with a partner, she would never be able to desert her own child, because "'I'll always belong to him completely.'"[71] Cixous and Irigaray similarly prioritise the inscription of the maternal relation in the symbolic. As Cixous suggests: "a woman is never far from 'mother'.... There is always within her at least a little of that good mother's milk. She writes in white ink."[72] Irigaray also insists:

> We also need to find, rediscover, invent the words, the sentences that speak of the most ancient and most current relationship we know – the relationship to the mother's body, to our body – sentences that translate the bond between our body, her body, the body of our daughter. We need to discover a language that is not a substitute for the experience of *corps-à-corps* as the paternal language seeks to be, but which accompanies that bodily experience, clothing

---

[69] Lurie, *The War Between the Tates*, pp. 124-5 [Ed.].
[70] Lurie, *The War Between the Tates*, p. 125 [Ed.].
[71] Lurie, *The War Between the Tates*, p. 300 [Ed.].
[72] Cixous, p. 251 [Ed.].

it in words that do not erase the body but speak the body.[73]

In *Foreign Affairs* patriarchal discourse is interrogated in ways that echo Irigaray's work on the possibilities for re-imagining femininity occasioned by a new "ethics of sexual difference." As we have seen, to re-imagine woman as more than man's lack, absence or (m)other entails for Irigaray an acknowledgement of woman in her own terms, as *different* rather than *other*. Recently she has become interested in the "wonder," rather than desire, that could be generated between men and women if their real difference from each other was celebrated rather than collapsed:

> This feeling of surprise, astonishment, and wonder in the face of the unknowable ought to be returned to its locus: that of sexual difference. The passions have either been repressed, stifled, or reduced, or reserved for God. Sometimes a space for wonder is left to works of art. But it is never found to reside in this locus: *between man and woman*. Into this place came attraction, greed, possession, consummation, disgust, and so on. But not that wonder which beholds what it sees always as if for the first time, never taking hold of the other as its object. It does not try to seize, possess, or reduce this object, but leaves it subjective, still free. This has never existed between the sexes since wonder maintains their autonomy within their statutory difference, keeping a space of freedom and attraction between them, a possibility of separation and alliance.[74]

---

[73] Luce Irigaray, *Sexes and Genealogies*; Gillian C. Gill, Trans. (New York: Columbia University Press, 1993), pp. 18-19.

[74] Luce Irigaray, *An Ethics of Sexual Difference*; Carolyn Burke and Gillian C. Gill, Trans. (Ithaca, NY : Cornell University Press; London : Athlone Press, 1993), pp. 12-13 [Ed.].

It is love (though not sex as the narrator is at pains to point out) with which Vinnie is unfamiliar, and it is this she encounters in the novel. Vinnie's nascent love for Chuck (whom she originally found repulsive) arises from the acknowledgement of his real *difference*, which has life-changing effects on her own personality and ethical position: usually selfish Vinnie makes the generous effort to struggle up to Hampstead Heath at dead of night to give Fred Turner a message from his wife which has the effect of saving their marriage. As she says: "Something has changed.... She isn't the same person she was: she has loved and been loved."[75] She asks: "Why shouldn't she imagine herself standing on the edge of some landscape as yet unmapped by literature: interested, even excited, ready to be surprised."[76] The suggestion of freedom from "overdetermination" by literary sources is equated with the "wondrous" freedoms occasioned by exploring previously uncharted territory.

Culture is textuality

What these key scenes suggest is that women characters resist patriarchal logic by asserting the value of the body, maternity, love and sensation. This may appear to endorse the association of women with the sensual and emotional spheres, to represent her as the "other" to the academic, logical, reasonable beliefs about the textuality of the material. However, it does so as an attempt, albeit a risky one, not merely to *remind* the symbolic order of how it functions but also to instate female difference and *jouissance* within it. As in the key texts of Cixous and Irigaray, it is through pregnancy, maternity and sexual difference rather than otherness that such a rewriting

---

[75] Lurie, *Foreign Affairs*, p. 278 [Ed.].
[76] Lurie, *Foreign Affairs*, p. 199 [Ed.].

possibly takes place. However, it is noteworthy that these interrogations are temporary: by the end of each novel they have failed to offer a lasting alternative to the patriarchal symbolic order of academia. The realist surface of Lurie's novel is, equally, never more than very superficially challenged by the linguistic and narrative experimentation that Cixous, for example, associates with "*écriture féminine*". Indeed, Cixous argues that novelists, unlike poets, are inevitably "allies of representationalism,"[77] although she includes novelists Colette, Marguerite Duras and Jean Genet as examples of "feminine" writing.[78] As *Love and Friendship* moves towards its close Emmy feels that her relationship with Will might as well not have happened because no one else acknowledges or discusses it. She feels "as if big sections of her life were being crossed out and thrown away."[79] By the end of the novel Emmy and Holman are back together and the status quo has been reasserted. To all intents and purposes the temporary feminine "challenge" to Hum C logic has been thwarted and revealed to be mistaken. Equally, *The War Between the Tates* concludes with the Tates' marriage reaching a détente. The solidarity Erica finds with Wendy and her friend Danielle, which was based on Wendy's pregnancy, turns out to be illusory when Danielle remarries and Wendy moves in with Brian, has an abortion, gets pregnant again by someone else, and leaves for a commune.

Foreign Affairs also demonstrates that Vinnie has a murkier personal ethics than her vivifying, if impermanent, relationship with Chuck implies. Vinnie's experience when recording playground chants has the potential to destroy her long-held theory about the

---

[77] Cixous, p. 250 [Ed.].
[78] Cixous, p. 248 [Ed.].
[79] Lurie, *Love and Friendship*, p. 209 [Ed.].

differences between English and American rhymes. This theory is, in itself, an Anglophile one: "the British texts do tend to be older ... they are also more literary. The American rhymes are newer, cruder, less lyrical and poetic."[80] Vinnie's thesis is contradicted by the crudity and vulgarity of the rhymes she is told by a little girl called Mary Maloney, who demands payment in return for them. Aware that "a few more of these and her theory ... will be down the tube,"[81] Vinnie decides not to record any more of Mary's rhymes. Although she tries to justify this decision to herself in various ways, it is obvious that Vinnie sacrifices objectivity when collecting research material to the demands of her preconceived theory. She twists language to make it construct a version of childhood that is amenable to her Anglophile way of thinking. Chuck's reading of her as "a good woman"[82] is arguably temporary.

She is not alone in being self-interested, however. Fred reads Lady Rosemary as a typical English rose but discovers that she is simultaneously Mrs Harris, the cockney charlady. Rosemary, a "flagrantly fictional woman"[83] develops the personality of Mrs Harris from imagining the language of a "typical" Cockney cleaning woman: "Rosemary slides into stage Cockney – 'and 'er dawg's worms and 'er cat's fleas and 'er budgie's molt, ooh, the pore dear, 'e's losin' 'is feathers somethin' awful.'"[84] It is Mrs Harris's choice sayings that define her, just as Rosemary's apparently "real" personality is eerily close to that of the role she plays on television. As Glendinning also comments: "The grotesque extent to

---

[80] Lurie, *Foreign Affairs*, p. 102 [Ed.].
[81] Lurie, *Foreign Affairs*, pp. 107-8 [Ed.].
[82] Lurie, *Foreign Affairs*, p. 174 [Ed.].
[83] Victoria Glendinning, "In Love with London," *The Sunday Times* (20 January 1985), p. 44.
[84] Lurie, *Foreign Affairs*, p. 114 [Ed.].

which Lady Rosemary herself is as much a 'dramatic construct' as the roles she plays on TV comes as a shock to Fred – but not to this reader."[85] It is as if, as Newman suggests: "there can be no real return to nature, not to some primary state of childlike [or feminine] innocence of language and culture. Culture is textuality."[86] In other words, Lurie's novels could be seen to offer a rather bleak critique of the idea that it is possible to challenge or rewrite patriarchal language. Like the work of Cixous and Irigaray, her fiction demonstrates the risks of an argument that constructs femininity as exterior to a monolithic and almost impervious symbolic order. For Lurie, writing and speaking means accepting the dominance of patriarchal law both conceptually and also creatively, in terms of her commitment to realism.

Foreign Affairs therefore concludes with the success, professional and romantic, of Fred, not Vinnie. He is described, resignedly, as "an example of Entitlement Psychology: he has been brought up to get, and think he deserves, all the good things of this world."[87] Fred is the son of Holman and Emily Turner in *Love and Friendship*, and certainly the same confidence, based on looks, money and class, is as apparent in him as it was in his mother. Unlike her, however, he also has the advantage of being a man. Securely part of the symbolic order, Fred can have it all: a career, a wife, a mistress while he is in England, and never come unstuck. The only minor inconvenience he endures is the unwanted attentions of his lovestruck students.

---

85 Glendinning, p. 44 [Ed.].
86 Newman, *Alison Lurie: A Critical Study*, p. 159.
87 Lurie, *Foreign Affairs*, p. 50 [Ed.].

The Academic Novel

The sense of an ending?

The reader may well reach the end of the Lurie novels examined here with a sense of frustration at their seemingly inescapable pressure towards closure and the restoration of conservative norms. Feminist theorists and critics have expressed similar concerns about the most influential ideas of Cixous and Irigaray, which arguably position feminine identity and writing as no more than a utopian possibility.[88] More recently, writers and critics have begun to see gender identity as a more flexible process or performance capable of disrupting patriarchal systems of power and language.[89] Lurie's stance is not, however, merely a consequence of the period in which the novels examined here were written and set. After a decade's break, Lurie's 1998 novel, *The Last Resort*, exactly resembles her earlier work in its final containment of challenges to convention. The novel's heroine, Jenny Walker, stays with her elderly husband out of pity and begins to drift away from her female lover, Lee Weiss. Similarly, Irigaray's latest book, *The Way of Love* (2002),[90] like *An Ethics of Sexual Difference* (1993) focuses on the differences between the sexes as fundamentally inescapable in the analysis of language.

Despite this rather negative conclusion, I would suggest that, to recast Frank Kermode, the "sense of an ending"

---

[88] See for example the chapters on Hélène Cixous and Luce Irigaray in Toril Moi, *Sexual/Textual Politics: Feminist Literary Theory* (London: Routledge, 1985).

[89] See for example Judith Butler, *Gender Trouble: Feminism and the Subversion Of Identity* (London: Routledge, 1990), and Judith Butler, *Bodies That Matter: On the Discursive Limits of "Sex"* (London: Routledge, 1993).

[90] Luce Irigaray, *The Way of Love*; Heidi Bostic and Stephen Pluhácek, Trans. (London : Continuum, 2002) [Ed.].

must be considered.[91] If poststructuralist feminist theory tells us anything, it tells us to be suspicious of phallocentric, or phallogocentric thinking: linear, or phallic readings are not the only ones. This would mean that, rather than focusing on the conclusions of Lurie's novels, where challenges tend to be contained, we should instead read more *synchronically*. Such a reading against the grain, which this article has attempted, would pay attention to the significant parts of the novels where the primacy of patriarchal language in the symbolic is challenged by a writing of the female body into the text and the deployment of a new "ethics of eros."[92] *The Last Resort*, for example, concludes with an invocation to focus on the present moment and not the past or future: "Lee remembered something she had read once, that as you grow older and the future shrinks, you have only two choices: you can live in the fading past, or, like children do, in the bright full present."[93] Instead of thinking about Jenny's renewed loyalty to her husband, she imagines the moments when she will be with her at night as a sensuous epiphany fusing beautiful scenery with sexual exploration. If we pay careful attention to such moments and their implications it becomes clear that those critics who dismiss Lurie's work as merely entertaining "campus fiction" or see it only as stirring the dying embers of the Anglo-American realist tradition are missing out. In fact, her work offers a sustained exploration of the place of the feminine in the symbolic order, as it is represented by academia. It also interrogates the tenets of

---

[91] Frank Kermode, *The Sense of an Ending* (London: Oxford University Press, 1967).

[92] Tina Chanter, *Ethics of Eros: Irigaray's Rewriting of the Philosophers* (London: Routledge, 1995).

[93] Alison Lurie, *The Last Resort* (1998; London: Vintage, 1999), p. 253 [Ed.]: '

poststructuralist theory from a gendered perspective, in order to inquire further into the relationship between the textual, the sexual and the material.

ROBERTSON DAVIES AND THE CAMPUS NOVEL[1]

David Lodge

Robertson Davies has had a long and distinguished career, not only as a novelist, but also as theatrical director, playwright and academic. He is one of Canada's most distinguished men of letters, but I have to confess that the novel under review[2] is my first acquaintance with his writing. Since I am unable to place it in relation to his other work, I will place it in the context of the genre, or subgenre, to which it belongs, namely, the campus novel.

This is by now a form of fiction so well established that addicts of the campus novel, like addicts of detective stories and spy thrillers, relish its familiar and recurrent features almost as much as they enjoy whatever new twist or texture the novelist is able to impart. What are the sources of the campus novel's attraction, for both readers and writers? One reason, perhaps, is that the university is a kind of microcosm of society at large, in which the principles, drives and conflicts that govern collective human life are displayed and may be studied in a clear light and on a manageable scale. One of Mr Davies's characters is of this opinion: "The University is such a splendid community, you know, every kind of creature here, and all exhibiting what they are so much more freely than if they were in business, or the law, or whatever."

Freely, presumably, because of the institution of academic tenure, which makes scholars less afraid of their peers and superiors than members of other professions,

[1] Previously published in *Write On: Occasional Essays '65-'85* (London: Secker & Warburg, 1986), pp. 169-73.

[2] Robertson Davies, *The Rebel Angels* (Viking, 1982).

261

and therefore less conformist. Universities are notoriously rich in extravagantly eccentric characters – especially in Britain (where, significantly, tenure is much more easily and quickly obtained than in the United States) and, if *The Rebel Angels* is any guide, in Canada too. Stuart Sutherland, professor of experimental psychology at the University of Sussex, England, who wrote a courageous book about his own mental illness, *Breakdown*, observed that in any other social context people would have recognized much sooner that he was going mad (he had reached the stage of saving time by shaving while driving to work and dictating letters through the door of the toilet) but that in a university his symptoms were tolerantly regarded as mere eccentricities.

Inside, as outside, the academy, the principal determinants of action are sex and the will to power, and a typology of campus fiction might be based on a consideration of the relative dominance of these two drives in the story. The Cambridge novels of C. P. Snow, for instance, notably his classic study of a college election in *The Masters*, were primarily concerned with the struggle for power; while the novels of Alison Lurie, *Love and Friendship* and *The War Between the Tates*, are primarily concerned with sexual intrigue. Both themes have an essentially ironic tendency in the context of a university, whose members are supposedly dedicated to the disinterested pursuit of knowledge and truth, but who are thus revealed as slaves to ignoble instincts and passions. Sometimes the two drives are evenly balanced, as in Malcolm Bradbury's *The History Man*, whose anti-hero uses sexual seduction as a primary means of imposing his will on campus politics. More often, sexuality is opposed to the scholar's professional life, and threatens its stability. An affair between teacher and pupil, for instance, even in today's permissive society, violates some deep-seated taboo and thrusts both parties into a realm of moral danger, excitement and deception, generating the stuff of fiction. "We all know what happens in universities," says another character in *The Rebel Angels*. "Nice girls turn up, professors are human, and bingo! Sometimes it's rough on the girl, sometimes it may be destructive to the professor."

Should we perhaps rather say, "Professors would like to convince themselves that they are human?" The successful academic has usually succeeded by dint of sacrificing a certain amount of libido in youth, and in middle age may feel a sudden urge to make up for lost time, to prove that he is not a totally cerebral being after all, but a man of passion and feeling; while the young student who offers a convenient focus for the desire may be unable to disentangle sexual attraction from intellectual awe.

The exercise of power in academic life was classically analysed by F. M. Cornford in his little pamphlet *Microcosmographia Academica: Being a Guide for the Young Academic Politician* (1912), which includes such gems of definition as "'sound scholar' is a term of praise applied to one another by learned men who have no reputation outside the University" and "a lecturer is a sound scholar who is chosen to teach on the grounds that he was once able to learn." According to Cornford, the academic exercise of power consists almost as much in exploiting the democratic system of university government to frustrate others as in advancing oneself. Things have changed a bit since Cornford's Cambridge days, but it is still true that to the worldly eye the issues which preoccupy academics often seem comically disproportionate to the passions they arouse. And here we perhaps approach the ultimate secret of the campus novel's deep appeal: academic conflicts are relatively harmless, safely insulated from the real world and its sombre concerns – or capable of transforming those concerns into a form of stylized Play. Essentially the campus novel is a modern, displaced form of pastoral, as

Mary McCarthy recognized by calling her classic contribution to the genre *The Groves of Academe*. That is why it belongs to the literature of escape, and why we never tire of it.

The Rebel Angels is certainly a novel whose characters scarcely seem to belong to the modern world, even the modern university world; but the fact that it is a campus novel makes us readier to accept and enjoy its mannered style and archaic atmosphere. It is set in one of the constituent colleges of the University of Toronto, an institution that Mr Davies knows well, since he recently retired as master of Massey College there. But I find it hard to believe that academic life at Toronto in the 1980s can resemble Cornford's Cambridge quite as closely, or that the preoccupations of its members are quite as bizarre, as the novel suggests. *The Rebel Angels* reads like the result of an unlikely collaboration between C. P. Snow and Muriel Spark, with assistance from Thomas Love Peacock and the author of *The Anatomy of Melancholy*. Snow's relish for the cosy intrigues of academic politics is combined with Muriel Spark's zany supernaturalism, Peacock's love of good talk, and Burton's sardonic delight in esoteric learning and human eccentricity.

The novel begins well, quickly introducing the sexual theme. The narrator, a young research student of Polish-Hungarian gypsy background who rejoices in the name of Maria Magdalena Theotoky, is hurrying to see her supervisor, Clement Hollier, at the beginning of the academic year, and hears a report being passed from mouth to mouth that "Parlabane is back."

This was what I wanted. It was something to say to Hollier when we met after nearly four months apart. At that meeting he had become my lover, or so I was vain enough to think. Certainly he had become, agonizingly, the man I loved. All through the summer vacation I had

Robertson Davies and the Campus Novel

fretted and fussed and hoped for a postcard from wherever he might be in Europe, but he was not a man to write postcards. Not a man to say very much, either, in a personal way. But he could be excited; he could give way to feeling. On that day in early May, when he had told me about the latest development in his work, and I – so eager to serve him, to gain his gratitude and perhaps even his love – did an inexcusable thing and betrayed the secret of the *bomari* to him, he seemed lifted quite outside of himself, and it was then he took me in his arms and put me on that horrible old sofa in his office, and had me amid a great deal of confusion of clothing, creaking of springs and peripheral anxiety lest somebody should come in. That was when we had parted, he embarrassed and I overcome with astonishment and devotion, and now I was to face him again. I needed an opening remark.

The reader would be correct in inferring from this passage that Hollier is an essentially frigid man whose only passion is his subject – "paleopsychology," or the investigation of popular thought and belief in the early Renaissance period. The professor who falls genuinely in love with Maria is Simon Darcourt, clergyman and biblical scholar, who fancies himself as a new John Aubrey, memorialising the eccentrics of Toronto University in a contemporary *Brief Lives*. His narrative and Maria's are plaited together to form the substance of *The Rebel Angels*, often covering the same event from ironically different perspectives.

Hollier and Darcourt are nominated along with Urquhart McVarish, a historian who claims descent from the seventeeth-century translator of Rabelais, as executors of the will of a great collector, Francis Cornish, who has just died. Among his precious *objets d'art* and rare

265

manuscripts there was a hitherto unknown group of holograph letters from Rabelais to the Renaissance magus, Paracelsus. Hollier is dying to get his hands on these letters, partly to assuage his guilt about the seduction of Maria by giving her the task and academic glory of editing them. But Urky McVarish, a crotchety and malicious character, has snaffled this prize without admitting that he has done so, much to Hollier's anger and frustration.

The mysterious *bomari* referred to on the first page, quoted above, turns out to be a container filled with high-grade horse dung – a treatment to restore purity of tone to old violins, used by Maria's gypsy mother. Introduced to "Marmusia" to learn this secret, Hollier also has his fortune told with ominous results, while Marmusia, seeking to secure his love for her daughter by means of a philtre, succeeds only in binding Darcourt's affections more tightly to her.

The character who precipitates the dénouement is Parlabane, a reprobate with a great scholarly future behind him, who, after many sordid and shady adventures, has come back to Toronto to batten on his old friends, Hollier and Darcourt. He is a sinister figure, often compared to the devil, who finally brings about the restoration of the Rabelais letters in a bizarre climax which it would be unfair to reveal here.

The names of Rabelais and Paracelsus are not gratuitously invoked by the plot. There is a Rabelaisian quality, a combination of robust humour and satire on pedantry, in Mr Davies's own writing; while the hermetic and heterodox ideas associated with the name of Paracelsus are exploited in a fashion that is at once playful and serious. The mythology of Gnosticism runs through the novel and explains its title. Maria Theotoky, whose name means "bringer of God," is worshipped by Darcourt as "Sophia," the feminine personification of Divine

Wisdom, while she identifies him and Hollier as Samahazai and Azazel, two rebel angels in apocryphal scripture who: "... came down to earth and taught tongues, and healing and laws and hygiene – taught everything – and they were often special successes with 'the daughters of men'.... Surely it is the explanation of the origin of universities!"

The Rebel Angels is one of those novels that impart a good deal of information - in this case rather esoteric information - as well as entertainment to the reader. Its flavour will be a little too gamy for some tastes, its high spirits too redolent of high table; but as the production of a writer in his sixty-ninth year, it is a work of impressive vigour and vivacity, which no addict of the campus novel will want to miss.

"NOT A COMIC NOVELIST, EXACTLY":
THE ACADEMIC FICTION OF DAVID LODGE

Chris Walsh

Any critic surveying British fiction in the second half of the twentieth century might well pause when considering how best to sum up the achievement and gauge the reputation of David Lodge the novelist. Of his twelve novels, from *The Picturegoers* (1960) to *Author, Author* (2004), four may be described as "campus novels"[1]: *Changing Places: A Tale of Two Campuses* (1975), *Small World: An Academic Romance* (1984), *Nice Work* (1988), and *Thinks ...* (2001), though even that seemingly straightforward term immediately requires qualification: the first of these novels, as its subtitle announces, deals with more than one campus; the second novel deals with the notional "global campus"; the third contrasts sharply two very different worlds of work – the university and the industrial firm; and the fourth, although set on a "greenfields" campus, is not primarily about academic mores, but is Lodge's fictional reflection upon the study of human consciousness, a counterpart to his ground-breaking critical study, *Consciousness and the Novel* (2002). But Lodge's writings, rather like those of his friend and former colleague, the late Malcolm Bradbury, are thought of as being *mostly* about modern academic life – indeed, the very term "campus novel" is often defined by reference to his fiction. Here, for example, is Chris Baldick's definition:

---

[1] I am excluding *The British Museum is Falling Down* (London: MacGibbon & Kee, 1965). Although that novel revolves around the life of a postgraduate research student, it is not about University life as such (academic *staff* are largely absent), and there is no "campus".

"Not a Comic Novelist, Exactly"

campus novel, a novel, usually comic or satirical, in which the
action is set within the enclosed world of a university (or similar
seat of learning) and highlights the follies of academic life. Many
novels have presented nostalgic evocations of college days, but the
campus novel in the usual modern sense dates from the 1950s:
Mary McCarthy's *The Groves of Academe* (1952) and Kingsley Amis's
Lucky Jim (1954) began a significant tradition in modern fiction
including John Barth's *Giles Goat-Boy* (1966), David Lodge's
Changing Places (1975), and Robertson Davies's *The Rebel Angels*
(1982).[2]

That is an accurate and fair definition, but it is noticeable
that Baldick felt the need to qualify the definition's terms
("usually ... similar ... many ... usual ... including ...").
Defining something entails setting limits, drawing lines,
ruling certain things in or out. But when the thing to be
defined is the novel (or even a novelistic sub-genre),
drawing lines is not so easy, for the novel is quite the most
capacious and flexible of all literary genres.

A similar point might be made about reputations.
Reputations are oddly amorphous, intangible and protean
constructs, and by their very nature impressionistic. When
I observed that the writings of Lodge and Bradbury "are
thought of as being *mostly* about modern academic life",
like Baldick I was conscious of the need for a qualificatory
emphasis in adumbrating literary reputations so
laconically. But "mostly", although unfair in the sense that
both Bradbury and Lodge have cast their authorial nets far

---

[2] Chris Baldick, *The Concise Oxford Dictionary of Literary Terms* (Oxford: Oxford University Press, 1991), p. 30.

more widely than "mere" campus fictions, is apposite in the sense that even those novels which are not campus novels usually bear some relation to the academy – if only, for example, by virtue of their inclusion of academics in their character sets. This is hardly surprising, as both novelists were themselves academics, and (moreover) their published scholarly and critical work included discussions of their own, and others', academic fiction. For many years, Lodge alternated between writing novels and critical monographs, and fairly early on in his career the two began to grow closer together, each informed by the other. In the case of his novels, this has certainly strengthened the impression of Lodge as the academic novelist par excellence, who specializes in producing novels of a highly self-referential kind, knowing, allusive, ludic, even at times parodic. Lodge himself has conceded that "in theory, everybody disapproves of academic novels, as being too inbred and stereotyped"; though he goes on to claim that "in practice there seems to be a very big public for them. People like reading them".[3]

But there is a particular problem with acquiring the appellation "academic novelist". The connotations are clear enough: writers of campus novels, particularly if they are themselves academics, and especially if they write little else,[4] are prone to be regarded as having a very limited "two inches of ivory" for their subject matter (at best a thin slice of whatever is meant by "the real world"), about which they write knowledgeably, wittily, entertainingly, satirically, but ... Lodge's words "inbred" and "stereotyped" contain the rub. The ivory-towered

---

[3] As quoted in Merritt Moseley, *David Lodge: How Far Can You Go?* (San Bernardino, CA: The Borgo Press, 1991), p. 8.
[4] This is patently not true in Lodge's case. It would be as inaccurate to describe him as a "Catholic novelist", even though Catholicism features in most of his novels, and is a dominant subject in at least three of them.

academic world is indeed a small world, a world in miniature, a self-contained world with its own distinctive traditions and conventions. To return to Baldick's definition: "a novel, *usually comic or satirical*, in which the action is set within *the enclosed world of a university* (or similar seat of learning) and highlights *the follies of academic life* [italics added]". It is as if there is not only a narrowness, a deliberate self-delimitation, but something rather lightweight, not quite *serious* about such novels. They are, after all, comedies, satires ("usually"). They do not deal with major themes – just the usual academic sexual shenanigans, the odd political fracas, and so forth, but nothing weighty. Lodge himself remarked of *Small World* that it contained

> ... an element of pointing out affectation and hypocrisy, which I think of as the satirical edge of comedy ... I think I can stand back from the academic profession enough to see its absurd and ridiculous aspects, but I don't think it's really wicked or mischievous. That's probably why the overall impression of *Small World* is genial: fun-poking rather than denunciation.[5]

This element of "fun-poking" is what is stressed in the promotional and publicity materials, unsurprisingly, to help the novels on their way up the best-seller charts. The blurb on the back of the first paperback edition of *Nice Work*[6] quotes Kingsley Amis: "a feast of fun". And yet, reading his novels, we realize that Lodge offers so much

---

[5] As quoted in John Haffenden, *Novelists in Interview* (London: Methuen, 1985), p. 161.
[6] David Lodge, *Nice Work* (1988; Harmondsworth: Penguin, 1989). All future page references to this novel are to the Penguin edition.

more than that. He is hardly a Howard Jacobson, and certainly no Tom Sharpe: his novels are never merely "entertainments", to adopt Graham Greene's taxonomical distinction. In his own blurb alongside, Anthony Burgess strikes a rather different note to Amis, describing the novel as "a work of immense intelligence, informative, disturbing and diverting ... The book confirms David Lodge's right to be taken *very seriously indeed* as one of the best novelists of his generation [italics added] ".

This note seems more apt. Lodge is surely a writer of *literary* fiction, of *serious* literary fiction, closer to the Julian Barnes and Ian McEwan end of the writerly spectrum than to the John Grisham and Dan Brown end, or (more tendentiously) closer to Amis *fils* than to Amis *père*. While he aims to be read widely (are there writers who aim to be read by few?), he is no populist. Or is this perhaps a false distinction? Here is Clive James:

> The last step, and the hardest to take, in assessing any comic writer, is to assert what should be an obvious truth: humour is not an overlay to seriousness. Humour is the thing itself, compressed and intensified into a civil code ... Comedy has to be astonishing or nothing, and Amis was astonishing enough to make even the obtuse realize that there are truths which only comedy can state.[7]

In the course of this review, James takes a sideswipe at John Carey who, in *his* review of Zachary Leader's *Life of Kingsley Amis*, focused on Amis's life at the expense of his literary achievement (hardly a crime for a biographer,

---

[7] Clive James, 'Public accounts': [a review of Zachary Leader's *The Life of Kingsley Amis* (London: Cape, 2007)], *The Times Literary Supplement*, 2 February 2007, 3-5 (p. 5).

admittedly). But Carey, in his impressive study of perhaps the greatest popular entertainer the English novel has known, has this to say:

> Dickens is essentially a comic writer. The urge to conceal this, noticeable in some recent studies, can probably be traced to a suspicion that comedy, compared to tragedy, is light. Comedy is felt to be artificial and escapist; tragedy, toughly real. The opposite view seems more accurate. Tragedy is tender to man's dignity and self-importance, and preserves the illusion that he is a noble creature. Comedy uncovers the absurd truth, which is why people are so afraid of being laughed at in real life.[8]

Comedy *or* seriousness? Comedy *and* seriousness? Comedy *above* seriousness? How might Lodge's academic fiction be best understood? The term "serio-comic" is a cheat, and must be rejected. It would rightly be thought as absurd to apply that term to Dickens as to the campus novels of Tom Sharpe (to take two very different examples). Moreover, Lodge is not a formulaic novelist: he experiments in each novel, and across his oeuvre there are clear lines of development and evolution.[9] Thus, reviewers of Lodge's later novels, quoted in the paperback blurbs, acknowledge how he has extended the boundaries of comedy, and refer to his "wit" rather than to his humour (or his humour is referred to as "dark"), and to his pathos, and a more "sober" view of reality. Whatever else he is, Lodge is not a novelist to be neatly pigeon-holed.

---

[8] John Carey, *The Violent Effigy: A Study of Dickens' Imagination*, 2nd edn (London : Faber and Faber, 1991), p. 7.
[9] Merritt Moseley's apt phrase for Lodge is "an experimental traditionalist"; see Moseley, p. 11.

The Academic Novel

A reviewer of the anonymously authored *A Campus Conspiracy* (2006) pronounced:

> The received wisdom in the English literature community is that the campus novel has had its day. Certainly, it has changed since the heyday of Lodge and Bradbury. Zadie Smith's *On Beauty* was set in the fictional Wellington University, just outside Boston, but is more than a campus novel. Philip Roth's *The Human Stain* is a campus novel that is satirical but not comic. This new book should show, however, that maybe there is life left in the slapstick comic genre first created by Kingsley Amis.[10]

This is a familiar perspective, according to which the campus novel is at best a limited fictional sub-genre, specialising in "slapstick" humour, and the very topicality which explains its (temporary) appeal will ultimately mean that it will be forgotten by all but literary historians. Campus novels, far from being fictional classics, are mere ephemera, amusing period pieces.

There may be some truth in that observation in general terms. Perhaps Tom Sharpe's *Porterhouse Blue* (1974), for all its moments of side-splitting uproariousness, will be as little read in centuries to come as Cuthbert Bede's *The Adventures of Mr Verdant Green* (1853-7) is today. But such a judgement looks distinctly shaky when applied to the "academic fiction of David Lodge. It is worth noting that his first academic novel, *Changing Places*, is still in print more than thirty years after it was published in 1975. Indeed, none of his academic fictions has ever been out of

---

[10] Lucy Hodges, 'In the footsteps of "Lucky Jim"': [a review of *A Campus Conspiracy* (Exeter: Impress Books, 2006)], *The Independent*, 19 October 2006 <http://education.independent.co.uk/higher/article1897762.ece> [accessed 28 June 2007].

print. Their popularity, it would appear, is not merely "of the moment". This is not to deny that these novels, by their very nature, have an inbuilt potential obsolescence. Consider, for example, a remark of Morris Zapp in *Small World*: "There are three things which have revolutionized academic life in the last twenty years, though very few people have woken up to the fact: jet travel, direct-dialling telephones and the Xerox machine".[11] That was nearly a quarter of a century ago. In today's even smaller world, one could imagine citing cut-price airlines, mobile phones, and (inevitably) email as equivalent examples, and no doubt these more up-to-date references will themselves seem hopelessly dated in twenty-five years. A similar point might be made about some of those theoretical debates in Lodge's novels (about post-structuralism, for instance) which may strike today's readers as rather quaint. But the presence of such time-rooted characteristics does not seem to have cannoned the novels post-haste into an ominous obscurity. Indeed, it may even be the case that these so-called period features may actually strengthen the novels' appeal with the passage of time. *Nice Work*, for example, is even more replete with solidity of specification of a most solid and most specific kind. The sense given in its pages of the state of Britain under Prime Minister Margaret Thatcher is one of the novel's many strengths. This is no mere period backdrop – local colour – but part and parcel of an intelligent, informed analysis of the context of higher education and post-industrial capitalism in the closing decades of the twentieth century, and one suspects that

---

[11] David Lodge, *Small World: An Academic Romance* (1984; Harmondsworth: Penguin, 1985), p. 43. All future page references are to the Penguin edition.

future cultural historians of that inglorious phase of British history will derive as much benefit from a study of *Nice Work* as students of the mid-nineteenth century do from studying the social-problem novels of Gaskell and Dickens, Disraeli and Kingsley. Lodge's academic novels are nothing if not densely, intelligently informative about the world which they depict.

And these worlds are *not* small, narrow, inbred. Lodge was clearly fully intent upon evoking and interpreting the bigger picture with subtlety and acuity. The novels are never provincial, and there is never any sense of the wood being missed because all the attention is on individual trees. There is depth and breadth in Lodge's academic novels, as in his other works of fiction. This is self-evidently the case with the impressive *Thinks ...*, a novel that is a campus novel only in the broadest sense of the term. For although it is set in academe, academe itself is not examined here as in his earlier novels, other than incidentally. This is a novel about consciousness, and Lodge's exploration of the nature of consciousness is in part an expert demonstration of what literature can offer to today's cognitive scientists – Henry James for the twenty-first century in the light of our current knowledge and understanding. In this respect, *Thinks ...* does carry on from *Nice Work*, much as modernism is an extrapolation from realism: it rewrites the nineteenth- and early twentieth-century novel of consciousness, much as his earlier novel rewrote the Victorian and Edwardian social-problem novel. But the emphasis is on *today*. Lodge's novels are almost always thoroughgoingly contemporary (or were, until *Author, Author* bucked the trend, with its account of Henry James and George Du Maurier). There has been a proliferation of postmodernist neo-Victorian novels since the 1960s – by Peter Ackroyd, A. S. Byatt, Michel Faber, John Fowles, Charles Palliser, D. J. Taylor, and Sarah Waters (to stop there). But Lodge's imagination is not primarily historical. He is too intent upon looking out of the window to look back.

He looks out, but in *Thinks* … he looks *within* to an extent to which he had never quite done before. The seriousness of this particular fictional project is immediately evident from the acknowledgements, where Lodge refers to "the current scientific and philosophical debate about consciousness" and provides a list of some twenty-five bibliographical items (mostly books and articles) consulted.[12] But although it has its humorous moments, *Thinks* … is not a comic novel. "Witty", on the other hand, the first word on the dust-jacket blurb, is an accurate adjective to apply to the novel, for this is manifestly a serious, sustained, *intelligent* attempt to render and explore human consciousness as if to prove that literature has a valuable contribution to make to the study of consciousness and that scientists and philosophers ignore such a contribution to their loss. And in the process it gives much rich intellectual pleasure – witty, indeed.

As always in Lodge's fiction, the novel is continuously inventive when it comes to the various ways with which to represent consciousness, from Ralph Messenger's stream of consciousness recordings and Helen Reed's diaries, through the masterly use of third-person narrative (involving the deftest deployment of free indirect style), to specimens of creative writing exercises (including several amusing parodies and pastiches) and (tellingly) emails. The novel abounds with examples of "thinks", of thought in action "as it happens", of verbalized "qualia". And it

---

[12] David Lodge, *Thinks* … (London: Secker and Warburg, 2001), p. 341. All future page references are to the Secker & Warburg edition.

does manage to convey the qualities of *different* minds: the thoughts and speech and writing of Messenger and Helen are individuated with precision. Indeed, *Thinks* ... is replete with serious conversations and dense discussions about consciousness, and the novel offers an excellent distillation of some of the classic problems and issues, made accessible to the layperson in Lodge's customary clear-headed way: he is superb at conveying complex ideas simply and effectively. The novel's seriousness is evident on every page.

That Lodge's seriousness has not been taken seriously is partly his fault. In one interview, he disavowed seriousness, and stated categorically his comic intentions:

> ... I became interested in comedy and the whole business of making people laugh. When I began to think of writing a novel about the subject of Catholic hang-ups and problems over birth control it seemed to me that to write a serious novel about this would be deeply embarrassing, but that if it were represented as part of the comedy of human sexuality that it could work for a non-Catholic audience. So it just had to be a comic novel. That's what prompted me to write ostensibly comic fiction.[13]

But later in the same interview he sets out how he tried to combine the two modes:

> My next novel, *Out of the Shelter* (which I had actually conceived before *The British Museum*) was much more continuous with the first two novels – more realistic, sober – and it was a complete flop.

---

[13] Chris Walsh, 'An Interview with David Lodge', *Strawberry Fare* (Autumn, 1984), 3-12 (p. 9).

"Not a Comic Novelist, Exactly"

And that made me think that if I was to get my fictional career going again I ought to go back to the comic mode, so then I wrote *Changing Places*. Then I began to think that I didn't want to swing between serious, realistic novels and farcical, stylistically experimental novels, so I thought that in *How Far Can You Go?* I would try to combine both.[14]

If *Thinks* ... is unambiguously and self-evidently a serious novel, then *Changing Places*, as Lodge himself emphasizes, is a reversion (after *Out of the Shelter*) to a more purely comic mode. Indeed, it can be thought of as a kind of comedy of errors, full of entrances and exits, the very stuff of farce at one level. It is cunningly structured around not mistakes of identity, but *discoveries* of identity. The international academic exchange becomes the catalyst for profound psychological changes. The physical journeys of Philip Swallow and Morris Zapp entail emotional journeys. Each self becomes rediscovered through an encounter with cultural otherness. Transplant characters from their habitual environment to pastures new, sit back and enjoy the comedic prospect: this is Shakespeare and Jane Austen and Henry James (all of whom are quoted in the course of the novel) in an academic milieu. The various transgressions and transformations of the Swallows and the Byrds mark this out as a novel of becoming, the rationale for which is the metaphor of the "infinitely elastic umbilical cord of emotions, attitudes and values" of the novel's opening section, with its suggestion of Heideggerian *Dasein*.[15] But the novel is, first and foremost,

---

14 Walsh, p. 10.
15 David Lodge, *Changing Places: A Tale of Two Campuses* (1975; Harmondsworth: Penguin, 1978), p. 8. All future page references are to the Penguin edition.

a comedy: its thoughtfulness about lived experience and its insights into contrasting cultures and mores emerge through its comedic structure. As Lodge observes: "My novels are comic, not only in the sense of being funny, but also in structure".[16] Lodge writes revealingly about how important structure is when transforming the raw material of experience into fiction:

> For me a novel usually starts when I realize that some segment or plane of my own experience has a thematic interest and unity which might be expressed through a fictional story. Then I look for some structural idea which will release and contain that potential meaning.[17]

He elaborates further in another interview:

> I think I am by temperament tentative, sceptical, ironic, and so that reflects itself in the structure and texture of what I write. I am well aware that I tend to play off different ideological or moral attitudes against each other, and I can see that one could say it is evasive ... I do sheer away from strong resolutions of the narrative line in my novels which would affirm one position rather than another. I tend to balance things against each other; my novels tend towards binary structures – with, for example, opposite characters – and they very much leave the reader to make up his own mind.[18]

---

[16] As quoted in Bernard Bergonzi, *David Lodge* (Plymouth: Northcote House/British Council, 1995), pp. 60-1.

[17] David Lodge, '*Small World*: An Introduction' (repr. in David Lodge, *Write On: Occasional Essays 1965-1985* (1986; Harmondsworth: Penguin, 1988), p. 72.

[18] As quoted in Haffenden, p. 152.

This is certainly the case with *Changing Places*. *Small World*, his next academic novel of 1984 (and a sequel of sorts), is a rather more complex, ambitious, less easily definable novel. Lodge remarked of the novel that it is "a reversion to comedy primarily ... a comic-satiric novel about what I came to call the 'global campus'".[19] "Primarily", note. So what is it "secondarily"?

The issue of genre is alluded to many times in the novel, from the subtitle, *An Academic Romance*, through the epigraphs from Horace, Hawthorne and Joyce, to the parody of Chaucer in the "Prologue" – and onwards. At the novel's climactic conference, someone asks: "... if the organ of epic is the phallus, of tragedy the testicles, and of romance the vagina, what was the organ of comedy? Oh, the anus, Angelica replied instantly".[20] Again, the selection of critical comments in the blurb provides clues to the novel's mixed modes: while its entertaining qualities and comic inventiveness are stressed (Frank Kermode judged it to be "the funniest novel he has written"), so too are its "dark humour" and its "couplings touching, funny and frightful" (all from reviews quoted on the back cover). Although there are continuities with *Changing Places* in terms of character and theme, the structure is far more complicated, for in the later novel there are multiple transformations and mistaken identities, and in place of the Swallow/Zapp binary exchange we are presented with a much more extensive gallery of characters, all of whom are on their own quests: "... everyone is looking for his own Grail".[21] The very first (of many) witty set pieces – Morris Zapp's keynote lecture[22] – offers an appropriate

---

[19] Walsh, p. 10
[20] Lodge, *Small World*, p. 323.
[21] Lodge, *Small World*, p. 12.
[22] Lodge, *Small World*, pp. 24-7.

hermeneutic: reading anything (not merely written texts) is part of an endless quest for interpretation and meaning ... "Each of us is a subject in search of an object", as Michel Tardieu remarks much later.[23] This gives the organising framework for the story (or stories), but it also allows Lodge to explore something more serious. For what are all these quests? What are we – all of us – looking for?

One answer is given quite early on: "Intensity of experience is what we're looking for, I think", suggests Philip Swallow[24] in a sudden moment of philosophical profundity, which follows a poignant exchange between Hilary Swallow and Morris Zapp, and precedes the introduction of one of the novel's numerous, and cleverly intertwined, sub-plots, illustrative (in Freudian or Lawrentian terms) of the competing sex and death instincts. "I felt I was defying death, fucking my way out of the grave", comments Philip Swallow.[25] A few pages later, the precise variety of intensity we all crave is narrowed down further by Swallow, and identified as sexual passion in relationships: "Perhaps *that's* what we're all looking for – desire undiluted by habit", which is the cue for Zapp to take us back to reading literature and defamiliarization: quoting Viktor Shklovsky, he explains how "*Art exists to help us recover the sensation of life*".[26]

This is a theme which Lodge pursues productively throughout the novel. Later, for example, as Philip is hurriedly catching an early morning taxi to take him to the airport (another conference beckons, this time in Turkey), he experiences just such a shock of defamiliarization, but in life, not in art:

---

[23] Lodge, *Small World*, p. 200.
[24] Lodge, *Small World*, p. 66.
[25] Lodge, *Small World*, p. 74.
[26] Lodge, *Small World*, p. 77.

"Not a Comic Novelist, Exactly"

But then an extraordinary thing happens. Hilary's old coat falls open, the neckline of her nightgown gapes, and Philip glimpses the curve of her right breast. It is an object he knows well. He made his first tactile acquaintance with it twenty-five years ago, tentatively fondling it, through the impeding upholstery of a Marks and Spencer's fisherman's knit jumper and a stoutly constructed Maidenform brassière, as he kissed its young postgraduate owner goodnight on the porch of her digs one night after a Film Society showing of *Battleship Potemkin*. He first set entranced eyes upon its naked flesh on his wedding night. Since then he must have seen and touched it (and its twin) several thousand times ... during which time it lost its pristine firmness ... and became as familiar to him as an old cushion ... But such is the mystery of desire – the fickleness and unpredictability of its springs and motions – that this unexpected glimpse of the breast ... makes Philip suddenly faint with the longing to touch, suck, lick, nuzzle, etc. it again. He does not want to go to Turkey. He does not want to go anywhere at this moment except back to bed with Hilary. But of course, he cannot. Is it only because he cannot that he wants to so much? All he can do is to press his lips on Hilary's more enthusiastically than he had intended – or than she expected, for she looks at him with a quizzical, affectionate, even tender regard as the taxi, at last, inexorably moves away. Philip looks back through the rear window. Hilary stoops to pluck from the gutter a stray sock, and waves it forlornly after him, like a makeshift favour.[27]

---

[27] Lodge, *Small World*, p. 168.

Clearly, the mode of description in this well-judged and finely understated passage is *primarily* comical, but that does not prevent the moment from being mildly erotic, and indeed "tender" and "affectionate", not least in the context of what we have learned about the faltering Swallow marriage. The episode's detail, moreover, has the ring of authenticity about it: it is real, fully convincing. The prose is contrived, carefully modulated (the jokes would not work otherwise), but the underlying note of seriousness is unmistakeable – serious enough, perhaps, to take the reader by surprise, and in the defamiliarizing ambush to help "recover the sensation of life". It is not the first, nor the last, occasion in the novel in which Philip Swallow is "surprised by Joy", and what makes these (linked) moments both plaintive and perspicacious is the clear sense that Lodge *means* them to be taken seriously. They are "extraordinary" moments (rather like Emma's tears, "extraordinary as they were" after the Box Hill débâcle). Profound human passions should never be taken *wholly* lightly, and Lodge, while showing a sharp eye for every behavioural absurdity in *Small World*, is far too intelligent a novelist to be content with mere "fun-poking". For all its game-playing and reflexivity and self-consciousness, the novel never trivializes the big issues. As Morris Zapp observes: "... death is the one concept you can't deconstruct".[28] The climax of *Small World* – wonderful irony! – is the discovery of the parentage of Angelica and Lily Pabst, twin daughters (who have, very appropriately, opening and closing inverted commas for their respective birthmarks) of Arthur Kingfisher and Sybil Maiden, in a scene parodying (what else!) Wilde's *The Importance of Being Earnest*. Lodge is hardly earnest, but he is certainly serious.

---

[28] Lodge, *Small World*, p. 328.

With *Nice Work* we are back to Lodge's favourite binary structures.[29] If less rich, complex, diffuse than *Small World*, this is tighter, sharper, more authoritative – a mature, masterly achievement (to use a Dickensian analogy, more *Great Expectations* than *Bleak House*). The novel's allusiveness and intertextual richness are more focused: Lodge revisits Gaskell's *North and South* through E. M. Forster's *Howards End* as he shows off his own brand of romantic realism. But while several of the main themes from his earlier novels reappear in *Nice Work*, there is a quality of self-assurance which is new. His account of the marriage and sex-life of Vic and Marjorie Wilcox (complete with mid-life crisis *and* menopause), for example, is even more convincing (more *felt*) than that of Philip and Hilary Swallow's relationship. Consider the account of Vic and Marjorie having sex.[30] The free indirect narrative moves effortlessly between Vic and omniscience, before switching to Joycean stream of consciousness. The tone, too, is neither comical nor dourly realistic, but somewhere in between. The psychological verisimilitude is matched by a moral seriousness:

> It was years since he had felt any unforced desire for Marjorie, and now he couldn't even force it. When she seemed to be going off sex because of her time of life he'd been secretly relieved ...Vic had old-fashioned ideas about marriage. A wife was not like a car: you couldn't part-exchange her when the novelty wore off, or the bodywork started to go ...[31]

---

[29] Most of Lodge's fictions including his two most recent novels, *Thinks ...* and *Author, Author*, have binary structures.
[30] Lodge, *Nice Work*, pp. 165-7.
[31] Lodge, *Nice Work*, p. 165.

The Academic Novel

Recalling his meeting with Robyn Penrose in a bathrobe, Vic (in bed with Marjorie) develops an erection:

> To his surprise, and almost dismay, his penis stiffened at the recollection. Marjorie, reaching probably for his hand, to give it a friendly squeeze, found his penis instead, giggled and murmured, 'Ooh, you are interested after all, then?'
>
> Then he had no option but to go through with it, though as Marjorie gasped and grunted beneath him he was only able to come by imagining he was doing it to Robyn Penrose ... [32]

This is well done. Vic is only "almost" dismayed; Marjorie was "probably" reaching for his hand. Lodge manages to be nuanced *and* authoritative. The characterization is profounder than in his earlier academic novels: both Vic Wilcox and Robyn Penrose are more strongly realized than Morris Zapp and Philip Swallow – we see them from inside and outside, as they see themselves and each other and so, partly as a result of Lodge's mastery of free indirect style, the portraits really are rounded.

Nice Work constitutes an advance on his earlier academic novels in several respects. Most obviously, it shows Lodge moving well beyond his comfort zone, dealing with aspects of contemporary life relatively unfamiliar to him. Up to this point, all of his novels have transmuted direct personal experience into fictional form: Lodge's childhood and adolescence, his time in the army when on National Service, his Catholicism, and his professional career as literary academic all feed, and feed into, his novels fairly recognisably. In *Nice Work*, he turns

---

[32] Lodge, *Nice Work*, p. 166.

his attention to the wider world of work in 1980s Britain, and in particular to the private sector – manufacturing, trade, commerce and industry – and relates this bigger picture to the (smaller) academic world. The "Author's Note"[33] modestly hints at the learning curve Lodge had to follow in familiarizing himself with this other world: research had to complement autobiography in the writing of this novel. And the research paid off – handsomely. *Nice Work* is a relentlessly informative novel, substantial, laden with detail – and clearly the work of a critic and pedagogue turning his serious attention to contemporary, Thatcherite Britain. The novel has, therefore, a much stronger sense of place. Much is explained to the reader in succinct, deft, witty set-pieces (whether about "the Dark Country" or semiotic materialism). The Silk Cut set-piece, for example,[34] is representative of Lodge's method, interrogating the assumptions of both the academy and industrial capitalism (in the factory and the City) by *defamiliarizing* both. In this respect, Lodge's novel is quite different from Gaskell's *Mary Barton* and *North and South*, where one of her main aims was undoubtedly to *familiarize* her ignorant middle-class readers with the alien world of urban working-class culture and society in the interest of "overcoming prejudice": "That's what this Shadow Scheme is all about, overcoming prejudice"[35] – as good a rationale as any for the nicely worked-out structure of *Nice Work*.

"People mutht be amuthed", Sleary insists in Dickens's *Hard Times* – a remark appositely quoted in *Nice Work*.[36] The seriousness of this novel springs partly, of course, from contrasting opposed ideological world views (Robyn

---

[33] Lodge, *Nice Work*, p. 7.
[34] Lodge, *Nice Work*, pp. 220-4.
[35] Lodge, *Nice Work*, p. 333.
[36] Lodge, *Nice Work*, p. 77.

– idealistic, academic, socialist, feminist, literary, theoretical; Vic – pragmatic, commonsensical, practical, capitalist, industrialist), and from setting up the Victorian social-problem novel and associated criticism and pedagogy as a commentary on 1980s England (and vice versa). So, unlike *Changing Places* and *Small World*, a debate runs through the novel, very much in the *roman à thèse* tradition. Its contemporary concerns challenge the reader still more insistently and profoundly than his earlier academic fiction, as Lodge attempts to do for the culture and society of the late twentieth century what the Victorians had tried to do for the mid-nineteenth century. The question inevitably arises: whose side is Lodge on? Does he lean more one way, or is he even-handed? Who has more to learn, further to travel – Robyn or Vic? The moral and political and economic issues are made real in both private and public spheres – and this is something else new in Lodge's novel: his creative linking of the private with the public spheres. Lodge insists powerfully that one should not attempt to dissociate the public and the private, and in this he is in agreement with Dickens, Disraeli, Gaskell, Eliot – and Forster, whose dictum "only connect" is explicitly quoted at a key moment.[37] Private acts have public consequences (and vice versa). The most important moment is kept to the very end, to the last main paragraph in fact, which describes Robyn looking out of the window, in a passage with clear echoes of Dorothea's similar epiphany in chapter 80 of *Middlemarch*. What we are presented with here by Lodge is a serious vision of the potential for a *whole*, undivided society, even though Robyn recognises that: "There is a long way to go".[38] This reinterpretation of George Eliot for our own time is bold,

---

[37] Lodge, *Nice Work*, p. 381.
[38] Lodge, *Nice Work*, p. 384.

and apt, and packs quite a punch. This is not glib, or superficial, or simply the stuff of comedy: it is – seriously – the real thing.

The seriousness of a novel, patently, does not depend on how much research (historical, biographical, scientific) underpins and informs it. (Though it is interesting to note that *Nice Work*, *Thinks ...* and *Author, Author* are Lodge's most obviously researched novels.) Moreover, seriousness is not an alternative to entertainment or amusement. Neither is seriousness about dealing with suitably big themes and issues in an earnest, imposing way. Nobody would claim that Shakespeare's comedies lack seriousness and are trivial or lightweight. Seriousness is, or ought to be, about an attitude of mind, a mind which *thinks*. David Lodge *Thinks ...* He really does.

In an extract from her book *At the Same Time* (London: Hamish Hamilton, 2007), published posthumously in *The Guardian*, the late Susan Sontag wrote:

> I'm often asked if there is something I think writers *ought* to do, and recently in an interview I heard myself say: "Several things. Love words, agonise over sentences. And pay attention to the world."
>
> Needless to say, no sooner had these perky phrases fallen out of my mouth than I thought of some more recipes for writer's virtue.
>
> For instance: "Be serious." By which I meant: never be cynical. And which *doesn't* preclude being funny ...
>
> Serious fiction writers think about moral problems *practically*. They tell stories. They narrate. They evoke our common humanity in narratives with which we can identify, even though the lives may be remote from our own. They stimulate our imagination. The

stories they tell enlarge and complicate – and, therefore, improve – our sympathies. They educate our capacity for moral judgment.[39]

In his academic fiction, Lodge is serious, I would argue, in precisely Sontag's terms. He is never cynical. His novels do "evoke our common humanity". The stories he tells do indeed "stimulate our imagination ... enlarge and complicate – and, therefore, improve – our sympathies [and, ultimately] educate our capacity for moral judgment". Bernard Bergonzi observes acutely:

> Lodge is unusual and fortunate in being a best-selling novelist of wide appeal who nevertheless takes the art of fiction very seriously ... and is willing to challenge his readers as well as entertain them ... He is interested, too, in ideas about how civilization is maintained; in his novels comedy is interwoven with serious reflections on religion and society, literature and education.[40]

In *How Far Can You Go?* Lodge comments: "This book is not a comic novel, exactly, but I have tried to make it smile as much as possible".[41] Lodge's academic novels have the unarguable merit of making his readers smile; they also have the inestimable virtue of making thoughtful readers think.

---

[39] Susan Sontag, 'Pay attention to the world', *The Guardian* 17 March 2007, Saturday Review, 4-6 (p. 6).
[40] Bergonzi, *David Lodge*, p. 60.
[41] David Lodge, *How Far Can You Go?* (Harmondsworth: Penguin, 1981), p. 74.

CAMPUS *FUGIT*: HOWARD JACOBSON'S *COMING FROM BEHIND*

Glyn Turton

Where are the polytechnics of yesteryear? Easily answered
– gone to universities, every one. The modernist logos have
been replaced by heraldic shields, the terse corporate
mission statements with powerful overtones of change and
opportunity have given way to classical mottoes – and the
prosaically entitled directors have been transformed into
vice-chancellors, ceremonial regalia and all. More to the
point, what *were* the polytechnics of yesteryear? That
question baffles now as it has done ever since these strange
institutions were created in the late 1960s, sired by a
socialist government on the grudging municipalities of
large British cities as a way of expanding higher education
on the cheap. With their origins in local business and
technical institutions, the *raison d'être* of the polytechnics
was meant to be that they should differ from traditional
universities in their greater emphasis on vocational
education and their more experimental curriculum. In
some ways, that was their distinction. But it was in the
end, alas, distinction of another kind, the kind which goes
with name and status, which they really craved, a craving
which the British government finally satisfied in 1992
when it removed the so-called binary divide between the
polytechnics and universities. For every institution in
Britain, just like every citizen, is afflicted by a sense of
being inferior or superior to something or somebody. And
the polytechnics suffered from day one from an inferiority
complex towards the longer-established universities, from
a crisis of identity, from a nasty sense that, though their
courses might be more in tune with the spirit of

contemporaneity, they were, somehow or other, not quite *kosher* ....

The same could hardly be said of Sefton Goldberg, unapologetically Jewish hero of Howard Jacobson's comic novel of polytechnic life. Stuck fast professionally as lecturer in English at Wrottesley Polytechnic, an unglamorous institution in an unlovely Midlands setting, in his mental and emotional life Goldberg vigorously surfs the repeated waves of envy, frustration and contempt that surge through his being. Multiple alienation is the key to his and the novel's satiric energy. Sefton is a Jew among gentiles, a failure among successes, a would-be metropolitan intellectual mired in provincial philistinism, a child of the suburbs totally out of sympathy with the English pastoral tradition he is forced to teach, and a loather of the national game of football, whose employer has rented part of a neighbouring soccer ground in which to house his department. Worst of all, he is an undiscriminating partaker of insipid foreign lager beers, surrounded by a freemasonry of "real ale" enthusiasts. No estrangement so complete. Never such separation of the *mensch* from the *goys*.

Sefton Goldberg's essential impulses are directed outwards and upwards. His twin passions are application and fornication, the first to any institution, great or small (other than Wrottesley), which will clasp him to its bosom and the second with female ex-students who will do the same. His position is in all respects non-missionary. That is how we find him at the opening of *Coming From Behind*, eponymously astride Mrs Lynne Shorthall, newly graduated, mature, working-class student of the kind to which the polytechnic seeks to give access and who is now reciprocally providing the facility for her former tutor. And that is how Sefton Goldberg sees his pedagogic purpose in life – to unenlighten. For his contempt for students and their failure to respond to his bravura performances in lectures has passed beyond the merely retributive withholding of knowledge to the gleefully punitive dispensing of misinformation.

> At first he went no further than to keep things from them – his freshest insights, his most startling judgments, a trenchant phrase that had come to him in his sleep. He didn't tell them any more jokes either, and he didn't rip any more Penguin Classics. But deprivation on this scale soon struck him as being rather tame, especially as his students lacked the wherewithal to comprehend the magnitude of their loss, and so he stepped up his campaign to include deliberately leading them astray – confusing chronology, moving without their noticing it scenes and characters from one long novel to another, misattributing authorship, and finally, in order that they should remain forever in ignorance of the great tradition, informing them that the major English novelists were Bulwer Lytton, Charles Lever, Harrison Ainsworth, Mrs Henry Wood, and Angela Carter. He also told them that the greatest English poets were Francis Quarles and Namby-Pamby Philips, and that the greatest living critic was Bernard Levin.[1]

The British campus novel of the post-war period has usually featured as the central character either an innocent abroad, or a subversive, or, occasionally, a mixture of the two. Into the first of these categories falls Perse McGarrigle of David Lodge's *Small World*,[2] into the second Malcolm

---

[1] Howard Jacobson, *Coming From Behind* (1983; London: Penguin, 1993), p. 47. All future page references are to the Penguin edition.

[2] David Lodge, *Small World* (London: Secker & Warburg, 1984).

293

Bradbury's "History Man," Howard Kirk,[3] and into the third Jim Dixon of Kingsley Amis's *Lucky Jim*.[4] Each type affords different possibilities for satirising the solemn game which is academic life. And each of these characters has about him something of the temper of the particular time in which the novel was set. Thus the clowning of Jim Dixon catches the apolitical mood of the 1950s while the pursuit of left radicalism for personal ends of Bradbury's Howard Kirk reflects a time – the period from 1968 to 1979 – when every campus was in thrall to ideology. Jacobson's *Coming From Behind* conforms to this pattern: Sefton Goldberg's desperate efforts to deliver himself from Wrottesley Polytechnic into the arms of the University of Cambridge, where he was once a student, his consuming envy of his contemporaries who have made it, are symptomatic of the *sauve qui peut* Thatcherite 1980s. *Coming From Behind* has neither the trenchant and controlled satire of *The History Man*, nor the allegorical elegance of Lodge's mock-Romance comedy, *Small World*, and in those respects it might be thought a slighter work than either. But it handles its slightness dexterously, like a judo expert, managing to bring down some weighty cultural totems and contemporary shibboleths in quite heavy falls. In one sense, too, its tone of simmering skittishness marks it out as of its time, which is that of an absurd post-modernity where style jostles with style, ancient university with modern polytechnic, Cambridge brahmin with Yiddish suburbanite, high culture with low. Here the signifiers really have broken free of the signifieds. All promotion is self-promotion – in which regard there is nothing to distinguish Sefton Goldberg's desire to re-attach

---

[3] Malcolm Bradbury, *The History Man* (London: Secker & Warburg, 1975).

[4] Kingsley Amis, *Lucky Jim* (London: Gollancz, 1954).

himself to the august University of Cambridge from the Polytechnic's desire to attach itself to neighbouring Wrottesley Ramblers Football Club in a bid to ingratiate itself with the populace and their pursuits.

In the campus novels of Bradbury and Lodge, liberal humanism, even when it is on the defensive, is usually at work somewhere, explicitly or sub-textually, as a talisman against false doctrine. Tolerance, sympathy and openness, in a world of incongruities, are seen as the only things congruent with moral certainty. In the robustly parodic *Coming From Behind* culture in general, and literature in particular, flicker on as the shades of once supposedly real values. But they are comic ghosts. Again, the comparative reference point is Malcolm Bradbury's *The History Man*. The setting of this novel is the campus of one of the new universities of the 1960s, those institutions which represented the wave of expansion of higher education that immediately preceded the creation of the urban polytechnics. In *The History Man* sociology is portrayed as the normative academic discipline with liberal humanism, represented by the study of literature, as a rival doctrine forced to fight for its life within an intensely politicised academy. Bradbury satirises both camps, but the satire bears the weight of a deadly serious argument about academic freedom and the academy is at least still the forum within which competing world views contend over mutually recognised issues. In *Coming From Behind* mere (comic) anarchy is loosed upon the world. Sefton Goldberg, educated in the Cambridge of F.R. Leavis where belief in the saving, morally therapeutic value of literature had become an orthodoxy, cares passionately about books – to the point where he tears up in lectures those of which he disapproves.

... Sefton Goldberg was incapable of taking the idea of a book lightly. For him a book had magical properties. In a book the word was made holy. Why else did he disapprove of so many so vehemently or make such a ritual out of tearing them up in lectures? In a world where reputation was evanescent and human passions were transient, only the book was stable and permanent. Even to be remaindered was to be remembered.[5]

But a ludicrous world throws back at him the image of his own absurdity, sometimes with robust Oedipal mockery. For Sefton stands in the shadow not only of his spiritual father, Leavis, but also of his natural one, Sam Goldberg, the large, benign vulgarian, whose hobby is party tricks and whose passion for tearing up telephone books mimics his son's histrionic performances on the lecture podium. In fact, Sefton harbours the searing memory of the moment in his life when the two worlds between which he wanders collided, when the Upholder of the Great Tradition and the Destroyer of the Manchester Telephone Directory encountered each other on the day of his graduation. Sam Goldberg, having hired a large limousine for the day, descended upon the narrow streets of Cambridge, and knocked "some of the finest minds in Europe off their bicycles," inflicts the ultimate humiliation on his son by setting up his conjuring table on the college lawn and theatrically producing an egg from Leavis's ear.

This comic episode featuring one of the great cultural icons of the twentieth century as magician's stooge is, of course, in one sense, nothing more than that – comedy through absurd juxtaposition. But the accumulation of such absurdities in *Coming From Behind* conveys a sense,

---

[5] Jacobson, p. 17.

not so much of the world turned upside down, as of the world probably never having been the right way up. The serious point of this, like that of most comic works, is that nothing can be taken seriously and certainly not the idea that culture, higher learning, the life of the mind are proof of reason and proof against anarchy. Indeed, in the very name of enlightenment, a kind of managed lunacy and an increase in the sum of ignorance may occur – as that awesome creation, Wrottesley Polytechnic, proves by its existence and its ways.

In its dedication to the proposition that the world is probably mad, both locally and generally, *Coming From Behind* has as much kinship with a great satirical novel such as *Catch-22*[6] as with earlier British campus fiction. In fact, in its comic strategy – the simple account of the hero's effort to escape, used to carry the reader past a gallery of satirical types and through a series of comic episodes – Heller's novel is what it most resembles. These episodes are most effective where Jacobson's astringent comic critique of polytechnic life broadens and extends to reach into the recesses of Britain's cultural myths and its national malaise. At such points of satirical strength, the author brings the hero's Jewishness fully into play, deepening the focus so that the novel becomes not just about being an unwilling foot-soldier in the army of the new educational utilitarianism, but also about being a Jew in a culture to which you are only half-assimilated. For *Coming From Behind* belongs with the tradition of the literature of the wandering Jew in its modern manifestations. Looking at the novel intertextually calls to mind Malamud's *A New Life*,[7] in which the comedy of academic manners in West

---

[6] Joseph Heller, *Catch-22* (New York: Simon & Schuster, 1961; London: Jonathan Cape, 1962)

[7] Bernard Malamud, *A New Life* (New York: Farrar, Straus and Giroux, 1961; London : Eyre & Spottiswode, 1962).

coast, small town America is seen through the eyes of a Jewish loner, and – and this is not fanciful – *Ulysses*,[8] where the partially alienated Jew is used as a focaliser for "making strange" the gentiles and their culture. (Not, the reader understands, that the polytechnics needed making any stranger in the first place.)

Chapter Three of *Coming From Behind* is such an example of the way Jacobson is capable of modulating the whimsical into the sardonic and deploying a Jew's-eye view to create a dark-edged comic perspective. The chapter as a whole is an exceptionally fine *tour de force* of humorous writing, laced with sinister undertones, and merits attention for the richness of its comic brio. It sees Sefton Goldberg at the nadir of his fortunes; already bitter at the successes of his Jewish school-friend, Godfrey Jelley, as a media celebrity, and his colleague, Cora Peck, as an academic, and so far failing to interest a publisher in his own book on failure, he has experienced insult added to injury with the news that the polytechnic has done a deal with neighbouring football club Wrottesley Ramblers, which will see Sefton's department re-housed in the club's south stand.[9] The central character's mood of desperation and cynicism is the cue for the chapter to open with a glorious résumé, rendered in free indirect reflection, of Sefton Goldberg's loathing for two of the prominent totems, one high and the other low, of Anglo-Saxon culture, namely nature and football. Within a few glorious pages, the ground is running with the blood of cows, sacred to the English's sense of themselves and mercilessly

---

[8] James Joyce, *Ulysses* (Paris: Shakespeare and Company, 1922).

[9] This apparently fanciful development is actually patterned on a similar arrangement between Wolverhampton Polytechnic, where Jacobson once taught, and the Wolverhampton Wanderers football club. The Poly occupied premises in the football stadium.

sacrificed on the altar of Jewish wit. The effect is uproariously funny and immensely liberating to any Englishman who has been put to Wordsworth and Wolverhampton Wanderers at too early an age.

If all English literature was about country walks – and that was beginning to look suspiciously like the case – then what the fuck had it to do with Sefton Goldberg who was Jewish and who had therefore never taken a country walk in his life? That was a question to which Sefton had not got around to finding an answer, even now. What happened in the country was as impenetrable as it had ever been. He still couldn't, today, tell a brake from a bosk or a rill from a beck; he still didn't know whether one ripped one's clothes on a tor or tumbled headlong down a coppice; and he was no more certain than he had ever been that one didn't swim in an osprey or feed crumbs to a runnel.[10]

In the end, though, greater than Sefton's incomprehension of nature is his exclusion from the passion of the British gentile male for soccer. As Jacobson warms to his satirical theme of all things *goyisch* and moves to Sefton's dislike of the national game, the humour begins to take on a darker tinge and opens out insightfully into a contrast in racial histories, cultural attitudes and tribal psychology. For Sefton, while he relishes the sense of occasion of the big game ("He was as sentimental as Hitler about applause and crowds"), believes that the switch-back ride of emotions undergone by the gentile spectator of soccer, from elation to deflation, represents a profound misreading of fate to which no Jew would ever be susceptible. He recalls being taken unwillingly to a soccer

---

[10] Jacobson, p. 59.

match late in life and seeing two orthodox-looking Jewish boys watching the match. When their team scores first, the one turns to the other and says, "I don't like it, Myer – they've scored too soon." Sefton understands this doleful disquiet, judging that the capacity of the gentiles, players and fans alike, for being transported by successive emotions of triumph and despair represents the "unimaginativeness of irreligion" of a people who "knew nothing of retribution, learnt nothing from experience, feared nothing from providence." For to Sefton Goldberg, "in the strictest sense the game they played was heathen. For the *goyim*."[11]

To be breast-high amid the alien corn is bad enough but to be up to your arm-pits in heathen turf is a sorrier plight. These introductory perspectives on the icons of high and low Anglo-Saxon culture, symbolised by the insensitive soccer hooligan and the hypersensitive north country nature writer (Sefton's deficiency being that he "did not yet know - *know* in that Nottinghamshire way - that he did not belong to himself"[12]) create an appropriately sardonic mood for the central episode of Chapter Three, an episode which is both comic and disturbing. Sefton returns to the Wrottesley Polytechnic car park. He is world-weary, having spent the better part of degree day worrying about his professional future and whether or not his office door was locked during coitus with Mrs Lynne Shorthall. As he approaches his car, he is confronted by members of the Department of Modern Languages for Business, on whose parking patch he has unwittingly encroached. Building on the idea of the Jew as a rootless, cosmopolitan threat to an insular and bigoted people, Jacobson turns this scene of confrontation into a stinging satire on a society which is

---

[11] Jacobson, p. 63.
[12] Jacobson, p. 60.

parochial, xenophobic, fundamentally at odds with itself. In the full sense, he prepares the ground for this show-down by evoking the urban polytechnic car park of the early 1980s as a manifestation of the national gifts for squalor as art form and for confusing service with servitude. For it is a truth universally acknowledged that, in British life, amenities are often proffered in a form which seeks to punish you for wanting them in the first place.

Sefton notes, how,

> ... undeterred, the drivers washed their wheels and imposed an order of their own upon the rotting terrain, parcelling it out strictly, with a foot or two more for this department and a foot or two less for that, according to the number of doctorates in each.[13]

Jacobson's humour here shades into a significant insight into the national psyche. *Coming From Behind* is recognisably set on the cusp of distinct phases in British social and political history with the individualist nostrums of the Thatcherite new right emerging out of the degenerated collectivist ethic of the post-war settlement. The description of the polytechnic car park with cars "vacuumed and waxed and smelling of shampoo," jockeying for space on a piece of squalid waste land stands out as an apt metaphor for a society in which the conflict between the public and the private is fought out not as a civil war but as a war of civilities. It appears to be true that fault lines in the collective social unconscious register differently from people to people. In France, the nation's argument with itself erupts in massive seismic upheavals at periodic intervals; in Britain it is present as a permanent, low-grade tectonic rumbling, so muted the natives can

---

[13] Jacobson, p. 64.

hardly hear it. Jacobson, with the ear of a Jewish ironist, picks it up well.

On this darkling plain of the polytechnic car park Sefton Goldberg clashes with the ignorant army of the Department of Modern Languages for Business who have pasted stickers over the windscreen of his car. Their ostensible quarrel with him is that he has parked in their space – and their real one that he is a smart-arse, a sender up and putter down of others in front of students, a dangerous cosmopolitan whose arrogance reflects the sense of superiority of the subject he teaches. The terms of the dispute are as much of their time as those which governed the conflict between sociology and literature in *The History Man*. The battle of the 1970s for the ideological high ground has given way to a 1980s battle for the low ground of territorial status, reputation and political correctness. The clash of the Grand Narratives recedes and the complex politics of the Single Issues emerges. One of Sefton Goldberg's accusers, the new lecturer, Walter Sickert Fledwhite, reputedly a structuralist, sports an anti-Nazi League badge, which the Jewish Goldberg paradoxically finds threatening while the homosexual Fledwhite's real grudge against Goldberg turns out to be that he has spent an hour inveighing to his students against the modern misuse of the word "gay." The car park row – and the chapter – conclude not with someone breaking someone else's jaw but with Goldberg breaking the ultimate modern taboo of the educating classes and calling Fledwhite a "little poofter" in an attempt to wrong-foot the encircling linguists. This bout of mutual taunting and persecution, linking the appropriation of parking space with the appropriation of words, satirises the contemporary academy's preoccupation with the inscription of power relations in language and the accompanying spatial metaphors through which meanings are conceived of as "sites."

But, acrimonious as it is, this dispute between the earnest, tap-water-drinking Linguists for Business and the Jewish Scholar Gypsy over where the latter rests his caravan (and his incautious words) is but a minor peninsular skirmish in the grand verbal conflict which is being fought out within Wrottesley Polytechnic. The commanding heights are occupied by the polytechnic's *apparatchiki*, who, "mindful of its obligations to a technological society and anxious not to be confused with Oxford or Cambridge"[14] have adopted a form of educational Newspeak , intended to assert the triumph of efficiency, modernity and managerialism over a played-out tradition of the gifted amateur. To this end, the polytechnic has renamed the Department of English Literature the Department of Twentieth Century Studies. Sadly, the department's staff remain unreconstructed, particularly their head, Charles Wenlock, old-fashioned humanist aesthete.

In this Swiftian battle of Ancients and Moderns, Charles Wenlock's *bête noire* is the sinister Dr Gerald Sidewinder, polytechnic bureaucrat, whose project of twinning the institution with the town's neighbouring soccer club has the subsidiary and, to him, entirely desirable aim of academically cleansing the polytechnic by relocating Twentieth Century Studies/Literature to the club's south stand. Sidewinder, a Strangelove figure of indeterminate function and qualifications, and Charles Wenlock, exasperated, comic-heroic and doomed to lose, act out a Darwinian struggle for the survival of values. The portrayal of the awesomely misanthropic and totally fire-proof Sidewinder is one of the most memorable

---

[14] Jacobson, p. 38.

achievements in Jacobson's gallery of polytechnic types. Even the most ardent post-structuralist, committed to the conviction that literature is not referential, would be compelled, provided (s)he had served time in a polytechnic, to suffer doctrinal lapse and recognise the Death-in-Life figure of Sidewinder, part-carpetbagger, part-commissar, as eerily familiar.

> Sefton had always prided himself on being, in so far as a proper worldliness demanded it, something of a cynic.... But Sidewinder taught him that he knew nothing at all of that perfect carelessness of the feelings and the opinions of men, that pure indifference to their regard or their execration, which is cynicism proper. Watching the slow movement of Sidewinder's tongue; listening to the flat vowels of his Chorley accent, Sefton realised that all along he had only been dabbling in misanthropy, which is a passion.[15]

The machinations of Sidewinder (the novel's baroque comic sub-plot) and the single-minded quest for recognition of Sefton Goldberg (its essential narrative) converge as the story draws to a close. It transpires that the deal brokered between Ramblers and the Polytechnic has been made possible through Sidewinder's friendship with the egregious Kevin Dainty, club captain, author of the autobiographical novel *Scoring* and Sidewinder's hang-gliding partner. When Kevin Dainty falls to his death from a hang-glider, a joint polytechnic-football club memorial service is arranged for the start of a big match between Wrottesley and Dainty's former London club, East Ham. Sefton, adulatory crowd junkie and the poly's "long novel" man, is made an offer he cannot refuse – to give the

---

[15] Jacobson, p. 43.

memorial reading from Kevin Dainty's book at the start of the game. The opportunity presents Sefton with the choice between a career sent soaring off into the wide blue yonder and a kamikaze dive, which might just sink the polytechnic. Should he ingratiate himself with Sidewinder and the poly's Director, who flank him as he stands before the forty thousand restive fans, by paying false homage to Kevin Dainty? Or should he strike a blow for his benighted colleagues and true culture by ritually tearing up *Scoring* as he has torn up so many despised books before? Summoning up his father's tips on directory destruction, he stands poised to come down on the side of the angels when a tomato-hurling pitch invasion by his sworn enemy Fledwhite distracts both fans and television cameras from Sefton's moment of glory.

Reduction to the absurd, all of this. And yet, the episode succeeds, as does the novel generally, in combining robust comedy and mordant satire. For in contemporary Britain those lower down the pecking order of higher education are right there in the market place, ever ready with stunts to persuade the punters that learning is as necessary as bread and as exciting as circuses. Strong double-glazing salesmen might blench at Jacobson's evocation of an inner city polytechnic open day – but it falls only just on the parodic side of the real.

> The younger, more junior staff were escorting groups of unbelieving school children around the building explaining the organization of courses, discriminating between modules, pointing out the generous provision of stair-cases and toilets, slighting the universities, hinting at pleasures not in the prospectuses. Enticements such as, "If you lean to your left and stand on tiptoes you can just see Wales" and, "Yes, field trips are a compulsory component of unit GEO II and they are subject to a … well, a form of assessment; but mainly we all

The Academic Novel

go to the Lake District and get pissed" floated across to Sefton Goldberg as he made his way to the room.[16]

At the opposite end of the spectrum to this effortful inferiority, lies the effortless superiority of Holy Christ Hall, Cambridge, more solicited against than soliciting, and recipient of a highly speculative application from Sefton for the prized Disraeli Fellowship. The depiction of Holy Christ Hall, its Fellows and its Master, is just as important an ingredient as Wrottesley in a fictional concoction which blends the real and grotesque in well judged measure. Whatever power the wheeler-dealing Sidewinder may have over Sefton Goldberg, it is as nothing compared to the ability of Sir Evelyn Woolfardisworthy, Master of Holy Christ, to reduce a Jewish ex-grammar school boy to a clammy-palmed wreck. Urbane, patrician and utterly poised, Woolfardisworthy is caught by Jacobson in a set-piece description as witty and memorable as that of Sidewinder.

Against all the odds, though, and aided by a display of intellectual showmanship over dinner at high table, Jewish local boy makes good. Sefton comes from behind to win the Disraeli Fellowship, and escape from Wrottesley, thus ensuring for himself – and the novel – a climax which is also a withdrawal.

Coming from Behind is a sharp and richly entertaining comedy of professional and sexual manners. It anatomises satirically the British higher education system at a moment of change and uncertainty, with its insights into the brazenness and insecurity of an upstart institution set against the sleek and no less absurd complacency of an ancient one. It hardly needs stating that Jacobson himself has had experience of both; indeed, a reading of *Coming*

---

[16] Jacobson, p. 20.

From Behind as a *roman à clef* for those on the inside might not be unprofitable. But for most readers, academic or general, the pleasures of this text will be, simply and delightfully, both cathartic and intellectual. Like David Lodge's campus novel *Changing Places*,[17] it is a book which sends tap roots into the contradictions and absurdities of society beyond the academy and draws them to the surface. It would not do to diminish the comic energy of the novel by crediting it with the deadweight of too much moral import. But, by lampooning notions of humanity and enlightenment alongside absurdity and irrationality, Jacobson does scrape away the encrustations that have accumulated on those ideals and cleans them up for future use. Satire succeeds if it gives us the measure of the otherwise incommensurable. And it can be counted effective if, through the vicarious process of engagement with the fictional, it converts vexation and outrage into reconciliation with the actual. By these tokens *Coming From Behind* takes its place not just as a notable example of the campus sub-genre, but as a satire on human behaviour which applies and appeals beyond the increasingly blighted Groves of Academe.

---

[17] David Lodge, *Changing Places* (London: Secker and Warburg, 1975).

NAME AND TITLE INDEX

Name and Title Index

Churchill, Winston 37
Cixous, Hélène 233, 234, 239, 250, 252, 254-5, 257, 258
Clark, Walter Van Tilburg 44, 62
Closing of the American Mind, The 10, 141
Coetzee, J. M. 111, 160
Coffin for Pandora, A 129-30
Colette 255
College Novel in America, The 3-4
Coming From Behind viii, 19, 106, 124-5, 158, **291-307**
Company She Kept, The 184-5, 186-7
Concise Companion to Contemporary British Fiction, A 3
Concise Oxford Dictionary of Literary Terms, The 268-9, 271
Confusions 46
Connery, Brian 11
Consciousness and the Novel 268
Consuming Fictions 6
Contemporary Novelists 83
Cool Million, A 50
Cooper, William 33
Cooper-Clark, Diana 109
Cornford, F. M. 98, 263, 264
Crampton Hodnet 136-7
Crispin, Edmund 116, 118, 119, 122-3
Criticism and Ideology 85
Crumey, Andrew 112
Culture Shock 130-1
Cuts 110
Dames' Delight 133-4
Darwin, Charles 74, 303
David Lodge 280, 290
David Lodge: How Far Can You Go? 270, 273
Davies, Andrew 157
Davies, Robertson 160, **261-7**, 269
Davis, Lennard J. 109
Dawson, Judith 113

311

Name and Title Index

Greene, Graham 272
Gregory, Philippa 111
Grisham, John 272
Groves of Academe, The 6-7, 8, 34, 43, 50-1, 53, 110, 142, 143, 150-1, 153, 155, **184-207**, 264, 269
Grudin, Robert 112-13
Grumbach, Doris 184-5, 186-7
Guardians, The 114, 122
Haffenden, John 271, 280
Hamilton, Roberta 242
Hamlet, Revenge 123-4
Hard Times 287
Hardy, Thomas 23-4
Hawkes, John 44, 62
Hawthorne, Nathaniel 45, 281
Heilbrun, Carolyn 109
Heller, Joseph 297
Hemingway, Ernest 46, 47, 60
Hers 34, 41
History Man, The 7, 10, 11, 13, 18, 42, 43, 80, 81, 85-6, 91, 94, 95, 97, 110, 129, 154, 156, 159, 206, 262, 293-4, 295, 302
Hobsbaum, Philip **20-32**, 100-1
Hodges, Lucy 274
Holbrook, David 4, 10-11
Horace 281
Horned Man, The 109
How Far Can You Go? 279, 290
Howards End 285
Howl 60
Hoyle, Fred 128
Hoyle, Geoffrey 128
Hughes, Thomas 7, 22
Human Stain, The 111, 162-3, 274
Hynes, James 111
I Am Charlotte Simmons 154

315

The Academic Novel

Women's Oppression Today 242
Wonder Boys 161
Woolf, Virginia 68
Write On 16, 261, 280
Writer's Place, The 76-7, 79, 83
Writing Dangerously 186, 190
Yorke, Margaret 135
Young Pattullo 137-8
Zuleika Dobson 7, 101, 155